Advanced
Case
Management

SAGE HUMAN SERVICES GUIDES

A series of books edited by ARMAND LAUFFER and CHARLES D. GARVIN. Published in cooperation with the University of Michigan School of Social Work and other organizations.

Advanced Case Management

New Strategies for the Nineties

Norma Radol Raiff
with Barbara K. Shore

SHSG SAGE HUMAN SERVICES GUIDE 66

*Published in cooperation with the University
of Michigan School of Social Work*

SAGE Publications
International Educational and Professional Publisher
Newbury Park   London   New Delhi

For information address:

SAGE publications, Inc.
2455 Teller Road
Newbury Park, California 91320

SAGE publications Ltd.
6 Bonhill Street
London EC2A 4PU
United Kingdom

SAGE Publications India Pvt. Ltd.
M-32 Market
Greater Kailash I
New Delhi 110 048 India

Printed in the United States of America

Library of Congress Cataloging-in-Publication Data

Raiff, Norma Radol.
    Advanced case management: new strategies for the nineties/Norma
Radol Raiff, Barbara K. Shore.
       p. cm.—(A Sage human services guide: v. 66)
    Includes bibliographical references.
     ISBN 0-8039-5308-9 (cloth).—ISBN 0-8039-3872-1 (pbk.)
     1. Social case work. I. Shore, Barbara K. II. Title.
III. Series.
HV43.R35   1993
361.3'2—dc20   93-20715

93 94 95 96 10 9 8 7 6 5 4 3 2 1

Sage Production Editor: Diane S. Foster

CONTENTS

Chapter 1

ADVANCED CASE MANAGEMENT
A Concept for the '90s

> Case management can be defined as a client-level strategy for promoting the coordination of human services, opportunities or benefits
>
> Moxley, 1989

Case management is in the forefront of a vigorously debated critical juncture. Alternatively described as one of the oldest, yet at the same time as one of the most innovative fields of contemporary social work practice, many newly designed and often heavily funded approaches have emerged in the past two decades as major program and policy reforms. The dissemination of these "case management" models, designed to resolve issues of inadequate service access, insufficient coordination, and skyrocketing costs of care has been spectacular, providing intuitive evidence of the depth of unmet need. Perhaps even more interesting is that these thrusts have been supported both by the public sector and private philanthropies and by alliances between businesses and the insurance industry. Yet even its most ardent supporters agree that the arena is in flux, and that program adoption has often occurred before rigorous field testing and without widespread grass roots or broad-based academic support.

The 1990s, then, are poised to provide answers to certain earlier policy choices. There are still many unresolved issues about the efficacy, professionalism, and efficiency of case management, both as a practice and as a systems approach. This book proposes to begin to address these issues by focusing on selected cutting-edge models: programs and practices that many consider to be in the forefront and that have gained credence among case management supporters and dedicated frontline practitioners. While this is not a surrogate for a

1

tested practice base, it begins to outline the shape of an emerging frame of reference that is likely to set future standards of care.

PURPOSE OF THE BOOK

This book provides an overview of state-of-the-art issues permeating advanced case management services. It illustrates the diversity of solutions that case managers, their supervisors, and administrators have developed in an emerging practice context. Many of these approaches have been endorsed by peer professionals, by consumers, and policy makers; others are controversial. This controversy provides both opportunities and challenges.

This guide describes *advanced* case management, defining case management both as a practice and as a program or system of care. Innovative approaches used by case managers as part of their everyday work are spotlighted: for example, new forms of outreach and assessment, alternative methods for engaging family members and natural supports and for upgrading their skills, state-of-the-art "wrap around" service plans that use flexible dollars, and emerging strategies that are more responsive to the needs of a culturally diverse constituency.

Case management also occurs within an organizational and environmental context. Program issues include the size and authority of staff, the degree to which existing services are available to meet clients' comprehensive needs, and intraprogram variation in target population, service philosophy, and resource base. Identification and discussion of those exemplary design features that are thought to support direct practice or to enhance program achievements is our secondary purpose.

Our approach is both eclectic and generic. Examples from many practice settings are included to illustrate case management's adaptability and its recent, rapid dissemination. For continuity, however, illustrations are consistently cited from the "Big Three" case management areas of aging, children's services, and mental health.

This book represents an effort to aggregate provocative advances, which are mainly reported in conferences and networking sessions and in scattered articles. While the advances are sometimes only anecdotally supported, these are widely viewed as exciting features of the case management landscape. This book should be most useful to those who have mastered the "basics," either through previous reading of such solid introductory texts as *The Practice of Case Management* (Moxley, 1989), or by course work, training, or on-the-job learning. Although not essential, prior experience will help readers to adapt noteworthy practices to their own setting.

It is our hope that this book will be useful to different levels of staff and learners seeking to go beyond an initial orientation. It is designed to meet practitioners' needs for an advanced academic sequence, and for supplementary on-the-job training or self-paced learning. A second audience consists of supervisors and administrators interested in human resource development (HRD) issues, such as personnel standards and quality programming guidelines.

CASE MANAGEMENT DEFINED

Until recently, professional skepticism about the role of case management within contemporary social work was often framed as denial: The term was criticized as overused, subject to too many program-linked interpretations, or so lacking in "operational clarity" (Johnson & Rubin, 1983, p. 49) as to defy meaningful comparison.

Some of these issues reflect case management's recent renaissance. The field was poorly studied before the early 1970s; it entered a period of growth only after a series of federal initiatives, especially in aging and mental health, resulted in a proliferation of community-based services that came to be disparagingly described as highly complex, fragmented, duplicative, uncoordinated and inaccessible. As a result, the role of the case manager as a "systems agent" or broker of services was increasingly seen as essential, and model demonstration projects were funded to determine the best mix of personnel and administrative supports. The fact that many programs were setting-specific and used their own terminology and personnel standards added to the field's ambiguity, as did the fact that no single profession could demonstrate a monopoly of skills (Ozarin, 1978). Early proponents were also often unclear about whether their emphasis was on case management's direct practice or on its administrative and systemic implications. These dynamics resulted in a literature that emphasized program description and outcome studies rather than scrutiny of the timing and pacing of optimal interventions. In spite of reservations about the efficacy and parameters of case management, and considerable dialogue about whether it represents a "new" or a conveniently rediscovered intervention, there is consensus that it consists of a core set of functions. These core elements flow out of recognition that people in high need may require outside help in identifying, accessing, sustaining, and updating an individualized "package" of services and resources. The *Encyclopedia of Social Work* encapsulates this by referring to case management as a quintessential "boundary spanning approach" (Rubin, 1987, p. 212), the purpose of which is to achieve continuity of care and to ensure that persons receive appropriate services in a timely fashion.

The most common definitions of case management practice divide its components into a series of analytically discrete yet overlapping set of functions that includes initial client outreach and engagement; assessment and diagnosis of needed services, programs and resources; developing a service strategy (referred to as the plan of care or the service plan); linking clients to services and community resources identified in the plan; implementation and coordination of effort to ensure that programs are implemented in logical, stepwise fashion and that they jointly address identified needs, which are "pooled" in the plan; and monitoring and evaluation to determine the goodness of fit between the client's state of being and current service deliverables. It has been proposed that a continuum of case management models co-exist, ranging from those that provide "minimal" services (e.g., outreach, assessment, planning, and simple referral) to more comprehensive programs that incorporate client and resource advocacy, direct casework, development of natural support systems, monitoring of program quality, education for self-care or teaching Activities of Daily Living (ADLs), public education, crisis intervention and, possibly, medication management (Baier, 1987; Korr & Cloninger, 1991).

Case management has been described as grounded in social work tradition as a problem-solving activity (Grisham, White, & Miller, 1983) and as an intervention with roots in the profession's value base, including its hallowed principles of respect for the individual, client self-determination, and equal access to resources (Modrcin, Rapp, & Chamberlain, 1985; Rapp & Chamberlain, 1985). Social work views of the person-in-environment and the singular importance of the casework relationship are also comfortable in contemporary descriptions; for example, case management has been defined as "short-term, task-centered work" that "focuses on helping clients identify and resolve concrete problems in their everyday lives" (Roberts-DeGennaro, 1987, p. 468), yet it is also something that "endures and provides continuity as the client moves back and forth across institutional, community, and agency boundaries" (Rubin, 1987, p. 215).

Finally, many recent definitions continue to reflect a more long-standing and unresolved social work dilemma: Is case management synonymous with client advocacy, or is it primarily intended as an approach to societal resource management (Netting, 1992; Weil &

Karls, 1985)? Conceptual confusion about case management's purpose has continued to the present, co-mingling client-focused and cost-containment expectations and creating ongoing tension for staff and for the greater professional and lay communities (Loomis, 1988).

THE NEW CASE MANAGEMENT

RECENT HISTORY

The new case management, in our terminology, refers to those concepts and models of service intervention that have emerged in the past two decades as a generalized response to shifts in the locus and financing of the health and human services. As community-based programs have dramatically expanded, accompanied by increased funding restrictions and escalating costs, the case manager's role as a broker of services to provide for continuity of care, both vertically across time and horizontally across service sectors, has been given greater centrality.

Several landmark movements are linked to the new case management's emergence, providing ideological and programmatic support. Among the earliest were the War on Poverty and the Model Cities programs (1960s) that brought the issues of service fragmentation and inaccessibility to national consciousness. In the 1970s, the Department of Health, Education and Welfare funded several "service integration" projects, which featured such precursors to contemporary case management as one-stop service centers, information and referral, computerized client-tracking and management information systems, and interagency agreements (Intagliata, 1982). The deinstitutionalization movements in mental health and mental retardation (1960s and 1970s) provided hard lessons that service availability could not be taken for granted, nor was it equivalent to automatic service use. Although well motivated, these thrusts often discharged individuals into inadequately serviced and unprepared communities. When local programs did exist, they were criticized as nonresponsive to some of the more needy populations, such as the young "chronic" or mentally ill homeless (Geller et al., 1990; Glasscote, 1978; Stein & Test, 1982). Concern with these hard-to-reach and "treatment resistant" groups continues, and it is precisely these individuals whom the new forms of case management are often expected to target (Axelrod & Wetzler, 1989; Bachrach, Talbott, & Meyerson, 1987).

Case management became a more empirically tested practice at about the same time that its utility was first recognized. Since the early 1970s, the Health Care Financing Administration (HCFA) has jointly funded several long-term care demonstrations in collaboration with state, county, and local agencies. Although designed to test alternative approaches to financing, initiating, and providing programs for the frail elderly, the demonstrations all included case management and an expanded smorgasbord of in-home and community-based services (Humphreys, Mason, Guthrie, Liem, & Stern, 1988). Professional "discovery" of child abuse as a major social problem in the mid 1970s prompted a landmark series of Child Abuse and Neglect Demonstration Projects that systematically studied the best practices (Berkeley Planning Associates, 1978). By the 1980s, family-centered case management initiatives in children's early intervention and mental health extended the right to case management services already established in the adult sector to our nation's neglected youth, while sparking interest in the role of caregivers as contributors to the case management process (Stroul & Friedman, 1986).

Expansion of case management services was often ideologically driven, but it was also fueled by the availability of private and federal dollars. Most notably, case management has been a critical ingredient in several recent, managed health-care demonstrations. These have included the Social/Health Maintenance Organization (S/HMO), a congressionally mandated demonstration that provides capitated (paid according to a uniform per-person payment), prospectively fixed program funding for functionally able as well as disabled elderly Medicare-eligible persons (Abrahams, Nonnekamp, Dunn, Mehta, & Woodard, 1988) and the 24 sites of the Robert Wood Johnson Hospital Initiatives in Long-Term Care (HILTC), which attempted expanded, vertical integration of hospital, continuing-, and long-term-care services (Applebaum & Austin, 1990; MacAdam et al., 1989). Most recently, the Robert Wood Johnson Foundation Program on Chronic Mental Illness provided funds to nine U.S. cities to establish local, centralized mental health authorities that combine administrative, fiscal, and clinical responsibility for the delivery of services to persons with chronic mental illness. Each city is expected to set up "a comprehensive system of care" or an integrated case management system that would control a full range of services, operate all hospital- and community-based programs in its jurisdiction, expand housing options, and have access to funds from state, county, and local resources (Goldman, & Lehman, 1990; Rothbard Hadley, Schinnar, Morgan, & Whitehill, 1989; Shore & Cohen, 1990).

Federal support has been critical to the spread of case management nationwide. In the area of aging, case management approaches were tested in over 15 federally funded demonstrations between 1973 and 1985. In more than 40 states, federal waivers under the Medicaid

Program, Section 2176 of the Omnibus Reconciliation Act of 1981, P.L. 96-499, permit reimbursement for case management in waiver-funded programs that provide for specialized home- and community-based services to help deinstitutionalize or to divert clients. By 1988, 19 states had approved Medicaid state plan amendments for case management to targeted groups, with many more states aggressively pursuing this option (Humphreys et al., 1988; Vourlekis, 1992).

P.L. 99-660 (Title V, State Comprehensive Mental Health Services Plan, Omnibus Health Act of 1986) now requires case management services for all individuals with serious emotional illnesses who receive substantial amounts of public funds or services. Similar legislative thrusts mandate case management services for: the developmentally disabled (Developmental Disabilities Act of 1970, P.L. 91-517), children with special needs (Education for All Handicapped Children Act of 1975, P.L. 94-142), handicapped and at-risk infants and toddlers and their families (Education of the Handicapped Act Amendments of 1986, P. L. 99-457), children in foster care (Federal Adoption Assistance and Child Welfare Act of 1980, P.L. 96-272), the homeless (Stuart B. McKinney Homeless Assistance Act of 1987, P.L. 100-79), and the elderly (Older Americans Act, revisions of 1978, P.L. 95-478). In general, federal legislation permits great flexibility in service design and presents a window of opportunity for states and localities to build innovative, diverse, and responsive case management systems (Zipper, Weil, & Rounds, 1991).

Given the large demonstration of need, the growing cast of players, the pyramiding of research findings, and the lure of added dollars, it is little wonder that case management is now recognized as a core service. It has been called "perhaps the most essential unifying factor in service delivery" and "the energizing factor that has propelled the service plan into the reality of service delivery" (Behar, 1985, p. 194).

At the same time, the new case management is nurtured by the harsh reality of escalating costs. As a result, some settings have interpreted case management as synonymous with "managed care" or "cost containment," as a program with a system-oriented, fiduciary focus, and as a macro-level intervention designed to alter the profile of community, region, or state services. Several managed-care approaches, such as the S/HMO and the HILTC, have already been cited. In general, managed-care programs are designed to stimulate the growth of a broader array of services (especially a continuum of less expensive options), to promote quality and efficiency, to enhance service coordination, to target the most-at-risk individuals, and to contain costs by controlling client access to services, especially high-cost programs. These system-focused thrusts are often considered to be case management's advance guard.

Managed-care approaches have also sensitized programs to quality assurance and cost-of-service issues and to the need to develop information technologies that can systematically track multi-service users and program outcomes (Rapp & Poertner, 1980). Yet even as policy makers are enticed by promised cost containment and just-in-time programs, there is an awareness that the service relationship and local programming will be affected by realignments in frontline staff's "portal of entry" authority. Some warn that promised cost containment has been dangerously oversold to policy makers and that we cannot yet definitively state that case management will provide a less expensive surrogate for service delivery "as usual" (Ashley, 1988; Franklin, 1988).

SOCIAL WORK AND THE NEW CASE MANAGEMENT

It is generally agreed that case management descends from social work's historical tradition and the work of Mary Richmond and the era of the early settlement houses and charity organization societies (Greene, 1992, Weil & Karls, 1985). Although the discovery of "case management" as a national- and state-level practice is relatively new, contemporary thrusts are highly compatible with traditional social work's emphasis on the importance of understanding of "the person in the environment" and the potential of the "environment as a helping resource" (Sullivan, 1987; Weick, Rapp, Sullivan, & Kisthardt, 1989). Allied areas include skills associated with client engagement; assertive follow-up and troubleshooting; individual, family, and environmental assessment; comprehensive planning; resource identification and resource consultation; fiscal accountability; system spanning; measurement of the quality of life; and program evaluation (Vourlekis & Greene, 1992a).

Dissimilarities between the new case management and turn-of-the-century social casework also need to be recognized, although the difference is often one of degree. The new case management programs often have a more sophisticated assessment and intervention repertoire, are more "ecologically" oriented, are less wed to a medical model, are more likely to adopt a social rehabilitation perspective, and are more apt to highlight individual, family and social network strengths rather than perceiving these as harmful influences (Abramczyk, 1989). Similarly, contemporary case management practice has certain emphases that make it "more distinctive" (Rothman, 1991, p. 521). These include a different profile of service activity that emphasizes information and referral, community-based skills, assisting clients to sustain community tenure, and a here-and-now focus. Nor is case management solely associated with social casework; it has been enriched by other professions. These dynamics "have prevented and will continue to prevent a straightforward meshing of case management and social work practice" (Vourlekis, 1992, p. 7).

The role of social workers in nationwide case management development is controversial and reflects serious concerns about ownership, faddism, ethical dilemmas, and professional responses to developing agency-related and other policies (Kane, 1988). Some social work professionals have provided significant national leadership as case management policy makers and consultants (Austin,1983; Behar, 1985) and as academic and frontline trainers influencing the newest cohorts of direct service workers, supervisors, and senior administrators (Ballew & Mink, 1986; Billig & Levinson, 1989; Stern, Serra, & Raiff, 1990). Others, however, remain ambivalent about whether this is truly an advanced practice specialty, sometimes interpreting it as a generic method most suited to undergraduates and occasionally dismissing it with a sense of deja vu (Moore, 1990). Reservations have also been expressed about the neoconservative aspects of the new case management (Schilling, Schinke, & Weatherly, 1987) and about the danger of a premature "professional flirtation" (Vourlekis, 1992, p. 7).

For its partisans, the new case management is "the state of the art" with the potential to remediate serious deficiencies in the organization of service while enriching the profession's knowledge and practice base. Advocates point to developments in aging, mental health, and children's services, and to a host of second generation programs, including private practice and health insurance administration, as *de facto* evidence of case management's broad-based utility and far-flung impact. In fact, one hallmark of the new case management is its ubiquity: trial programs and practice advances have been reported in practically every human service sector. These include *health* (Leukefeld, 1990; Polinsky, Fred, & Ganz, 1991), *mental health* (e.g., Degan, Cole, Tamayo, & Dzerovych, 1990; Kurtz, Bagarozzi, & Pollane, 1984; Sanborn, 1983), *aging* and *long-term care* (e.g., Applebaum, 1988a; Dobrish, 1987; Steinberg & Carter, 1983); childhood *early intervention* (Dunst & Trivette, 1988), *developmental disabilities* (Hare & Clark, 1992; K. Kaplan, 1992), *AIDS* (acquired immunodeficiency syndrome) programs (M. Kaplan 1992; Piette, Fleishman, Mor, & Dill 1990), the *homeless* (James, Smith, & Mann, 1991; Ridgway, Spaniol, & Zipple, 1986; Rife, First, Greenlee, Miller, & Feichter, 1991), *children and youth services* (Brindis, Barth, & Loomis, 1987; Kamerman & Kahn, 1990), *child abuse and neglect* (e.g., Klee & Halfon, 1987); *drug and alcohol* (Graham & Timney, 1990); *vocational rehabilitation* (Roessler & Rubin, 1982), and *probation and parole* (Porporino & Cormer, 1982). These efforts constitute a pragmatic truth test of case management's essential interface with social work's traditional mission. Brieland & Korr (1989) have provided a life-cycle schematic for understanding the contribution of case management components throughout the major human service sectors from infancy to young adulthood (see Figure 1.1).

THE "NEW" CASE MANAGEMENT

In spite of reservations, there is a growing consensus that there is a new case management or, perhaps more accurately, a variety of contemporary approaches that depart from the prototype of social casework or the more limited effort traditionally provided as an ancillary intervention.

1. The new case management is a child of its time. Although sometimes promoted as a ubiquitous element of service delivery, its greatest thrusts have occurred in selected populations that have benefited from public and privately funded initiatives. Aging, mental health, and youth services associated with early intervention and childhood disability have been more affected than others.These sectors are case management "enriched" or "lead" settings, which influence spin-offs and often have the most specializations. The new case management is also heavily influenced by current theories of helping. Although there is marked variation in work and community environments, all of the major thrusts embrace theories of consumer rights, the importance of social supports and informal helpers in the case management process, and the need to respect cultural diversities. These awarenesses expand the historical definition of what the case management relationship involves.

2. The new case management is often considered a core or pivotal service, one that under some circumstances may "drive" the service package rather than playing a secondary role. Under certain political or organizational arrangements, case managers are viewed as powerful forces for systems intervention with potential authority to affect the balance between institutional and community-based care, either by virtue of staff's ability to allocate local resources directly (Schwartz, Goldman, & Churgin, 1982) or indirectly in the course of assessment, referral, and service planning.

3. The new case management is not synonymous with "old-fashioned casework" but is a hybrid that includes "varieties of specializations, concentrations and practice settings" (Austin, 1988, p. 5). A melding of historic events, including social work's movement into more clinical settings, deprofessionalization in the public sector, and technical advances associated with occupations and expertise, has neutralized claims to a

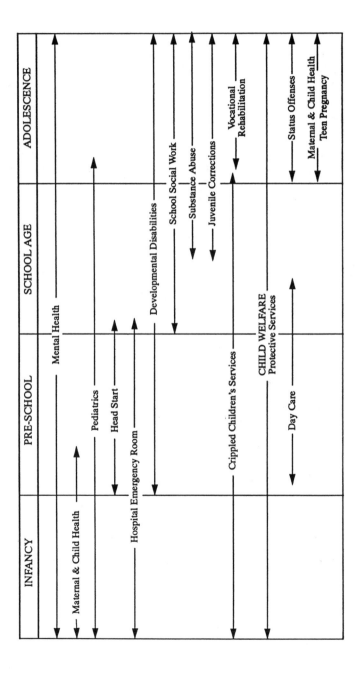

Figure 1.1. Overlapping Service Components by Age Level
SOURCE: Brieland (1989). Initially suggested in material prepared for a symposium paper, "Education & Training for Social Workers Serving Mentally Ill Children." Charleston, SC.

11

social work practice monopoly (Aaranson, 1989; Moeller, 1991) and opened the field to new partnerships.

4. The new case management has been widely promoted as a cost-containment and a public policy tool. Although this may have created unrealistically high program expectations (Callahan, 1989; Holloway, 1991), "top down" approval has meant incredibly rapid dissemination of models and, in some states, has meant building entirely new coordination systems for assuring that consumers, family members, service providers, and legislators are represented in system planning and design (National Institute of Mental Health, 1987). As a concomitant, many recent programs also require client and program tracking, which links interventions to explicit outcomes.

5. Although virtually all direct-service providers report managing their cases, programs vary tremendously in their authority and ability to command resources. As a consequence, some programs are far more comprehensive and able to provide specialized, advanced interventions. Applebaum and others (Applebaum & Austin, 1990; Applebaum & Wilson, 1988) suggest that state-of-the-art programs may have unique provision for service intensity, breadth, and duration. *Intensity* refers to the amount of time staff spend with their clients. Its indicators include the time allotted for intervening with clients and their significant others and a small caseload size that permits intense involvement. *Breadth* refers to how broadly staff is allowed to view the scope of the client's problem and the range of services staff can access. *Duration* refers to an open-ended expectation that staff will remain involved with the client as long as the need exists and the client agrees to services. This type of long-term-care model is considerably different from the case management programs typically provided by hospital discharge planners or county social service departments, which may include one, but generally not all three of these criteria. A "substantial increase" in more comprehensive case management programs has been reported in many local delivery systems, although this is by no means a majority approach (Applebaum & Austin, 1990, p. 6).

6. Model building provides further evidence of the field's coming of age. Case management prototypes can be loosely classified as either "client-focused" or "system-focused." The more client-focused models emphasize the microrelationships between the client/consumer and the case manager and the interface of their interventions. System-focused models highlight the perspective of the service environment, organizational structure, and the resource base as determining features.

Robinson and Bergman (1989) are key analysts of client-focused models. Their examination of mental health case management identifies four primary approaches: expanded broker, personal strengths, rehabilitation, and full support. The *expanded broker* model emphasizes the case manager's traditional linkage function. It exceeds the traditional "broker of service" prototype in that it not only assumes responsibility for assessment and referral, but also for ensuring the availability of services. The *personal strengths* or developmental acquisition model highlights the case manager's relationship as a personal "travel companion" in helping client/consumers to achieve a better quality of life. The worker's relationship to the client in providing support and mentoring and creating opportunities for personal growth is considered pivotal to community reintegration (Rapp & Wintersteen, 1985; Sullivan, 1992). The *rehabilitation* model, associated with Boston University's Center for Psychiatric Rehabilitation (Cohen & Nemec, 1988; Cohen, Nemec, Farkas, & Forbess, 1988a, 1988b, 1988c), places emphasis on client-centered needs assessment and goal development to enhance discharge planning. It focuses on identifying the individual's strengths, goals and deficits; analyzes the individual's level of skill functioning for what is needed for goal attainment; and uses the outcomes of this assessment to teach direct skills or to provide consultation for program referral and/or new program start-up (Freeman, Fischer, & Sheldon, 1980). The *full support* model is a derivative of the PACT (Programs in Assertive Community Treatment) (Stein & Test, 1985) model and combines traditional service planning and coordination with advocacy, supportive psychotherapy, clinical case management, and pro-active direct provision of treatment and rehabilitation services.

O'Connor's (1988) observation that case management programs addressing similar populations are better compared than an across-the-board spectrum is illustrated in long-term care programming. Quinn & Burton (1988) identify three long-term-care case management models using the narrower criterion of recurring combinations of funding mechanisms and resource controls: brokerage, prior authorization screening, and consolidated direct service. *Brokerage* programs link clients to a network of providers and can include expanded dollars for service coverage. The widely disseminated *prior authorization screening* model emphasizes case management screening as a decision point for nursing home diversion versus placement. There are many variations of the *consolidated direct service* model (Abrahams & Leutz, 1983); however, all involve a pooling of funds and the provision of a comprehensive range of services.

As yet, efforts to develop more universal models of case management are better described as rudimentary. One exception is Merrill's (1985) global typology of social, medical, and medical/social programs, which analyzes programs according to their intended constituency and funding base. *Social* models are time-limited, prevention-focused programs that target well individuals whose primary needs are for supportive services rather than health care. *Medical* case management services are synonymous with managed care and many efforts of the health insurance industry. A growing employment area for social workers, these programs share an interest in cost containment, utilization review and risk sharing and treat the service provider rather than the client as their primary constituency. The types of familiar public social work programs, such as long-term care and mental health, are classified as *Medical-social* programs. They target at-risk populations and provide a mix of interventions designed to address acute episodes while balancing concern with overall costs and the individual's life-style preferences.

ADVANCED CASE MANAGEMENT

The new case management includes different program constellations, ranging from traditional simple broker services to those with more sophisticated goals, structures, or operations. Innovation can be limited or broadly based and can include linking services to cost containment; creating staff, consumer, volunteer and family partnerships; building interagency and community-level coalitions; or developing quality assurances. To allow for diversity, we propose a multidimensional scheme that contrasts "beginning" or everyday" case management, and "advanced" case management.

Advanced case management is only *one* subset of the new case management. The criteria for identification are purely pragmatic: What do the literature and knowledgeable practitioners identify as cutting edge or as worthy of dissemination, or which model programs are borrowed or adopted by others? Based on a computerized literature review and analysis of existing models, we propose that a program or practice may be characterized as "advanced" if it displays innovative behavior on five possible dimensions: client, practitioner, organization, model of service delivery, and/or attention to quality assurance.

THE "ADVANCED" CLIENT

Many of the first case management advances grew out of a policy need to lessen risks, to provide superior service integration or more comprehensive service delivery, or to reduce the costs associated with "high-user" populations. Targeted clients typically included those with the most severe, potentially long-term disabilities who were likely to require extended contact. Described as "treatment resistant" or as exhibiting "revolving door syndromes," they were not only the "most expensive" to the system but were also seen as able to be served in the community with proper supports. Other targeted populations included generational groups, such as youth, whose needs are more effectively met in secondary or in "natural" settings associated with life stage activities; individuals with a "dual diagnosis" whose disabilities required joint service planning and coordination by two or more specialized (and often independent) service sectors (Fariello & Scheidt, 1989; Kaufman, DeWeaver, & Glicken, 1989; Landsberg, Fletcher, & Maxwell, 1987); or emerging populations, such as AIDS victims, whose need for case management services was absolutely critical.

In brief, we begin with a client-focused definition: Advanced case management is defined as a specialized practice designed to bring together a vast array of services needed to sustain the most vulnerable and "difficult" populations that are at the greatest risk.

One consequence of the level-of-need criterion is that case management interventions are "intensified" rather than casually conducted. As Applebaum and others (Applebaum & Austin, 1990; Applebaum & Wilson, 1988) note, intensity involves a time dimension and implies a sufficiently small caseload to maintain frequent contact. On the practice level, intensive case management often includes the expectation that services will be open-ended and available for the duration of need, or that they will be frequent (e.g., contact is provided anywhere from daily to once every two weeks). Many of the newer programs also specify that contacts occur in person rather than on the telephone and in the community or home (*in vivo*) rather than in the office, thus lending an interactive intensity to the process (Hodge, 1990).

In addition to intensity, some advanced programs have a "just-in-time" aspect. That is, although staff involvement is not expected to be open-ended, the case manager's gatekeeping functions are extremely critical to the client's immediate maintenance of status or continuation in a least restrictive environment. AIDS case management and hospital diversion programs with strong case management components fall into this class.

A second aspect to the client dimension is the development of expanded services to "secondary" consumers, most commonly parents, family members, or significant others. These services may be directly supportive or may incorporate educational and advocacy activities designed to enhance the case management knowledge and skills of the client's caregivers. Legitimating a secondary constituency reflects new

policy awareness of limited program resources and greater respect for
lay individuals as gatekeepers, sustainers and partners in case management.

THE "ADVANCED" CASE MANAGER

In spite of the common professional view of case management as a
"generic" activity (Minahan, 1976), case managers have varying levels of
attained competency. Consequently, there is increased attention to the type
of academic preparation and to the desired kinds of integration of theory
and practice that distinguish "advanced" from "everyday" practitioners.

Advanced case managers are pragmatically identified as persons who
are expert in the conduct of comprehensive case management functions.
The more advanced staff will display greater autonomy, self-awareness,
and diversity in their skills, knowledge, and attitudes. Their "scope" of
expertise will extend to greater proficiency in the work of case management, that is, client and systems advocacy, crisis intervention, home
visiting, *in vivo* outreach and assessment, practical counseling, the
ability to access services and entitlements, and innovative collaboration
with informal support systems and the formal service community. Adept
movement between the roles of broker, enabler, educator, or advocate,
and skilled pacing of the more effective interventions, also signal
expertise.

Although case management programs are most associated with "ecological" models, there is growing consensus that advanced staff will
be able to synthesize "clinical" approaches into their practices (e.g.,
Bachrach, 1992; Harris & Bergman, 1988c; Kanter, 1989; Lamb,
1980). Familiarity with other frames of knowledge is essential to
engage in meaningful relationships with "system resistant" clients and
to have a greater impact on the multidisciplinary settings in which so
much advanced practice occurs.

Finally, advanced practitioners are associated with "autonomous
practice, broad responsibility, and high task complexity" (O'Connor,
1988, p. 98). *Autonomy* refers to the degree of staff's freedom and
self-direction in organizing and performing assignments. The autonomous practitioner is someone who works under supervision, but due to
the field-emergent nature of practice and its need for immediate decisions,
this is more by way of supervisory consultation to legitimize practice.
Responsibility refers to the advanced practitioner's mastery of a broad
range of tasks, and *complexity* refers to the level of difficulty of the
work. To put it simply, advanced case managers "are expected to deal
with problems and issues that are complicated, irregular, and risky at

the client or system level" (O'Connor, 1988, p. 99). Although the principle of self-determination continues to be paramount, and clients are philosophically encouraged to make decisions related to their own care, as programs gain experience in working with more impaired and in need populations, the evidence is that decisions are sometimes left to the case manager (Ryndes, 1989).

THE "ADVANCED" PROGRAM

Some programs are more complicated than others in their structural arrangements, fiscal accountabilities, and control over needed resources. "This is not to suggest that client advocacy will be overlooked, but that the case management job is becoming more complex, involving not only advocacy and service coordination, but also financial responsibility and gatekeeping functions" (Applebaum & Austin, 1990, p. 12).

Advanced programs are best located through demonstrations and reported models. These need not be large or well funded. They are characterized by their administrative support of cutting-edge services and the ability to anticipate change and to provide staff with well-developed manpower arrangements, such as that found in PACT or other team case management environments (Arana, Hastings, & Herron, 1991; Johnson, 1990).

Although a low staff-client ratio, such as 1:10 to 1:25 and even lower, is sometimes considered a surrogate measure of program accomplishment, raw caseload size can be misleading. The more advanced programs have the capacity to match staff and client, to successfully assign different levels of staff to tasks requiring different baseline skill levels, and try to assign caseloads to accommodate different levels of need or disability (Goldman & Ridgely, 1990; Kanter 1987b).

Advanced case management services are also sophisticated users of program data. Whether relying on manually collected or computerized data, these programs use financial and management information (Rapp, Gowdy, Sullivan, & Wintersteen, 1988) to help the program to monitor client status, "movement" through intake and discharge, and the pattern of service provision and its link to individual outcomes.

Human resource development (HRD) issues are a priority for advanced case management programs, which attach urgency to staff development and supervision. These programs seek the highest as well as the most appropriate level of professional staffing (Atshuler & Forward, 1978), and may be in the forefront of such personnel innovations as consumer case managers (Sherman & Porter, 1991). Advanced systems also often rethink traditional role assignments to explore hybridization and role sharing (Applebaum & Wilson, 1988; Walden, Hammer, & Kurland, 1990). Mandated training is a common feature and can be required by program-funded initiatives working with an advanced clientele (Bromberg, Starr, Donovan, Carney, & Pernell-Arnold, 1991).

"ADVANCED" MODELS OF SERVICE DELIVERY

Many programs display a striking ability to articulate a frame of reference that drives the program design, molds service delivery, and provides staff with a professional identity. Although some models are relatively rudimentary, they all identify a targeted client group, a system level goal, and some preferred mechanism for intervention. These are typically pragmatic, mid-range conceptual constructs. As Bachrach indicates, when two or more models serving a single population are compared, "Differences in philosophy and concept are sufficiently marked that they appear to weigh more heavily than the similarities" (1989, p. 884). Competition between alternative models is one of the indicators of the field's vitality, yet it may also create additional confusion for clients, service providers, third-party payers, and the public at large, who are already struggling with case management as a concept.

The positive aspects of a philosophically driven program are important in helping staff to explain their function to their clients and the community. Certain models, such as the Madison model in mental health (Stein & Test, 1980), and other large-scale government or privately funded experiments, such as the Living-at-Home program in aging (Bogdonoff, 1991) or the Channeling Projects in aging (Applebaum & Christianson, 1988; Carcagno & Kemper, 1988), have also been tested in several national and international sites. This has made it possible to discuss under what conditions models can be transferred or must be modified to suit local needs or community infrastructures.

Continuous program change reflecting cross-fertilization and program borrowing, expansion of the knowledge base, changes in societal perceptions, and shifts in society's social agenda are common. Some field-derived models are already in their second or third reincarnation. In articulating the history of the Madison model, Thompson et al. (Thompson, Griffith, & Leaf, 1990, p. 631) write that the "changes in the scope and content of the model should not come as a surprise. . . . There is no universal quick fix for the problems of designing service systems for the severely mentally ill and . . . what solutions exist are only partial at best." These authors suggest that "a model of care must actively court the process of change on multiple levels" and imply that "assertive adaptability" and the "ability to transcend professional dogma" are needed for system endurance. Similarly, Bachrach (1979) states that effective planning requires idealism, vision, and a sense of reality. The most responsive case management programs are not those that have been developed out of needs assessment based on understanding of communities as they are today but those based on an understanding of communities as they will be in the future.

Well-developed models of service delivery are found in all the lead case management sectors. The "strengths approach" (Modrcin et al., 1985; Ronnau, Rutter, & Donner, 1988) and PACT (Programs in Assertive Community Treatment; Stein & Test, 1980) models in mental health, the Living-At-Home program in aging (Bogdonoff, 1991), and the CASSP (Child and Adolescent Service System Program) federal initiative for children and youth services (Street & Friedman, 1984a; Stroul & Friedman, 1986) illustrate programs with strong conceptual identities.

A QUALITY APPROACH TO PRACTICE

Attention to quality service provision is the last dimension of advanced practice. *Quality* has several meanings, but ordinarily alludes to a plan of evaluation plus attention to assurances incorporating standard setting and monitoring (Panzarino & Wetherbee, 1990). The basic objective of quality assurance is the provision of excellent case management services to the most needy individuals in the most efficient and effective way possible (White & Goldis, 1992). This requires up front identification of what the case management process is expected to achieve and effective monitoring to ensure that the program has been carried out as designed and that standards of practice were upheld.

Quality case management incorporates at least three dimensions: structure, process, and outcome (Collard, Berman, & Henderson, 1990; Henderson & Collard, 1988; Donabedian, 1966). *Structural* measures assume that individuals or agencies meeting certain structural standards can provide the expected quality level of care. These include standards related to individual licensure, training and professional credentialing, staffing arrangements, the best "mix" of personnel, and staff and client "matching" issues. These are basically surrogate measures of the organization's capacity to provide care. Because data to answer these questions are relatively easy to track, structural indices have been widely used in local- and state-level quality indicators. These should be considered necessary first steps, but are not enough by themselves to guarantee that a service will be of high quality or cost-effective (Shueman, 1987).

Inquiry into quality *process* refers to the sequence and coordination of case management activities, an area that has been poorly studied.

Process indicators focus on "how we do what we do" and review the scope of the service, its most important aspects, and what is commonly thought of as of good performance (Vourlekis, 1991). Process issues include timeliness, comprehensiveness, involvement with secondary consumers, and teamwork.

Quality *outcomes* are generally taken to mean a systematic approach to studying the net changes that have occurred in client status as a result of the provided activity. Common indicators include measures of client improvement and satisfaction, enhanced compliance with the service plan, indicators of continuity of care, and the interaction between these variables. Whereas evaluation research is most strongly needed in these areas, even the most advanced programs are only still striving to meet the rigorous standards of experimental research design.

DESIGN OF THIS BOOK

This book is intended to provide a compendium of approaches associated with advanced practitioners and advanced case management systems. It is organized to capture some of the many exciting recent developments and to highlight issues of quality or what are now considered best practices. Chapter 2 explores certain innovative procedures that are changing the face of traditional efforts associated with service plan development, delivery, and review. The practitioner focus continues in Chapter 3, which targets more holistic, "meta" dimensions of activity that represent broadly accepted, albeit controversial, views of how case management services ought to be delivered. Human resource development (HRD) issues such as training, supervision, and employment of alternative case management providers and "extenders" provide a bridge to programmatic concerns and are discussed in Chapter 4. The concluding material in Chapter 5 examines advanced case management as a program and as a system of care.

Chapter 2

THE ADVANCED CASE MANAGER
A Quality Approach to Best Practice

Among the many and often conflicting models of case management that have recently proliferated, the presence of the case manager as a constant and accountable individual working to ensure continuous coordination of services has remained a given (Clark, Landis, & Fisher, 1990). Yet even as case managers are increasingly recognized as pivotal "boundary-spanning" (Rubin, 1987, p. 212) agents, there is a lack of research about what is good practice, or even about what case mangers "actually do" (Baker & Weiss, 1984, p. 925). This gap reflects long-standing system features, including a greater concern for case management as a policy strategy (Austin, 1983), the lack of a common language (Aaronson, 1989; Kenyon et al., 1990), and widespread dismissal of case management as an unsophisticated and, hence, easily accomplished activity.

The process of case management is complex and involves time and relationship issues that have not been extensively studied. There are many unanswered questions: How are case management functions actually delivered in the field compared to a program's more formal description? What is the relationship between specific interventions and desired client outcomes? How does the timing and pacing of specific interventions make a difference? Only a handful of authors (e.g., Chamberlain & Rapp, 1991; Fiorentine & Grusky, 1990; Hargreaves et al., 1984) have begun to provide empirical answers to build recommendations for a research-based micropractice.

A PROPOSED MODEL OF QUALITY
CASE MANAGEMENT PRACTICE

The development of a conceptual prototype that can organize review of the case management process and describe its component relationships is a prerequisite for quality assurance. This chapter proposes a two-dimensional model (see Figure 2.1) that defines advanced practice as incorporating function-specific and generic elements.

The Function Axis organizes discussion by examining what is professionally known or accepted as good practice in each of case management's recognized tasks. Six core functions cited in the *NASW Standards and Guidelines for Social Work Case Management for the Functionally Impaired* (1984) are selected as surrogates for professional consensus: (a) *assessment,* (b) *service/care planning,* (c) *implementation of the service plan/plan of care,* (d) *coordination and monitoring of services,* (e) *advocacy,* and (f) *termination.* The approach is generic and assumes that these functions are more similar than different in the variety of fields in which case management is being emphasized. In real life, however, practice is also codetermined by (a) the specialized nature, needs and projected futures of the target population; (b) technical mastery requirements associated with the field of practice, such as knowledge of specialized assessment and intervention techniques; (c) the support systems and the community in which the practice is carried out; (d) the organizational structure of the practice setting; and (e) funding and reimbursement requirements. For this reason, illustrative tables are scattered throughout this chapter to present some of the different issues that affect field-of-service case management practice delivery.

The Meta Axis provides a synthesizing framework. It identifies four "meta" initiatives thought of as corollaries of excellent practice throughout the delivery cycle: (a) *cultural competency,* (b) *consumer enablement and empowerment,* (c) integrated *clinical frameworks,* and (d) advanced *multidisciplinary* or *transdisciplinary practices.* This axis is less well-defined because it is newer. It is also more linked to specific fields of practice and has only recently shown wider dissemination.

We treat this model as an organizing framework suggested by a review of the literature and by exemplary program descriptions. These dimensions provide a working definition of advanced micropractice: It is superior conduct of specified case management tasks that incorporate at least some aspect(s) of the underlying meta standards. This chapter

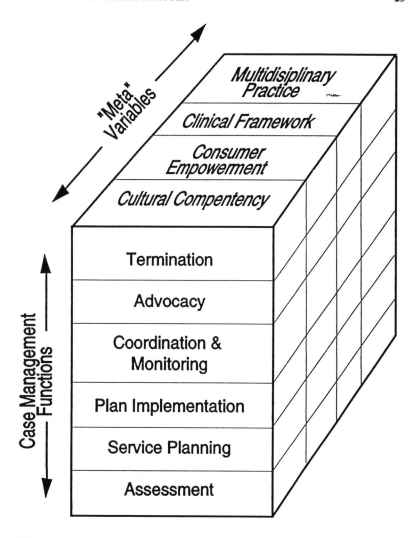

Figure 2.1. Matrix of Quality Case Management Practice: A Model

discusses the Function Axis is greater detail; description of the Meta dimension continues in Chapter 3. An illustration of best practices in the conduct of the case management cycle, from the area of child abuse and neglect, is summarized in Table 2.1.

TABLE 2.1 Quality Standards of Practice (Case Management With Children and Youth)

In 1974, the Office of Child Development and Social Rehabilitation Services of DHEW funded 11 projects to test alternative models for the treatment of child abuse and neglect. Berkeley Planning Associates (BPA) subsequently evaluated these projects to provide guidelines to local communities. An area of BPA's interest was the development of standards for quality case management. These were identified through review of the professional literature, random chart audits and personnel interviews. Descriptive and multivariate analysis were used to establish minimal standards and to describe the relationship between specific practices and client outcomes.

The following practices were cited as making a difference:

1. Small caseloads: Under 25 when possible, for professionally trained workers; fewer than four for lay or part-time workers.

2. Quick response time between report and first client contact: One-day response in emergencies, within a few days for all other reports.

3. Follow-up with the reporting source to gather information and to discuss client progress: Seen as necessary to reduce duplication of effort and to build program trust.

4. Frequent client contact: At least once a week in early stages, once or twice a month after the case had stabilized.

5. Sufficient time in treatment: Defined as between 6 months and 2 years. Termination linked to specific criteria tied to treatment goals, with post-discharge referral occurring on an as-needed basis.

6. Multidisciplinary team (MDT) reviews: Complex cases should be staffed with MDT intake; all cases should be reviewed at some point in the treatment process. Each staff member should present a minimum of one case for MDT review every 6 months for the case manager's own professional development.

7. Outside consultants should be used for the more serious/complex cases.

SOURCE: Berkeley Planning Associates, 1977, pp. 126-129.

A HOLISTIC VIEW OF QUALITY TASK PERFORMANCE

Advanced practice includes an integrated performance as well as accomplishment of task-centered activities. Three global factors characterize exemplary practice regardless of task focus: virtuosity, a knowledge-based practice, and degree of professional autonomy.

Case management *virtuosity* refers to the fact that advanced practice should be understood as an entirety and not merely as completion of discrete tasks. This is important because field-based research (Grusky, 1990) shows that many case managers are not proficient in all functions.

Instead, they limit their activities to a handful of preferred interventions such as intake, monitoring, crisis management, and supportive counseling, while neglecting certain "midstream" activities such as teaching social and life skills or providing linkage, referral, and advocacy. Because workers spend as much as two-thirds of their time in indirect services (Wright, Skelbar, & Heiman, 1987), competency in case load management also indicates virtuosity.

Advanced practice is also *knowledge-based* and displays competency in three related domains: (a) knowledge of the biopsychosocial features of the target population, (b) in-depth familiarity with the community's formal and informal service sectors (e.g., regulations, admission criteria, funding and reimbursement issues, natural gatekeepers, community influentials), and (c) an associated repertoire of function-related skills (Pittsburgh Program for Affordable Health Care, 1989). In addition, expertise in communication and rapport building, problem solving and conflict resolution, and knowing "when to intervene and when not to may, in some ways define the effectiveness of the case manager" (Bush, 1988, p. 40).

Several authors (O'Connor, 1988; Roberts-DeGennaro, 1987) have characterized advanced practitioners as having an *autonomous work style* that is comfortable in being entrepreneurial and taking risks related to case finding, assessment/evaluation, and multi-service coordination. As Rapp and Poertner (1980) suggest, a major difference between new and traditional forms of case management is that staff are now often expected to assume quasi-administrative responsibility for making case decisions. This is becoming both more commonplace and more difficult in the face of continued fragmentation in the service environment.

PROCESS OF CASE MANAGEMENT

Case management practice is best understood as a phased process with sequential, and often overlapping, functions (Rothman, 1991). Although programs differ in how they implement specific functions (Kurtz, Bagarozzi, & Pollane, 1984) and in their control or access to ancillary services (Korr & Cloninger, 1991), there is consensus about the profession's core elements. Illustrations of these six functions are listed in Table 2.2, which presents a somewhat artificial, linear view of the process for the sake of illustration.

TABLE 2.2 Six Case Management Core Tasks: Suggested Components

Assessment	Service Planning	Implementation
Engagement and outreach to those with limited access to services [Optional]	Ensure client input and feedback	Strengthen/build on client autonomy and capabilities to link clients to resources
Collect information about client's needs and resources	Set long- and short-term goals compatible with client's values and strengths	Contact and broker individually tailored "wrap around" services
Establish baseline status by *in vivo* observation and collateral contact (when appropriate and with permission)	Develop positively stated, achievable, measurable, goals	Provide direct counseling and support to empower clients to participate in services
Conduct formal assessments (e.g., functional or social network assessments)	Consult with multidisciplinary team for input and review	Provide crisis services if needed
Ancillary assessments as needed (e.g., risk and lethality, housing needs)	Establish who (staff, client, other) is responsible for specific functions	
Integrate case management assessment with clinical and testing data	Establish clear success criterion (e.g., what actions or behaviors will occur)	
	Establish time lines for objectives and plan review	
	Establish crisis plan in advance	
	With client's input, provide timely updates based on changes in conditions	

System Coordination/Monitoring	Client Advocacy	Termination
Develop process for joint client and case manager evaluation	*Case Advocacy*	*Case transfer*
	Explain client's perspective to others	Help client assess need for continued services and intensity
Use purchase of services control and authority	"Market" client to program	Provide options for meaningful choice
	Intervene on client's behalf	Schedule transition meetings
Develop interagency agreements, continuity-of-care arrangements	Help client to collect evidence of need and qualify for benefits	
Monitor service provision for appropriateness, intensity, quantity, quality, efficacy	Support attendance at advocacy training	*Termination*
	Encourage clients through role play and support to advocate for themselves	Help client assess options, maximize choices
Develop mechanism to systematically document unmet needs and gaps in services/resources	*Class advocacy*	Allow ventilation of feelings
	Document categorical need	Mutually review and assess progress and goal achievement
Develop mechanisms to monitor outcomes (e.g. quality of life, number of acute/long-term care episodes, client satisfaction)	Participate in needs assessments	Provide follow-up services to clients,
	Staff an advocacy committee or group	
	Identify effective community leaders and resources	
Develop mechanisms to monitor fiscal cost, services rendered; track high service users/missed appointments; other exceptions from expected standards		
Follow-up monitoring		

SOURCES: Adapted from Grisham et al., 1983; Harrod, 1986; Moxley, 1989; Netting, 1992; Rothman, 1992; and Steinberg and Carter, 1983.

ADVANCED CASE MANAGEMENT TASKS
AND PRACTICE CONSIDERATIONS

ASSESSMENT

Both social work (Vigilante & Mailick, 1988) and case management (Lebow & Kane, 1992) have recently emphasized the importance of assessment as a first stage of goal planning and intervention. Comprehensive assessment is the initial step in the service allocation process (Applebaum & Austin, 1990), although Gwyther (1988) suggests that it is a helpful clinical service in and of itself. Although programs may broadly define case management assessment to include a separate screening or preliminary assessment, the related functions of intake, assessment, and goal planning often occur together.

Assessment introduces, engages, and ultimately establishes the relationship between the provider and the client. Its functions include program description and solicitation of the client's opinion of need, and determination of a possible match between the program's services or gatekeeping requirements and the client's or principal caregivers' wants (Lebow & Kane, 1992). Assessments also collect baseline data against which client change is to be measured and develop a framework for later decisions about the service mix and needed benefits.

Prescreening Assessment

In some organizations, case management staff conduct an initial prescreening or intake review that establishes the client's eligibility and appropriateness for service. This brief procedure often uses client self-report (Downing, 1985) or in some cases is accomplished through group orientation (Rothman, 1992).

Prescreening is frequently the least professionalized case management function (Applebaum, 1988a; Berkeley Planning Associates, 1985). However, innovative programs sometimes use recent technology such as computerized screening instruments or mail and telephone surveys to routinize data collection and to predetermine eligibility. Programs that use entry-level staff or even interactive computer software to provide this function may also deploy advanced staff to provide supervision and quality review.

Decision bodies composed of empowered agency representatives, such as state and local Interagency Coordinating Councils (ICCs) that prioritize referrals to children's mental health and early intervention case management services (Stroul & Friedman, 1986), lie at the other end of the human technology spectrum. Good practice associated with these gatekeeping functions includes significant community organization skills and expertise in the art and politics of persuasion.

Assessment

The comprehensive assessment is the vital first step in the case management process. Its timing and location are a professional decision based on an evaluation of the client's needs, stability, and situation (Pittsburgh Program for Affordable Health Care, 1989). Assessment often includes solicitation of client opinion; *in vivo* observation; contact with significant family members, informal caregivers and other providers; review of agency records; and testing (Moxley, 1989). It is a recurring procedure completed early in the initial contact and at intervals to satisfy accountability requirements. Table 2.3 illustrates some of the variations common in case management assessment practices in the fields of aging, mental health, and child health services.

Quality Standards of Practice

The assessment cycle often includes discretionary elements that rely on staff's ability to independently coordinate and manage data, to pace the inquiry and encourage accuracy, and to anticipate client queries. Assessment is a periodic activity typically conducted at several "trigger" points that act as standards for review. These trigger points include: (a) at intake, (b) at admission to or discharge from a more restrictive environment, (c) following marked changes in the client's symptomology, level of functioning and social environment, or at social "transition" periods, (d) at the consumer's and/or caregiver's request, (e) when providers alert staff to changes in the client's program status, and (f) as periodically required by agency policy or public regulation.

The case management interview occurs in an ambient environment. Staff's ability to maintain the client's level of comfort and to sustain what Gwyther (1988) calls the meeting's "amenities" (e.g., attention to confidentiality, privacy, and dignity) is important. Much of the challenge comes from the fact that sometimes the client is not seeking any change and does not want to be "managed." Case managers must also help consumers understand that assessment is conducted to determine service referral and benefits entitlements and is not an automatic guarantee of services or program acceptance. Because people often delay seeking help until they are in crisis, being able to successfully explore client expectations, to engage clients or caregivers, and to coherently interpret the program's agenda are important front-end issues. Staff should be able to discuss

TABLE 2.3 Assessment Factors in Selected Case Management Fields of Service

Field: ELDERLY	*Field:* CHRONIC MAJOR PSYCHIATRIC DISORDER	*Field:* CHILD HEALTH
Subfield: Permanent Frail Elderly		*Subfield:* Spina Bifida
Target Population Criteria: — Abused, neglected — Multiple hospitalizations — Chronic illness — History of mental illness exacerbated by aging — Impaired ADLs, decline likely — Lives alone or primary caretaker ill or unable to provide care	**Target Population Criteria:** Homeless — Recurrent MH hospitalizations — Medication noncompliance — Suicidal risk — Chemical dependency — Needs multiple community-based services — Impaired ADLs — Confused, inappropriate behavior	**Target Population Criteria:** Spina bifida coupled with recurrent hospitalizations for allied congenital anomalies — high-risk infant or prematurity — developmental delay
Assessment: *Demographic* — Identify caregiver, contact, guardian, or who has power of attorney — *Medical/Physical* — Health history — Multiple physicians & treatment plans — Nutritional assessment — Medications & over-the-counter drugs — *Functional items* — Baseline ADLs — Use & effectiveness of devices & medical equipment — *Cognitive/Emotional/Behavioral* — Orientation, judgment — Mental status, depression — Drug/Alcohol abuse — *Social Assessment* — Possible abuse by caregiver or others — Social isolation — *Environment* — assess mobility, safety hazards — Access to pharmacies, grocery stores, transportation, programming —	**Assessment:** *Demographic* — Contact persons — Previous hospitalizations — Involvement & satisfaction with providers — Involvement with law — History of violence — *Medical/Physical* — Recent medical exam — Insurance coverage — Psychotropics, side-effects — Medication noncompliance, failure to keep appointments — *Functional items* — Ability to conduct ADLs — *Cognitive/Emotional/Behavioral* — Illness denial — Chemical dependency — Self-esteem — Suicidality — Danger to self & others — *Social Assessment* — Adequacy of social skills — Social isolation — Homelessness — *Environment* — Housing & neighborhood safety — Adequate housing or supervision	**Assessment:** *Demographic* — Family support persons — Hospital history & clinic attendance — *Medical/Physical* — Urological tests — Bowel function — Skin integrity — Neurologic testing — Proneness to osteoporosis — *Functional Status* — Access to early intervention, rehabilitation, & vocational training — Impact of aging on mobility — *Cognitive/Emotional/Behavioral* — Developmental & social delays — Ability to use language & to reason — Self-esteem and self-perception — Social & sexual issues, especially at adolescence — *Social Assessment* — Family & sibling reactions — Parent work schedules — Caregiver arrangements —Child's school

Financial — Knowledge of programs & entitlements — Family willingness to contribute —Adequacy of health insurance —*Support Systems* — Caregiver respite — Ratio informal to formal supports — *Possible Client Goals* — Prevent nursing home placement — Maximize pain — *Discharge Potential* —Service continued until nursing home placement or death

if in group setting — Proximity to transportation & services — *Financial* — Eligibility for SSI, other entitlements — Interest in vocational rehabilitation — *Legal* — Involuntary or outpatient commitment —Need for guardianship — *Support System* — Family understanding of illness — *Possible Client Goals* —Independence of living — Increased understanding of illness & symptom control — *Discharge Potential* —Open-ended, intermittent –

& neighborhood friendships — Parental marital difficulties — Parental education & age — *Environment* — Necessity for modification of home environment — Adequacy of educational services — Parent awareness of education handicapped rights — *Financial* — Family resources — Adequacy of health coverage — Application for SSDI — Long-term financial planning — *Support System* — Family coping patterns — *Possible Client Goals* — Adequate physical rehabilitation — Psychological support services — *Discharge Potential* — Ongoing need for service coordination

SOURCE: Adapted from Pittsburgh Program for Affordable Health Care, 1989.

their program's philosophy and any policies, procedures, or other restrictions that may interfere with the worker's ability to follow through. Without these explanations, clients may feel victimized, angry, or self-defeated, or think they are being given a bureaucratic runaround (Krieger & Robbins, 1985).

Good process also requires special alertness to indicators of client fatigue and disengagement-engagement. Because most assessments are structured as open-ended interviews, staff's ability to use vernacular, to reframe, and to know when to probe are important (Abrahams & Lamb, 1988).

Assessment is a vital means of engaging clients and helping them to anticipate future role sharing and next steps. This process can be enhanced by such behaviors as providing anticipatory explanations and client-friendly written materials while offering assurances of the worker's continuing active intervention. The ability to engage the more difficult-to-reach clients, to conduct on-site assessments under demanding circumstances, and to selectively provide for immediate gratification of the client's personal needs before the assessment and service planning processes are completed are advanced capabilities.

Comprehensive and supplementary assessments should be tailored to capture the dimensions of the individual's presenting problems and also to gather data related to the program's mission. Comprehensive assessment is multidimensional and involves a "sharpening of problem identification" (Rothman, 1991, p. 522) to know which informal and formal resources should be accessed on the client's behalf. Well-done assessments incorporate a case management history that clarifies the client's physical and mental status, involvement with social support systems and level of social well being, degree of family involvement/cooperation, current socioeconomic or employment status/history, recent living arrangements, and immediate and past financial situation and participation in entitlement programs (Clarke & Anderson, 1988).

Good assessment includes determining which of the resources initially identified are accessible, available, and acceptable to the client (Moxley, 1989) and whether existing caregiving arrangements are viable or are overly stretched. Staff may also need special skills in engaging and earning the trust of informal and "natural" helpers, especially when cultural or religious value systems differ or when staff try to meet needs that the informal sector does not think are necessary (Hoeman & Winters, 1988). Staff should also be careful not to assume that what the caregiving network is providing is sufficient and that expensive, formal services can be bypassed for the sake of cost containment (Chatman & Turner-Friley, 1988).

Social network assessments are often needed to round out the picture. Typically these assessments incorporate information about the number and mix of network resources, what services the network is already providing, and the "size" of the caregiver's responsibility (e.g., the client's need for extensive personal care or constant supervision). Other probes should help determine the network's effective coping strategies, identify precipitants to the breakdown of network routines, explore caregiver capacity (e.g., age, health, income, employment status, other family obligations), and estimate the client's and caregiver's long-range welfare (Seccombe, Ryan, & Austin, 1987).

Recent interventions with deinstitutionalized (Hogarty, 1979) and with minority, underserved populations (Greene & Monahan, 1984) have also underscored the importance of taking a good medical history and of incorporating *biomedical assessment* (Honig, Tan, Weenick, Pop, & Philipsen, 1991). Other recommended supplementary assessments include *environmental assessment* or *in sito* observation of client functioning; *"risk" assessment* (e.g., risk of lethality, violence, precipitants to institutionalization), *caregiver "burden"* (Etten & Kosberg, 1989; Kosberg & Cairl, 1986; Lefley, 1989), *housing need* (Ridgway et al., 1986), *use of drugs and alcohol* (National Association of Counties, 1989), *mental status* (American Psychiatric Association, 1987) and *history of sexual or physical abuse or domestic violence* (Rose, 1991). Staff's clinical sophistication (Kanter, 1985d), accumulated experience, and familiarity with community resources and contact persons, especially those providing anticipated allied services to the target population, also help determine the extensiveness and conduct of the assessment (Ryndes, 1989).

Measurement of the client's *level of functioning* as part of the assessment package to individualize planning and to manage costs is a recent innovation (Borenstein, 1990; Goldstein, Bassuk, Holland, & Zimmer, 1988). Since persons with similar diagnoses may have very different abilities, functional assessment is becoming increasingly popular as a targeting strategy—a means of identifying those in likely catastrophic circumstances in order to monitor them and to free up service dollars for the most in need. This should be balanced with a client-centered focus: "While a functional assessment may suggest problem areas to explore with the client, the level of functioning alone does not indicate the client's unique difficulties, nor does it reflect the client's perspective about the difficulties" (Cohen & Nemec, 1988, p. 11).

Standards of the Written Assessment

Quality assessments are complete and timely, in keeping with the client's needs, and reflect adherence to standards of documentation (Harkness & Mulinski, 1988). The assessment should include: (a) an exploration of the person's living, working, and social environments; (b) a goal statement for each environment where there is dissatisfaction and recognition of a problem; and (c) an assessment of a person's skills, strengths, resources, and needs in relation to each goal. The assessment should also try to specify under which conditions the identified area has either been successfully addressed by the client or has proved to be troublesome. Well-done assessments also try to describe the individual's current and previous "highest level of functioning" (Levine and Fleming, 1985) as well as to make predictions for the near future. Table 2.4 indicates several quality criteria for model case management program assessment.

SERVICE PLANNING

Service planning is widely recognized as the crux of case management effort; it involves tailoring a package of programs and services that reflects the client's identified needs, preferences and strengths. Although resource management and fiduciary know-how are signatures of a more advanced practice, the key to service planning with the more difficult-to-reach and highly needy consumers is the establishment of the case management relationship (see Table 2.5). Research has clearly shown that involvement in service plan development is closely related to successful service goal achievement (Wasylenki, Goering, Lancee, Ballantyne, & Farkas, 1985). A client's experiencing of problems (Cohen & Nemec, 1988), especially at critical transition stages, may facilitate client acceptance of services. Specialized expertise may also be needed to engage "involuntary" clients, those who are under court commitment or other legal mandate to participate in the case management process (Weick & Pope, 1988).

Staff should pace service planning discussions so consumers feel comfortable in disclosing information. In some programs, the plan may be delayed for a month or longer while relationships are established. Plans, which can address environmental and/or more psychologically supportive issues, should be incrementally developed. A working rule of thumb is that it is less threatening to clients to begin with a focus on concrete needs. Early opportunities should also be created to allow the individual to express his or her feelings about dependency and independence and to react to the immediate and long-range implications of

TABLE 2.4 Quality Standards of Case Management Assessment

1. A comprehensive assessment is performed and documented on every client entering the case management system.

2. A determination will be made of the need for any medical, psychiatric, or other specialized assessment. If this need exists, is there recent information (e.g., within the past 3-6 months)? In the absence of current data or depending on the stability of the client, refer the client to an appropriate provider for assessment.

3. Assessments will be done within several working days of referral, depending on the client's situation and the program's internal policies.

4. Assessments should incorporate an evaluation of the client's home/living situation.

5. Assessments should be provided by an interdisciplinary team.

6. Authorization must be obtained from the client, or family if appropriate, to secure services on the client's behalf.

7. A signed authorization for release of records must be obtained.

SOURCE: Pittsburgh Program for Affordable Health Care, 1989.

service acceptance, especially if service entry requires acceptance of a "most impaired" label. Possible changes in the service relationship's intensity should also be discussed early, so clients can be helped to understand that staff availability is not always synonymous with an absence of limits. Finally, the planning process should be treated as an opportunity to develop problem-solving skills as well as a vehicle for growth. To this end, the more sophisticated service plans are those that incorporate steps to help develop the client's capacity to self-manage and to grow (Kane, 1988b).

Higher-level service planning is accomplished when a more comprehensive and intimate knowledge of the community's resources is brought to the planning process. Staff should know what is available, what programs cost, how programs differ in quality, and the proposed service package's expected immediate and long-range expenses. Most case managers have multiple ways of collecting this information, including informal networking and personal and office resource files (Rothman, 1991). Client and caregiver opinion should be solicited to identify resources and to elicit consumer-oriented information about a program's ambience and services. Such input is essential if the plan is to address what resources and supports will be acceptable to the client or what the caregiver requires for maintenance. This approach is congruous with the view of the case manager as a consultant rather than a knowledge expert (Bernheim, 1989; Friesen et al., 1990; Hatfield & Lefley, 1987; Kanter, 1985c; Silva, 1990).

TABLE 2.5 10 Ways to Encourage Client Involvement in the Service Plan

---

1. Pay attention to the relationship and the process of relationship building.

   Pace the relationship; introduce the service plan only after there has been psychological engagement.

2. Involve the client from the beginning.

   Solicit the client's wishes; educate clients about their rights as consumers.

3. Pace the development of the service plan.

   Take the time to learn about client preferences and change goals as well as gaps in needs and resources.

4. Plan in parts.

   Develop the plan in increments, using several sessions as needed.

   Don't overwhelm the client by promising too much or asking for too much change.

5. Emphasize client strengths rather than problems.

   Help the client own the plan by emphasizing what the client can do, rather than what he or she is unable to accomplish.

6. The plan should reflect the person, not just the disability.

   The plan must be holistic and community oriented, not just disability-specific.

7. The plan must be individualized.

   Have the client specify what he/she wants to achieve and how this fits into long-term goals.

8. The plan must be client-centered.

   Do not confuse agency-established criteria with what the client actually wants and needs.

9. Anticipate the possibility of failure.

   Don't give up if objectives aren't met. Use failure as an opportunity to assess the objective as stated. Is the objective realistic, valued, appropriate? What have you learned from the experience?

   Reinforce the client's ability to change and your willingness to help.

10. Remember: There is no such thing as the one ideal treatment.

Good practice also dictates that the plan be fiscally accountable and that some mechanism for tracking costs of service be developed. Good planning is prudent, and some programs "cap" community-based services at the cost of equivalent institutional care. Fiduciary responsibility also means that case managers should be vigilant in trying to reduce monies spent on unnecessary or ineffective care.

Quality Standards of Practice

Exemplary plans are dynamic and should be modified to reflect alterations in the client's wishes and status or in the environment's resource capacities (Bachrach, 1991). Plans should also be client-driven to the extent possible. Therefore, if a client rejects a problem area as unacceptable, exploration in that direction should be discontinued for a time (Cohen et al., 1988b). Best practice also dictates that responsible case managers will attend to the "law of diminishing returns." That is, planning tries to match the intensity of interpersonal and resource investment to the expectation of desired outcome. Although the strengths perspective is an effective strategy for engaging clients, many field workers also stress "the importance of a realistic outlook" (Rothman, 1991, p. 524), which balances open-ended "hope, rational optimism, and empowerment" (Harding, 1990) with the recognition that sometimes community maintenance to stabilize the individual is a primary goal.

A criterion of good practice is that the plan demonstrates a relationship to the wants, needs, strengths and limitations documented in the assessment. Research from the National Long Term Care Channeling Demonstration (Schneider, 1988) provides distressing evidence that as much as 20 to 30 percent of the problems identified in the assessment are later ignored in the plan. This may be due to staff's unilateral dismissal of the validity of client perceptions, the assessment instrument's utility, the provider's ability to respond, or a feeling that some issues are the family's rather than the program's responsibility.

Two keys to good planning are continuity of care and comprehensive services. Properly continuous plans provide as-needed and/or long-term access to services that are client-friendly as well as geographically accessible and affordable. This can be difficult in resource-poor environments where staff are confronted with relatively few service or program options. In these situations, staff may elect to "stretch" their repertoire of functions so as to provide the individual with needed support or types of brief counseling in lieu of accessing traditional programs. Staff may also use aggressive educational tactics to advocate with existing providers or with other "generic" community resources to modify schedules, entry requirements, or other program or structural barriers that interfere with access. On-site consultation by the case manager and linking more limited programs to other resources (e.g., arranging for on-site service delivery by allied consultants and specialists) are alternative ways to bolster a sketchy resource infrastructure.

A second expectation is that planning will address the consumer's transitional needs as well as the most immediate service requirements. Transition planning is frequently difficult, especially when referrals involve discontinuous services and specialized, often conflicting, eligibility requirements. Case manager interventions to ease the transition

between programs include arranging for joint program discussions with
sufficient lead time to develop an orderly transfer, and helping clients
or families to collect and appropriately present the records and information they will need to successfully demonstrate eligibility for next-
stage services. Transition planning may also involve education and role
rehearsal with the consumer or family member to learn the new
program's way of doing things, arranging for pre-site and trial visits, and
providing sufficient lead time for the client to reflect on the perceived
impact of the program change on his or her self-image and the conduct of
everyday, taken-for-granted personal and/or family routines.

"Comprehensive" services are the "viable substitutes" (Bachrach,
1986, p. 172) for the needs package associated with the tenets of the
National Institutes of Mental Health's Community Support Programming: They provide access to housing, treatment, crisis intervention,
leisure, recreation, and social supports (Tessler, Bernstein, Rosen, &
Goldman, 1982). This can require unusual persistence, extended outreach, community education, or recruitment of case management "extenders" as adjunct helpers with the activities of everyday life.

Process elements are important in service planning, and quality plans
reflect negotiated agreements between case managers, clients and family members, and the other professionals represented on the service
planning team. As the plan's guardian, the case manager is responsible
for advocating for the consumer and for ensuring parity among the
players in the decision-making process. This means that service planning should be consumer-centered rather than program-driven and
reflect needs-based decision making.

Client self-determination is a tenet of good service planning. However, case managers working with seriously impaired populations may
need to make difficult choices about a client's ability to develop his or
her own plan versus assertively recommending specific plan options.
In general, the principle of extending self-determination "to the greatest
extent possible" should be followed, with the client being provided with
the most complete information about alternatives and the implications
of choice. When the client's impairment places the individual at serious
risk, the case manager should seek the assistance of either a family
member or guardian and should work jointly with them to develop a
plan of service. At the same time, the case manager should continue to
assess changes in the client's ability to resume more complete participation in the case management process and should attempt to structure
experiences that reinforce both the client's and the caregiver's capacity
to self-manage while signaling the case manager's willingness to remain in partnership and to be an ongoing resource.

The best service plans incorporate steps that help develop a client's capacity to self-manage and to grow. It has been suggested that the four guiding principles of plan development include helping each client: (a) move from a position of dependence toward a position of independence, (b) move from having little control toward gaining increasingly more control over one's life and environment, (c) move from negatively valued behaviors to more positively valued behaviors, and (d) move from simple to more difficult behaviors that permit the individual to adapt and cope with increasingly more complex situations (Texas Department of Mental Health and Mental Retardation, 1985).

To ensure that service plans address the client's perspective, case managers should inform consumers or their caregivers of their rights to "fair hearings" and any existing legal right to request additional consultation or to refuse services without jeopardizing access to other programming or entitlements (e.g., those protected by P.L. 99-142, the Education of All Handicapped Children Act). Consumer and family participation in the planning process are discussed in more detail in Chapter 3.

Finally, expert case managers should be proficient in conflict mediation so that holistic and reasonable plans can be developed with multidisciplinary as well as consumer input. Flexibility and a sense of humor can be helpful (Zipper et al., 1991), and process monitoring to ensure that plans are not superficial but reflect real consensus is important. Symptoms of process breakdown include the development of plans that satisfy no one but are agreed to in order to present a "united front" to clients or caregivers. They may also result from a "conspiracy of silence" on the questionable grounds that it is better not to confuse consumers with declarations of knowledge insufficiency (Sands, Stafford, & McClelland, 1990). When these are persistent features of the service-planning environment, requests for outside consultation or for program review are appropriate.

At the highest level of expertise, Kane (1988b) and Schneider (1988) have suggested that master practitioners have a mandate to develop rationalized *decision trees*—procedures that indicate which case management responses are optimal in specific, recurring situations. Some progress toward *criteria mapping*—establishing standards of appropriate care—already exists in medical case management programs (Henderson & Collard, 1988). On a more immediate basis, service plans should be audited with reference to standards of professional practice related to the client's diagnosis; social, physical, and environmental statuses; and the case manager's demonstrated knowledge of the service system (Applebaum & Austin, 1990). Highly skilled case managers can help their programs to establish program- and population-specific quality review standards.

Standards of the Written Plan

Baseline standards writing requires that service plans incorporate at least five elements. There must be (a) prioritized, long-range goals initially identified in the assessment; (b) at least one operationalized, short-term objective linked to each goal that is to be immediately addressed; (c) specification of action steps or the planned intervention; (d) assignment of individual responsibility for goal accomplishment; and (e) a time frame for completion and/or review. These are frequently grouped in the document according to the functional domains of life. (See Table 2.6.)

A bedrock criterion is that the goals reflect the client's priorities. Although programs differ in their attention to long-range goals and some authors (Steinberg & Carter, 1983) do not believe that goal development affects a program's outcomes, goal writing can hone professional self-awareness. Goals should meet the criteria of being manageable, current, neutral, and clear (Cohen et al., 1988b). Modrcin and Chamberlain (1985) have also suggested that a goal's reality focus is less important that its affirmation of the client's potential for personal growth and change.

Although long-range goals are not directly measured, they generate specific measurable statements, called *objectives*, which are short-term goals articulating the client's immediate priorities. These narrower objectives are ultimately used to rate client progress. Standards of writing expect that short-term goals will be positively phrased and meet the criteria of being observable, outcome-oriented, desired by the client, and realistic (Cohen et al., 1988b; Hodge, 1990). Because goals can easily proliferate, practice wisdom recommends initial selection of the goals most highly desired by the client or that are easily achieved, highly urgent, or positively supported by significant others. More sophisticated plans may also document issues that were mentioned but are not being immediately addressed, and the reasons for putting these on inactive status. This provides a "tickler file" for future reference.

The plan's immediate purpose is to specify what the client wants and needs from a service provider or from environmental resources. Depending on the circumstances, case managers, caregivers and other family members can contribute alternative, attractive strategies for goal attainment; however, the ultimate choice is the client's. Input from these supportive individuals should also be documented, along with the case manager's optional comments.

Plans should specify the service arrangements and identify preferred providers, such as programs and/or informal helpers. What will be provided is typically written as units or hours of service for formal providers, or frequency of contact for informal agents. Assignment of responsibility incorporates the identification of agents who will assist in planning, linking, or providing direct service. The case manager will often be this agent, although the most skilled practice involves "doing with, not for." At its ultimate, the plan may identify capacity-building goals and steps the case manager and consumer will take to increase the client's own case management. Quality standards also require that persons identified as ancillary helpers be willing and able to help, and be preapproved-approved by the client.

Time lines are important as benchmarks for testing the plan's utility and sufficiency. Quality data include the projected date of referral, start of service provision, and projected date of goal achievement or date of goal review. In general, it is better to select a longer time line than risk failure because of insufficient time. Additional standards of documentation include: assurances that the plans meet applicable accreditation, certification, and licensure standards and are consistent with the program's mission; that they are a separate component of a unified record; and that they are written in client-friendly language.

SERVICE PLAN IMPLEMENTATION:
REFERRAL, LINKAGE, BROKERING

Implementation incorporates several closely related functions: referral, linkage, and brokering (See Project WrapAround, Table 2.7). Front-end negotiations can include contacting formal and informal providers to arrange for services and contracting for individualized services or negotiating for cost effectiveness. In some programs, case managers are accountable for demonstrating that they have balanced client need with being "prudent buyers" of service (Humphreys et al., 1988, p. 158).

K. Kaplan (1992, p. 92) makes the point that "linking" competencies may also involve "unlinking" skills to "wean" a client from the use of a resource in order to avoid prolonged dependence. Exemplary practices of linking include: assisting the important persons in the client's life to be unintrusively helpful in supporting the recommended plan of action; providing problem solving to agencies to individualize programming to better meet the client's need; and preparing the client through anticipatory discussion and role play to maximize implementation of the plan's prescriptive recommendations (Stein & Test, 1980). In-depth knowledge of the client's current level of functioning, the client's attitude toward change, and the availability and demand for program resources are co-determinants of decisions to unlink.

TABLE 2.6 Five Quality Standards for Service Plan Development

1. *Service planning is a logical process.*
   It must be demonstrably linked to the service assessment.

   It must be linked to the recommended interventions.

   It must be linked to the case management agency is mission.
2. *Service planning starts with an initial set of long- and short-term goals.*
   Long-term goals reflect what the client wants his or her life to be.

   Long- and short-term goals should reflect a client's priorities.

   The case manager should help the planning team to understand what these goals represent behaviorally and descriptively to the client.
3. *Short-term goals should be realistic and attainable.*
   The goals should be specified so they are understandable, with necessary steps formulated clearly in advance.

   Goals should have a high probability of being achieved; otherwise they should not be implemented.

   Goals should be attainable. If they involve other people's time and energies, the case manager should verify that others are willing to do what required.

   Goals should be measurable. Specify exactly what will take place, what is to be accomplished.

   Goals should be capable of being observed.

   Intermediary steps should be specified, so that incremental achievements can be noted and celebrated.

   It is better to err on the side of client optimism to reinforce a "can do" attitude. If the immediate goal is not accomplished, the client's willingness to take chances can be affirmed.
4. *Standards of goal documentation.*
   Only one goal at a time should be considered.

   The goal should be stated in positive terms: what the client is expected to do, rather than to stop doing.

   The goal statement must be constructed properly and contain an action verb, a single key result or behavioral and measurable standard, and a target date.

   Adjectives and adverbs will be avoided.
5. *Standards of the service plan.*
   The service plan will be completed in timely fashion.

   It will be appropriate.

   It will be thorough (e.g., identify desired goals, action steps and accountabilities).

   It will identify specific interventions or steps intended to accomplish the short-range goals.

   It will demonstrate the client's involvement in the plan's development, implementation, and evaluation.

   It will identify which steps are the client's and which are the case manager's responsibility.

   It will identify who else (relative, friend, other program) will play a role in implementation.

   It will specify what is expected to happen.

TABLE 2.6 Continued

It will establish criteria and a time line for review.

Updates will be timely and based on changes in the client's condition or need.

The client will be involved in the update.

Input from other service providers and the client's social network will be solicited when appropriate.

Activities of service arrangement include brief telephone referral, letter writing, case record sharing, attending conferences, and pretrial site visiting. Allied skills include persuasion, friendly advice, escort, interpretation, and coaching. "Marketing" the client so that the receiving program is encouraged to view the individual as a desirable service candidate also involves taking the time to learn about a program's style and its stated and implicit admission criteria (Cohen et al., 1988a; Perlman, Melnick, & Kentera, 1985).

Although these brokering activities have been described as among the most rewarding and important to professional identity (Caragonne, 1980), preliminary research indicates that relatively little time and priority are attached to these tasks (Fisher, Landis, & Clark, 1988; Grusky, 1990; Intagliata & Baker, 1983). This has been the source of considerable academic commentary. There is agreement that more data are needed on how everyday practice is affected by staff's learning curve, staff's ability to manage workload and crises, and the availability of resources.

A major determinant of linkage and brokering is whether the intended intervention is directed toward the informal (e.g., family), the "generic" (e.g., churches or voluntary associations) or the "formal" (e.g., designated helping agency) sector. A growing literature supports the importance of integrating the client's informal supports into the case management plan of action (Collins & Pancoast, 1976; Kurtz, Mann, & Chambon, 1988; Maguire, 1991). Social supports are increasingly recognized as *gatekeepers* to case management services (Emlet & Hall, 1991; Intagliata, Willer, & Egri, 1988; Kanter 1985b, 1985c; Warren, Dunn, & Jackson-Clark, 1991), as *co-interventionists* (Bond, Mcdonel, Miller, & Pensec, 1991; Cornish & Nelson, 1991; Parks & Pilisuk, 1984), as the client's *advocates* (Lamb & Oliphant, 1979), and as influential persons in planning *follow-through* (Grella & Grusky, 1989).

Case managers are often mandated by the program to maximize the use of informal community resources to normalize the client's environment and to control costs. These involve different sets of skills and

TABLE 2.7 The Alaska Youth Initiative: Individualized Service Planning to Avoid
Out-of-State Placement (Case Management in Mental Health)

The Alaska Youth Initiative (AYI) represents an ongoing statewide attempt at coordinated case management services. AYI was initiated in 1987 as a joint endeavor by the Alaska Department of Education, the Division of Family and Youth Services, and the Division of Mental Health and Developmental Disabilities to focus on 34 children who were placed out of state. It was funded in part by each agency. Based on Kaleidoscope, an urban model, and the national CASSP (Child and Adolescent Service System Program), AYI service principles include unconditional care, the least restrictive environment, child- and family-centered care, flexible care, flexible funding, and interagency care.

The agencies initially pooled $1.8 million dollars formerly spent on 28 children and brought them back home for treatment. These flexible dollars could be used to buy "whatever it takes." The major agencies provide assessments for each child and develop individualized plans that aim for normalization and economic feasibility. Services continue as long as there is a need.

AYI children are served in their families and in regular classrooms before they are placed in more restrictive programs. Sometimes individualized service models have to be created. For example, a small rural Alaskan village may not have a day treatment program, so a flexible school program will be developed using the school's current resources and supplementing as necessary. Family assistance coordinators (case managers) have the authority to use flexible dollars. The money for purchasing needed services follows the child and is available to serve the child regardless of the program the child is in.

AYI has developed two procedures to facilitate sustained interagency involvement in the plan. One is that no expenditure can be made without the signature of two team members; the other is the Proactive Child Tracking System (PCTS). It consists of weekly subjective assessments staffed by each adult team member and relevant service providers.

After 2 years of individualized care, almost all the youth served in the program who had been in out-of-state residential placement are being served in less restrictive programs within Alaska.

SOURCE: Burchard and Clarke, 1990.

applications of social-support-system theory (Maguire, 1991). Linking to appropriate network members requires sensitivity in helping clients decide whom to involve in helping and "the ways in which these individuals will be involved," plus creative interventions to strengthen, expand, or to forge new network links (Biegel, Shore, & Gordon, 1984, p. 54). Once this has been established, individual network members must be approached to elicit cooperation and support for the service plans devised.

The organizational context of the case management program is an important determinant of its linking and brokering (Grisham, White, & Miller, 1983; Robinson & Bergman, 1989). Hiring policies will determine whether these functions are provided by well-trained, clinically informed case managers (e.g., Lamb, 1980), by lesser-trained case management aides (Johnson & Rubin, 1983), or by volunteers (Challis & Davies, 1985). The more professionally prepared staff are more likely to exhibit role virtuosity and to provide role coaching, rehearsal and modeling, resource development, and program education and consultation. Knowledge of government funding programs and the more common insurance reimbursement policies is increasingly important in those areas of practice where expensive courses of treatment are anticipated. Expense containment is also at the heart of more sophisticated *financial control* case management programs (Applebaum & Christianson, 1988). In these settings, workers may have responsibility for financial planning and resource allocation and for independent contract of services. These require skills in gatekeeping, rate setting, and fiscal accountability. Advanced interventions may also include limited responsibility for development activities, such as staff education, to upgrade a provider's service capacity. This can also be a way to access less costly programs that ordinarily do not provide the specialized services some clients need.

Quality Standards of Practice

Good practice includes skills in referral and assertive follow-through. Many high-need consumer populations have an abysmal record of not connecting with recommended services. Others may drop out after a brief initial trial or may attend a program but fail to engage in a meaningful way. The plan's failure to address what the consumer was requesting, and rigid or unrealistic programming, can be causal factors in premature termination. To avoid this, good practice requires that staff be skilled in problem identification and issue resolution.

Many staff members and programs develop informal criteria for case-by-case referral. Review of a provider's potential may include assessment of its service reputation, whether its programs are considered accessible and available, analysis of staff language capacities and experience with the particular population, and perceived ability to keep records and to comply with funding standards (Torres, 1988). Consultation with colleagues who are considered to have expert knowledge about local programs and community needs, is a common way of obtaining this information.

Several strategies are available when a primary obstacle to plan implementation is the poorness of fit between needed resources and client preferences. One is to persuade providers of the client's positive attributes to negotiate a trial visit or program modification. If unmet need is widespread, the program administrator can be approached about developing memoranda of understanding or contracts to create special partnerships between the case management program and providers. These arrangements may include clauses guaranteeing program access—a guaranteed number of "slots," priority consideration, or a "no eject" agreement. Best practices suggest that informal linking and fact finding should be initiated while the plan is being developed. This requires in-depth current knowledge of programs and their most preferred clients. It also involves providing assurances and a profile of the individual that closely matches the organization's mission and most desired service recipient (Cohen et al., 1988a), paying attention to what Moxley (1989, p. 99) labels the agency side of the "referral equation." If the client is someone with an extremely poor reputation (e.g., a "revolving door" client), staff should try to negotiate a "no failure" agreement by offering the provider assurances, such as a 24-hour crisis-management plan that either guarantees some form of program respite or the case manager's just-in-time on-site services (Bush et al., 1990; Intagliata, 1982; Stein & Test, 1981).

A program's willingness to accept high-risk clients can be strengthened by the case manager's demonstrated willingness to forge partnerships and to show good faith interest outside immediate service requests. Workers should also be prepared to compromise and to provide conflict resolution. Skills and attitudes associated with effective negotiation include clarity of communication, being positive but honest, and demonstrating a willingness to look at things from the other person's view.

Turn-around of referral and the capacity to deal with emergency situations, are two other signatures of good practice. Rapid turn-around in connecting clients to their referrals indicates staff efficiency. It is also at consistent predictor of client retention. Early research indicates that follow-up should occur within a few days to one week after community-based referral, or within one month if the individual is in an institutional or custodial setting (Berkeley Planning Associates, 1978; Tessler, 1987). At the arrival or trial-visit stage of linking, immediate staff feedback to the program and client to assess mutual perceptions and comfort with the arrangements is recommended. A telephone contact and a file note, followed by some form of written acknowledgment, may meet this requirement. Each program should develop quality standards for feedback time lines.

Having a reserve of emergency resources to meet unexpected situations is another quality indicator. Finding and negotiating fall-back resources requires unusual persistence, creativeness, a willingness to take measured risks, and old-fashioned "horse trading." Anticipatory planning for the possibility of a crisis and the practice of alerting "likely resources to be on standby where particularly unstable client situations exist" (Kaplan, 1992, p. 103) are proactive interventions with high-risk clients.

There is evidence of growing interest in developing empirical standards to measure quality referral choices (Collard et al., 1990). New practices include formal checklist procedures to assess providers, and formal case-record review by outside staff and consultants from allied fields of practice. These are seen as an important protections against potential program abuses created by the zeal for cost containment. Another option is peer review of "single-case studies" to analyze the pathway and successes or failures of trial arrangements.

Finally, fiscal control and other broker models may employ financial expenditure reports normed to a client population as administrative measures of their case manager's performances, starting with the initial service package. This is common in programs that operate under client and/or agency budget caps where case managers are held fiscally accountable for the costs of their clients' service plans. Although such programs are becoming increasingly popular, especially in aging and in private case management, the ethics of this practice have not been resolved.

SYSTEM COORDINATION/MONITORING

System coordination and monitoring are quintessential elements of boundary spanning, yet the literature often gives short shift to these processes or merely assumes it exists (Weil & Karls, 1985). For the sake of distinction, *coordination* refers to the exchange of impressions or information and conjoint planning or review. *Monitoring* includes feedback derived from on-site visitation, review of service-related documentation, and client and caregiver reports.

Coordination and monitoring are continuous feedback processes used to determine whether or not the service plan is effectively meeting the client's needs and to assess if the client's condition warrants plan modification. "To accomplish these goals, the case manager must know the patient, services, and individual providers and must use this information to exert control over systems generally lacking appropriate accountability mechanisms" (Shueman, 1987, p. 315).

Service coordination has been called "boundary work," or intervention at the interface system (Hearn, 1969). Its three functions include: (a) ensuring that the different providers continue to view the client holistically and understand the contribution of their program to the client's overall functioning, (b) reconnecting to community support services in anticipation of discharge from more restrictive treatment settings and vice versa, and (c) making sure all the elements of the service plan have been implemented in timely fashion and that service duplication is avoided.

Service coordination may include informal approaches or formal methods, such as an interagency memorandum of agreement (Levine & Fleming, 1985). The most frequent informal coordinating methods include in-person or telephone contact with providers and review and discussion with the client and/or principal caregivers or other informal supports to verify changes in client status. Although coordination can occur through client conversations, during which time the individual's commitment to programs and services may be weighed and strengthened, most coordination involves formal interaction.

Coordination is typically accomplished through participation at regularly scheduled, interdisciplinary, service planning team meetings. This can take "months to achieve and requires ongoing effort to maintain" (Ridgway et al., 1986, p. 5). Typically, the case manager is responsible for identifying a cohort of professionals to work with a particular client over time or arranges for collaboration within an existing team. A cutting edge practice is the inclusion of advocates or *ombudsmen* (Blazyk, Crawford, & Wimberly, 1987) to be sure that the client perspective is adequately protected. This strategy has been widely disseminated in the children's mental health agenda (Knitzer, 1982; Stroul, 1992b) and in hospital discharge planning (Netting and Williams, 1989).

Monitoring refers to oversight practices: methods designed to judge whether a program is being implemented as designed, is a quality program, and whether it can be made more cost-efficient (Beinecke, 1986). It has been succinctly described as a continuous self-correction mechanism (Moxley, 1989) and as a potentially major force for improving the quality of care (Vourlekis, 1991).

Applebaum & Austin (1990, p. 24) note that responsiveness to changes in a client's needs based upon monitoring "can have a dramatic impact on service costs." As such, it is among the most frequently performed (Kurtz et al., 1984) and often unexpectedly time-consuming aspects of the case manager's work (Fisher et al., 1988). Monitoring frequency varies with the intensity of client needs, the stability of the situation, and the types of providers reviewed (e.g., whether they are more "visible" organizational programs or are private, home-based services, and whether the direct care staff are highly trained or lesser skilled). Activities include collection and review of financial, service and/or outcome records; site visits; and discussions of progress with client, staff, and caregivers. Nonetheless, monitoring is one of the "least well-specified" aspects of case management, with ambiguity existing about how it is actually conducted (Brekke, 1988), how often it should occur, and what type of verifiable information should be required (Vourlekis, 1991).

Preliminary research indicates that staff's ability to coordinate effectively and to monitor is greatly affected by the program's model of case management—whether the case manager works under the umbrella of a financial control model and is given authority to purchase services directly, or whether staff must predominantly rely on negotiation. Findings from the Channeling programs indicate that the financial control programs are better positioned to build in "training, supervisory, and monitoring provisions contained in . . . [their] contracts for leverage to bring about behavior changes" (Applebaum & Christianson, 1988, p. 230).

Monitoring can also be an impetus for program change even without specific organizational controls. Henderson and Collard (1988) suggest that monitoring can improve care by exerting a "sentinel effect"—that programs will voluntarily self-monitor because they know they are being watched. Professional and program reputation, competing job expectations and standards, and ingenuity in motivating others to provide better services are variables in this process.

Quality Standards of Practice

Although the relationship among case manager, client, and provider ought to be determined by service need, there is evidence that case managers are more responsive to certain client populations. The "most preferred" clientele appear to be those who are younger (Baker, Intagliata, & Kirchstein, 1980; Harris & Bergman, 1988b) or those who have less severe or chronic problems (Harris & Bergman, 1988c). Interventions are also more likely to be directed to "squeaky wheels"; individuals who are "demanding" or in crisis, rather than reflecting the degree of disability (Baker et al., 1980). Case managers also report greater success in forming partnerships when services are supplied by their own agency (Rapp & Poertner, 1980). Yet monitoring of service patterns and practices should ask if recipients are being treated equally.

Service coordination requires a delicate balance between satisfying the provider's autonomy and the need to encourage conjoint effort. (See Table 2.8.) Netting et al. (1990) distinguish between multiprogram cooperation and coordination. *Cooperation* occurs when two or more programs work toward similar, nonconflicting goals, sharing information but working independently. A higher level of practice involves *coordination*, when several programs work together to mesh efforts and to avoid duplication. Expert interventions include effective strategic planning and team building processes associated with coordinating the delivery of

TABLE 2.8 Steps to Ensure Quality Services Coordination

1. *Build in sufficient lead time.*
   Establish a joint task force to identify problems in coordination and the most common, shared issues.

   Conduct needs assessment to determine the scope of need.

   Explore solutions and their costs.

   Allow staff to voice concern about any perceived loss of professional control and barriers to sharing.

   Plan what is needed.

2. *Educate program staff about advanced case management.*
   Define the case manager's role and the role of the case management agency.

   Identify what case management can do to facilitate the process or to assist staff.

   Explain the lines of accountability.

3. *Develop formal working agreements that describe:*
   Who is the joint client.

   What are the service elements.

   Who can initiate the coordinating process.

   Under what conditions program functions will be performed, either jointly or separately.

   Who is responsible for seeing that records can be physically shared (e.g., who is responsible for ordering, copying, and coordinating the record exchanges).

   Where the elements of the case management record will be kept and what components can be shared.

   Who can institute closure of the arrangement.

4. *Develop advanced methods of coordinating services.*
   Cross train to develop a common knowledge base.

   Develop methods for joint review and decision making.

   Develop procedures for conflict resolution.

   Explore use of shared forms (e.g., joint referral form for a "single point of contact" inquiry no matter where the client enters the system).

   Explore joint information system, share computerized tracking.

SOURCES: Adapted from Netting and Williams, 1989; Netting et al., 1990; Moxley, 1989; Rapp, 1984; Wimberley and Blazyk, 1989.

independent programs that are accountable to different constituencies and that may have overlapping but nonidentical missions.

Role sharing and responsibility trading among case managers with a joint clientele are important elements of coordination. Conjoint planning may be used as a means to reduce duplication of effort and to limit the recipients' need to deal with multiple agents.

Coordination requires skills in time and records management, information gathering, personal networking, problem analysis and problem solving, group facilitation, decision making, and advocacy (Weil, Zipper, & Dedmon, 1992). Research indicates that although informal practices such as establishing personal networks of service contacts are important first steps, they cannot guarantee the client's long-term interest, especially if there is substantial staff turnover.

Formal agreements between providers support practice and work best when they are tailored to each program's mission, internal staffing patterns, and information system needs. Such contracts enhance a program's confidence in referrals, encourage information sharing, and help to build supportive relationships between parties. They also help alleviate conflict by spelling out the limits of staff's authority and describing the agreed-to steps for conflict resolution.

Monitoring is closely allied to coordination but involves different functional activities (See Table 2.9). The advantages of *qualitative* monitoring, that relies on staff judgment, and the more *quantitative* approaches that use standardized scales or performance-based criteria, continue to be debated. In either case, there is consensus that *some* aspect of the care process ought to be monitored to protect a service population that is often increasingly vulnerable "to fraud, abuse, and substandard treatment" (Applebaum & Christianson, 1988, p. 227).

Because of their "soft" nature, qualitative approaches frequently employ redundant mechanisms to check that services are being received and are of the nature promised (See Table 2.10). Mechanisms include periodically scheduled meetings between providers and case managers for routine exchange of opinions and information about the consumer's status, planned but informal performance reviews of the provider at the time of annual renewal of contract, and negotiated task sharing between case managers and the most trusted program staff working in allied settings (Ridgway et al., 1986). When given authority, the case management program staff may request that critical incident reports citing use of restraint or accident be reviewed to check that the service provider is "doing no harm" to clients in its care. On-site observation through home and program visits can also be used to confirm that claimed services or changes in client status are actually present (Torres, 1988).

Consumer contact and satisfaction reports are important for monitoring. Clients should be asked, either by phone or in person, if key elements of a plan were fulfilled. Did they feel that the services received were of good, average, or of poor quality? Do they feel their needs are being met, and do they see the service providers as competent and sensitive (Collard et al., 1990; Parker & Secord, 1988a)?

The quality of the case management relationship, the client's ability to report, and vulnerability to program abuse are important factors in

TABLE 2.9 Nine Examples of Quality Monitoring Practice

1. *The individual efforts of the case manager are paramount.*
   Be persistent, willing to cross-check and triangulate data, and to spend time developing a relationship in which information is freely exchanged.

2. *Develop and implement a monitoring schedule.*
   Use monitoring retrospectively (Has what was planned, happened?) and to project (Should the plan be changed?).

   Monitor on a planned schedule and develop a plan for critical incident reports.

   Include regularly scheduled provider performance appraisal.

3. *Supplement with unscheduled and as needed oversight.*
   Monitor services with a poorer or an unknown reputation more intensively.

   Monitor sites to confirm that services are actually being delivered.

   Monitor client behavior to see if program objectives have been transferred to everyday life.

4. *Use aggregate and computer generated reports.*
   Exceptionality reports (e.g. large numbers of no-show or canceled appointments, a large number of days without service, outdated service plan review dates), targeted high-user reports, and fiscal reports (expenses-to-date summaries, targeted higher-than-normal monthly expenses) help identify clients where special monitoring may be indicated.

   Know and become comfortable with using these mechanisms; help develop report mechanisms that will be helpful to you.

5. *Assist clients and caregivers to become knowledgeable consumers.*
   Provide access to literature and to other resources that enable the individual to become better informed about rights, standards of practice, and potential unwanted iatrogenic effects.

6. *Assist clients and caregivers in developing simple, low-effort monitoring systems.*
   Encourage consumers, family members and informal community caregivers to develop and use graphs, charts, and written checklists to account for services provided.

7. *Seek out client and caregiver perception of satisfaction.*
   Develop and implement client-friendly instruments that are suitable to the client's level of comfort, degree of literacy, and attention span.

   Ask:

   Did the client perceive the service as voluntary or was he or she pressured to join?

   Did the program work out as the client anticipated?

   Was the case manager friendly? Did the client feel comfortable in discussing concern?

   Did the case manager make a difference? If so, how?

8. *Administrative support for program monitoring.*
   Document successes, the complexity of monitoring; ask for sufficient time and allocation of resources to conduct this function.

9. *Monitor all services, whether or not you can directly influence change.*
   Where there is purchase of service authority, implement monitoring and encourage needed changes to ensure provider compliance.

   Continue to provide systematic input to the private sector and to generic community services about unresolved issues.

TABLE 2.10 Monitoring in Practice: The Ohio Quality Assurance Project (Case Management in Aging)

Ohio's community-based program for the elderly, PASSPORT, used team case managers to arrange for a variety of home-based care services. Most of these were personal-care activities that were largely unregulated and provided by homemakers and home health aides who were less experienced and less than professionally trained.

The Ohio Quality Assurance Project, a joint venture of the Scripps Gerontology Center of Miami University and Ohio's Department of Aging, was funded, in part, to design strategies to monitor the quality of service provision. Staff activities included direct contact with home care clients to monitor service provision. This included monitoring visits to observe and document directly the client's condition and adherence to the service plan and to assess service quality.

Case managers were also responsible for reviewing the client service progress report prepared by supervisors in provider agencies. Monitoring included review of forms that summarized the client's functional status, adherence to the care plan by workers, and client and family perceptions of service.

Client feedback was another component of monitoring. A consumer checklist and other client education activities were implemented to encourage good feedback. A home-care clients' bill of rights and responsibilities was also provided to help consumers to understand what providers were expected to do.

On the agency front, a provider feedback log was also developed to record clients' positive and negative feedback. This was designed to give providers information about the quality of their in-home services.

Finally, case managers assisted in reinforcing quality by identifying exceptional care and initiating letters of commendation. This was seen as a means of helping provider agencies to reduce turnover by recognizing outstanding contributions of their service personnel.

SOURCE: Atchley, 1989.

interpreting the client's answers (Challis & Davies, 1985). Continuity of staff contact (Shaw, Hargreaves, Surber, Luft, & Shadoan, 1990) helps pre-empt client silence resulting from fear of termination or perceived vulnerability (Applebaum, 1988a).

Tracking consumer satisfaction and quality of life is important to ensure service follow through. Consumers who are satisfied with their program are more likely to follow service plans, to remain in service, and to have improved outcomes (Collard et al., 1990). Eliciting this information requires skill in questioning, probing, and soliciting client and family or caregiver feedback; sensitivity to the potential influence of differences in age, race, status, or ethnicity in skewing client responses; and the ability to translate information into a reformulated plan or other action steps.

In contrast to these qualitative procedures, quantitative monitoring uses reported information or surrogate indicators to measure key aspects of care. Data that are naturally generated during service provision are preferred: dates and units of service, number of planned versus crisis interventions, number of no-shows versus kept appointments. These provide baseline data that are likely to be complete and available and that lend themselves to answer such program questions as: What is considered the most appropriate period between program termination and referral elsewhere? Do the programs provide an appropriate mix of spontaneous versus planned appointments?

Formal monitoring can include charts and audits to screen a service record and to assess how well program delivery matches the referral's expectations. Records can be reviewed for content, for goodness of fit between the case management service plan and the provider's treatment, or for evidence of client progress. More advanced programs may try to link client outcomes to amount and intensity of service delivery (Brekke, 1988).

Computerized case management programs are recent additions to staff's armamentarium of techniques. These help workers to track large numbers of clients and provide instant access to information, such as current level of functioning, identified problems and resources, and service pattern use (Wimberly & Blazyk, 1989). While not supplanting quality judgments, well-established information systems can provide thorough, immediate, and robust knowledge of cost and frequency of service; help case managers target and monitor the most costly program users; and provide the substrate for program and policy appraisal (Beinecke, 1986).

ADVOCACY

There are many definitions and uses of the term advocacy and its accompanying dilemmas (Blakely, 1991). Advocacy has been defined as a risk-taking activity (Brager, 1968), as a model for social policy formulation (Specht, 1968), as allied to the Consumer Movement (Orlin, 1973), as an effective technique for influencing legislation (Dear & Patti, 1981), and as a strategy involving demonstrations or protests (Pincus & Minahan, 1973). Although there are different positions about how advocacy is expressed, there is consensus that this function is among the most proactive of the case manager's activities.

Case managers become involved in advocacy when, in the course of monitoring or service planning, they become aware of a need for change. Cohen et al., (1988c, p. 12) define advocacy as a process designed to address deficiencies that clients encounter "when choosing, accessing, or using service providers." Similarly, advocacy has been defined as an activity designed to "to secure or enhance a needed service, resource, or entitlement" (McGowan, 1987, p. 92); and as "public benefits advocacy" (McGinnis, 1990). This means that case managers assist their clients in gaining access to all the benefits the consumer is entitled to. Examples of advocacy include steps taken: (a) to make existing services available to clients, (b) to make existing services meet a client's needs, and (c) to develop services to address unmet client needs.

Effective advocacy requires at a minimum that staff be thoroughly familiar with eligibility criteria, application processes, and appeals procedures for each needed service or program. In addition, the worker's interventions will be co-determined by the client's individual needs and expressed wishes, the structure and extensiveness of resources in the service community, and specific agency case management guidelines. On the level of intervention for a specific client, actions, will be ultimately driven by the clients' perspective about desired improvement in either the quality and/or quantity of services and by whether the case manager has attained at least a "minimum level of client involvement" (Cohen et al., 1988c, p.7). Most social workers agree that advocacy's long-range goal should be to develop clients' abilities to advocate for themselves and that the clients' interests should supersede the workers' personal choices.

Advocacy practice is affected by the program's organizational capacities and mission. Internal advocates work within and are supported by a targeted service system, whereas external advocacy is provided by persons who are not supported by the targeted service system in any way. Although it has been argued that human service workers function better as advocates if they are free of the constraints of agency policy and rules (Piliavin, 1968), others believe that internal advocates may be more credible and may have easier access to information and to first-hand knowledge of what strategies will work with key decision makers (Cohen et al., 1988c). Most case managers are internal advocates, although they may occasionally provide external advocacy by documenting a program's shortcomings or broader service gaps. In reality, external advocacy on the level of line and administrative staff frequently occurs by default, as a response to widespread public indifference or prejudice against the population of concern (Platman, Dorgan, Gerhard, Mallam, & Spiliadis, 1982).

The distinction between *case advocacy,* where efforts occur on behalf of a single client, and *class advocacy,* involving actions to change service programs and systems in response to documented deficiencies, is also widely recognized. Examples of case advocacy are difficult to identify because they are often embedded in everyday case management practice. Interventions may include strengthening and building on client autonomy, independence, and capabilities; conflict resolution; accessible and timely use of agency grievance procedures; and educating clients about their consumer rights. These micro strategies are described in greater detail in the discussion of consumer empowerment in Chapter 3.

Class advocacy is also important but is less commonplace. In addition to the forms of protest already identified, it can include coalition building within the advocacy community, case finding, and legislative class action appeal. Many authors believe that class advocacy should be used cautiously and that it is more properly an administrative or supervisory function. For this reason, class advocacy should be grounded in political expertise and the ability to work through the grass roots and the legislative processes, as well as in sensitive and informed use of the supervisory relationship. A growing number of currently available services, pro-client regulations, and law are the outcomes of advocacy efforts by ex-clients, consumers, family members, and coalitions of service providers.

There are few in-depth guidelines about how programs should be constructed to best serve clients' interests. "Because there are almost as many models for . . . case management as there are programs . . . generalizing about their activities as advocates can be difficult" (Blazyk et al., 1987). Among the various models of service delivery, consolidated case management programs—those given the authority to allocate resources—are generally viewed as being optimally positioned to bring about desired change. A number of grass-roots groups have also argued that the advocacy function is best protected when policy or regulation require that case management programs be "administratively discrete" (e.g., that the program not be organizationally housed in the structure of a direct service provider where there is a potential for a conflict of interest).

Finally, staffing patterns for advocacy remain open. Although some informants view case advocacy as a less skilled activity (Greene & Lewis, 1991) that can be provided by entry-level case managers, case aides, and volunteers (Moore, 1990), other programs expect this at all levels of staffing (Ridgway et al., 1986). The reality is that advocacy is probably the least frequently and least intensively carried out staff activity.

Quality Standards of Practice

Although advocacy is often an embedded activity, there are times when case managers must make hard choices about the continued investment of personal and professional resources. Even in programs where advocacy is considered a centerpiece function, a worker's decision to pursue change assertively will also be affected by such considerations as: (a) whether the need is for individual referral to legal advocacy, or for general (class) service improvement, (b) the likelihood of success, (c) whether the amount of time required is justified by the size of the problem, (d) whether there will be a radiating impact, and (e) personal passion (Cohen et al., 1988c). Experienced staff will balance these factors with awareness of the personal risks of being co-opted, having to face negative personal consequences, or the danger of putting the client or the service plan at risk or disturbing otherwise cordial relationships with providers (Gemmill, Kennedy, Larison, Mollerstrom, & Brubeck, 1992).

Advocacy requires skills in persuasion and power brokering, effective use of confrontation, risk tolerance, system education, bureaucratic know-how, resource mobilization and coalition-building (Vourlekis & Greene, 1992b). Decisions must respect the client's wishes, as mediated by the staff's perception of the client's capacity for informed consent and consideration of factors associated with "just resource allocation," which involve responsiveness and accountability to all those on one's caseload (Kane, 1988).

Advocacy often implies inherent role conflict between the worker's need to enjoy good collaborative relationships with providers and other resources, and the desire to accomplish the service plan's objectives. Case managers may feel reluctant to advocate because of concerns of backlash, a desire not to harm other clients with competing needs, or too little time. Advocacy can result in many important consequences for providers or other groups targeted for intervention, including loss of funds, or worker or administrative sanction. Mailick and Ashley (1981) suggest that advanced case managers will be able to balance the client's immediate needs with the program's long-range interest in intersystem collaboration.

Advocacy tactics can be adversarial or collaborative. Although case managers usually use collaborative activities at first to avoid negative consequences, even when tactics are not overtly confrontational, individuals in the targeted system may view them as such. For this reason, advanced staff should be skilled in nonconfrontational negotiation, using the principle of *least contest* (Weil & Karls, 1985) to resolve problems at the lowest level of confrontation possible (Moxley, 1989), that is, approaching someone at the organization's lowest level. This is recommended because if the intervention proves ineffective, remediation can be sought at a higher level. However, the reverse is not true.

Effective advocacy also calls for the principle of *least process,* using the least intrusive methods first, and escalating the stakes later. The order of intrusiveness of the various advocacy strategies ranges from: (a) education, to (b) persuasion, (c) bargaining, (d) negotiation, (e) political maneuvering, and (f) direct contest. (See Table 2.11 for a more extensive list of steps in case management advocacy.) Direct staff are generally permitted access to only the first two strategies: education, which involves making the target individual aware of such circumstances as a client's likes, needs, or history; and persuasion, which involves trying to convince the target individual of the needed change and to gain her or his support. Although these are the sole methods used when working in the informal sector, they can also be effective interventions with colleagues and formal systems.

In general, adversarial tactics are most effective as one-shot events and lose their impact if prolonged or repeated too often. Therefore, it is important that staff communicate their position as working to support a client rather than as opposing those not aiding their client. Because case managers must rely on other providers to help achieve the service plan objectives, workers should strive to keep a cooperative spirit intact while advocating for system change (Texas Department of Mental Health and Mental Retardation, 1985).

Effective advocacy "demands sensitivity, flexibility and imagination" (McGowan, 1978, p. 89). Best practice includes decision making that takes into account whether success is possible, the case manager's personal resources in time and energy, and whether the amount of effort needed to solve the problem is justified by its size. Consultation with case managers, clients, or other service providers helps to clarify the issue's dimensions and scope (Cohen et al., 1988c). The advocacy process should also be monitored to change any nonproductive strategies (Modrcin et al., 1985).

The consumer's rights within the case management program is an important but infrequently discussed ethical issue (Dill, 1987). Because many case managers are public-sector employees, a potential conflict exists when staff want to advocate for a client against their employer. Discussion of these issues is cursory at best. Client's rights issues include the right to refuse case management yet still receive other services, the right to request another case manager or consultant, and the right to reject the service plan's recommendations (Downing, 1985). There is an acknowledged need to develop program policies and procedures and to establish peer review and other quality assurance mechanisms.

Finally, advanced case managers may try to influence the larger scene by using destigmatizing frames of reference and by stated support for consumer empowerment. Systems advocacy can be accomplished by

TABLE 2.11 Steps in Case Management Advocacy

1. Explore the client's or caregiver's understanding of the situation's causes and what they want to see changed. Explore their preferred solution and what they will settle for. Encourage them to ask for everything on their priority list, rather than just the minimum they think they can get.

2. Develop a plan and decide on the advocacy strategies necessary to achieve the goals. Define how pervasive the problem or issue is in their lives.

3. Do your homework; know the issues, the services, and the people in the system. Be able to speak knowledgeably about the chances for success.

4. Review what roles the consumer or caregiver will play in the intervention beforehand. Discuss whether a neutral third party (e.g., an ombudsman, friend, client, or family advocate) should be present to provide the consumer with needed, additional support. This party can also raise pointed questions or offer statements of fact without having the case manager risk further alienating "the system."

5. Plan a formal or informal meeting with the most appropriate level of staff:
   - Begin by clarifying the meeting's objectives, stating the problems clearly and allowing all interested parties to discuss the problem.
   - Separate the person from the problem: recognize that staff need to be part of the solution and are often also frustrated by a situation.
   - Go "hard on problems, easy on the person." Reinforce your support for the other and identify the real or perceived barriers. Focus on the big picture; appeal to underlying ethical values.
   - Jointly develop a definition of needed changes and negotiate for these changes.
   - Develop a written statement (e.g., a draft memorandum that is circulated for approval, a change in the service plan, or a file note) outlining what has been agreed.

6. *If* agreement is not achieved and change not accomplished:
   - Reinforce that the client is not being abandoned and recall past successes.
   - Assure the client that the matter will continue to be worked on or that the next supervisory or administrative levels will be activated.
   - Document the meeting and prepare a clear presentation to the supervisor or administrator in anticipation of further action.
   - Continue to keep good records of all subsequent meetings, conversations, site visits, and surveys.
   - Attend or conduct workshops and conferences; and encourage family members to do this also.

SOURCES: Adapted from Fine and Borden, 1989; Texas Department of Mental Health and Mental Retardation, 1985.

challenging explanations that blame the victim, by encouraging the allocation of more resources for research and programming, and by being proactive in enabling clients and caregivers to have a more formal voice in the design and evaluation of the systems of care (National Alliance for the Mentally Ill, 1982).

TERMINATION

Disengagement and termination are rarely discussed in the advanced literature because the work of case management has been described more as a series of functions than as a process. This has been complicated by the fact that so many of the newer, exemplary programs have concentrated on the needs of very impaired, long-term clients. Thus the bulk of discussion has been on program retention rather than termination.

The older view of advanced case management as an indefinite relationship, however, is being increasingly challenged by system pressures, especially as programs find themselves with waiting lists and caps on caseload size and with a mandate to grow even with restricted funding. Newly expanding program thrusts, such as in children's case management and case management with dual populations, have also refocused interest in transition activities. On the macro level, case management options have been substantially augmented, with increased funding options paving the way for a broader continuum of choices, including advanced short-term practice (Sonsel, Paradise, & Stroup, 1988) and programmatically related, supported living services. These shifts have prompted reexamination of planned referral to less intensively managed (Bachrach, 1992), or to more conventional services, as well as a rethinking of termination.

Quality Standards of Practice

Planned termination of advanced case management services to targeted high-risk clients is often an ethically and a politically difficult decision, implying a judgment that a client's gains have been maximized or that a prediction of risk warrants this decision. Some research indicates that an individual's gains lapse when program support is removed (Stein & Test, 1980); however, other findings suggest that relapses can be avoided through proper planning. From the client's perspective, there are several, often overlapping, reasons for termination. Spontaneous client-initiated requests for termination or *de facto* "drop out" may signal incompatibility between the client and the worker or the program. This can represent either program expectations that are too rigid or a transitory testing of the case manager's and the program's commitment to the individual. Clients who wish to "fire" their case managers often "re-hire" them after a good-faith demonstration of worker outreach. In these cases, staff should follow program guidelines about attempts to recontact, standards of documentation, and keeping the case on active status.

A request for termination can also be a healthy sign of client gains and growth in self-confidence. Its dynamics can include: the client's or caregiver's perception that goals have been attained and that progress can be sustained independently or with reliance on an expanded network; a desire to assume responsibility for being the primary case manager; the fact that environmental or other life stressors have been successfully addressed or diminished; or the desire to graduate to a less intensive or time-demanding program.

Staff transfer recommendations can reflect a judgment that achievements have been maximized, that continuation of the relationship is likely to foster unhealthy dependence, or that the client is unable to tolerate the intensity of some of the more advanced programs (Harris, 1988; Kanter, 1989). There is also some indication that involuntary termination is occasionally used as a confrontational, last-resort tool to precipitate a crisis to reengage "uncooperative" clients (Steinberg & Carter, 1983).

The more skilled case managers will be alert to, and respect, indications of client movement toward autonomy. Ballew and Mink (1986) suggest three broad indicators of disengagement readiness: (a) presentation of an enhanced ability to make decisions and to resolve problems independently, such as making one's own referrals or initiating contacts without requesting the case manager's assistance; (b) behaviors that signal a lessened need for the partnership, e.g., requesting less frequent meetings, decreasing the frequency of phone contacts or need for home visits, or indications of a closer relationship with other key helpers; and (c) making more effective, spontaneous, or expanded uses of available network supports as case management extenders or as resources.

The process of disengagement includes relinking and follow-up to ensure that the client experiences a smooth transition, verification that the client's goals have been met and can be sustained, and leaving the door open to program return should changes in client status or a subsequent request for service occur (See Table 2.12). Decisions to terminate should consider the client's current level of functioning and extent of involvement in the other systems of care. Clients whose needs are being met successfully in direct programming and whose status appears stabilized are likely candidates for transfer of case management responsibilities. Typically, they are transferred to someone who is currently providing primary services that could be combined with case management. Transfer to less intense programs with larger caseloads may also be driven by fiscal reasons, by improvement in client status, or as a treatment recommendation.

TABLE 2.12 A Checklist of Quality Practices for Termination of Case Management Services

1. Is there a policy specifying criteria for termination and are the case manager and client aware of it?
2. Does the case manager's experience suggest that new policy is needed or that existing policies should be changed?
3. What steps has the case manager taken to prepare the client or caregiver for the possibility of termination? At what stage of the case management relationship has this occurred?
4. If termination is requested by either client or case manager, has the case manager explored what this means personally to the client, as well as the potential impact on client functioning and access to services?
5. If termination is requested, does the agency have a written review and discharge plan or some other mechanism to monitor these steps?
6. Does the agency allow clients to reaccess services without going through lengthy intake procedures, and has the case manager communicated this to the consumer?
7. If termination results in referral or transition to other services, has the case manager facilitated the process, including pre-site visits and making sure all necessary paper work is accomplished in a timely and complete fashion?
8. Does the case manager provide extended outreach to former clients or their caregivers? How is this accomplished?

Staff should approach caregivers as colleagues and try to recruit family or other network members to help provide explanations and encouragement. It is also important that both clients and their families be given the opportunity to vent any "guilt, sadness, and hostility" as well as any anxiety that the proposed change of status may cause (Abramson, 1990).

Termination planning should include evaluation of client progress and risk factors and an assessment of the robustness of the client's network. Staff should be skilled in fostering client self-determination and be able to separate from the client. Responsibilities for coordinating a multidisciplinary termination and/or transfer plan include identification of any continuing case manager, contacting programs to see if needed services and supports are in place, and documenting that all actions required for termination and/or referral have been taken. Termination plans should also consider potential risks to client safety and identify remedial plans of action. Finally, referral and consultation and liaison may be optionally offered to sustaining programs, along with monitoring to verify that referrals are followed through (American Hospital Association, 1988).

Other end-process skills are needed when the case management service is being involuntarily terminated, such as with clients who "age out" or who do not continue to meet program criteria for retention. Clients who express ambivalence should be encouraged to have an increased sense of control. This can be facilitated by giving them time to make decisions and arranging for previsits to other options, providing written materials and directions, and exploring if some window of return can be established. The case manager should also try to ensure that clients are provided with a sense of choice within existing parameters, such as a choice of alternative staff or programs with lead responsibility.

Depending on the program's resources, some method for sustaining access may be implemented once a client has been transferred or discharged. This can be done by allowing the case manager to continue seeing the client on a transitional basis, so that the client will experience "only a change of staff role, not the end of the therapeutic relationship" (McRae, Higgins, Lycan, & Sherman, 1990, p. 176); by providing pretransfer/termination referral to hotline access or other volunteer programs that can provide re-referral if necessary; by sending routine mailing of holiday, birthday, or "anniversary" discharge date greetings; by making routine offers of short-term service; and through periodic consumer satisfaction surveys or status checks (Steinberg & Carter, 1983).

Chapter 3

QUALITY STANDARDS OF CASE MANAGEMENT PRACTICE (CONTINUED)

AXIS II: THE "META" CRITERIA

As Gestalt psychology views the whole as greater than the sum of its separate parts, so the concept of expert case management implies a practitioner who can weave several well-conducted, discrete functions into a superior result. The intertwined meanings that provide a case management service gestalt are referred to here as *meta* variables—second dimension or background competencies that provide a value-added practice throughout the case management cycle. These competencies represent a creative side and are often borrowed from sister professions, uniting advanced case management with more recent trends in social work at large.

Because meta competencies come to life in the context of their functions, specification can be difficult. One approach is to identify cutting edge behaviors by their "tracks," that is, the noise raised in the broader professional realm. This can by done by analyzing issues debated in the literature, by spotlighting what model programs say is essential, and by listening to concerns raised by highly self-aware staff. While support for these positions is often rhetorical rather than well-tested, and the principles may not yet be consensually accepted, these factors are in the forefront of intellectual discourse.

Using such tracking methods reveals four advanced topics that meet the criteria of intellectual debate and model-program support. Analysis of current conference topics and a computerized printout and review of the last decade's case management literature identified four advanced areas that are in the forefront of intellectual debate. The areas are: (a) cultural competency, (b) consumer empowerment, (c) *clinical* case management (e.g., the reintegration of clinical insight into the case management relationship), and (d) more recent multidisciplinary models of practice. These factors are related in that each reflects attempts to engage groups that have traditionally been overlooked or given only minor or passive roles in the case management process.

CULTURAL COMPETENCY

America is a pluralistic society but not a country that is comfortable addressing the persistent effects of prejudice, racism, and non-mainstream cultures on personality formation, level of stress, and access to social supports and other resources that promote health and everyday well-being (Pinderhughes, 1984). Because these facts are the foundation of case management, good practice cannot occur without specific attention to the management of cultural diversity.

The term *cultural competence* has many meanings. However, within the case management literature it is frequently applied to four sociocultural groups of color: African Americans, Asian Americans, Hispanic Americans, and Native Americans. Although diversity concerns are also appropriate for other social groups—for example, the aged, sexual minorities, and women—people of color are most commonly the focus of discussion about culturally competent practice. This is often supported as a justice issue; that is, these are groups that have historically experienced the most severe and persistent discrimination and the most restricted access to economic and political power. It is also argued that one cannot understand cultural differences without looking squarely at the reality of racism.

Social work has been aware of racial and ethnic minorities as special populations with major stakes in social program outcomes since the early 1970s (Williams, Williams, Sommer, & Sommer, 1988). The profession still has to go a distance in consciousness raising, training, and developing practice-based culturally aware models of intervention (Adams & Schlesinger, 1988; Echols, Gabel, Landerman, & Reyes, 1988). The situation is made more urgent by the fact that not only is cultural competence ethically mandated—both the National Association of Social Workers and the Council on Social Work education established policies designed to end racism in the profession as early as 1969—but it is also becoming demographically necessary (Williams, 1988). Statistically, we are increasingly a nation of many colors, and our minority population is growing more rapidly than our majority population. It is projected that people of color will be nearly 40 percent of the service delivery system by the year 2000.

Case managers working in public settings can increasingly expect to work with people of color. These clients will often need extended interventions to coordinate long-standing service needs made worse by pervasive discrimination and restricted access to life chances. Service needs will often be complicated by experiences of migration/immigration, linguistic differences, and stresses associated with acculturation. If targeted case management were truly successful in outreach, clients of color would be overrepresented compared to the general population receiving services, and the per capita number of needed primary and ancillary services provided through case management would be substantially greater.

Minority group members are latecomers to many different systems of care. They are less served by preventive services, more often routed to punitive, custodial settings, and are more frequently ignored. They are our "invisible" (Knitzer, 1982) and under- and nonserved constituencies (President's Commission on Mental Health, 1978). This situation is compounded by "inaccurate assessment of ethnic and linguistic minorities, culturally insensitive treatment models, and inappropriate service delivery systems" (Guzman & VandenBos, 1990) that contribute to service underutilization. Although the minority community is often ill-served, some subgroups receive a less or lower quality of care than others (Padilla, Ruiz, & Alvarez, 1975). All of these factors challenge case managers' boundary-spanning and advocacy efforts.

Cultural competency can be defined in many ways; however, its major features include awareness of how individual and agency practice must change to accommodate to the history, culture, life-styles, and experiences of people of color (Hanson, Lynch, & Wayman, 1990). The bedrock of cultural competency is acknowledgment of the extensive effect of discrimination on self, program, and client behaviors, coupled with a recognition of the diversity of choices and life-styles present in minority communities.

Cross, Bazron, Dennis, & Isaacs (1989) propose a developmental model of cultural competence: a continuum ranging from cultural destructiveness and incapacity to the highest levels of cultural competence and proficiency. As envisioned, there are five elements: (a) valuing diversity, (b) having the capacity for cultural self-assessment, (c) being conscious of the dynamics inherent when cultures interact, (d) continuously expanding cultural knowledge and resources, and (e) being able to adapt one's practices to better meet the needs of minority populations. Several instruments based on this continuum are available for staff sensitivity raising or supervisory discussion (Mason, 1989).

Appreciation for "biculturalism," the adaptations that individuals use in learning to function well in their own environment and that of the mainstream society, is a major tool for understanding diversity (Padilla & Lindholm, 1983). Biculturalism can be a source of personal rootlessness and stress and an important human resource. Because biculturalism involves the ability to effectively bridge the gap between one's culture of origin and the host society, case managers need to understand how clients' behaviors take meaning in specific cultural contexts and be able to share this knowledge with other professionals. It is important that clients be encouraged to continue accessing their natural supports and indigenous community's resources while seeking services in the formal sector. Finally, good practice suggests that staff try to understand the individual's personal view and not merely assume that behavior has a specific meaning because of ascribed group membership.

Cultural sensitivity is especially vital for those with a community-based practice. Respect and familiarity with cultural norms governing "private" social space (e.g., homes, kitchens, family occasions) and personal space is essential if staff is to be ethnoculturally accessible and not merely physically available to clients. Attention to the norms of socializing, accepting food, taking the time to establish one's own family background, and spending time on "trivial" conversations, show respect for the host's culture.

Cultural respect begins with acknowledging that differences in social class, lifestyle, perspective, or expectation are potentially significant factors in the case manager-client relationship. Obviously, case managers must avoid equating dissimilarity in life-style with cultural inferiority (Castro, nd). The issue of building trust can be exacerbated when working with people of different racial or ethnic backgrounds whose feelings can range from caution to open hostility (Everett, Proctor, & Cartmell, 1983). Additional personal resources may have to be spent to overcome client distrust that emerges as an indication of a language barrier, a desire to be with familiar others, a wish to avoid being in a threatening environment or being given a bureaucratic run-around, or finding the service strange (Sue, Allen, & Conaway, 1978).

Shrewd practice dictates that case managers should expect lengthy periods of testing where delivering on promises to expedite appointments, to arrange for services, or to provide accompaniment are seen as evidence of trustworthiness. Interviews can be scheduled to take place on the client's own turf (e.g., at home) to encourage clients to have a greater sense of control and to ease perceived differences in status.

Good practice also recommends taking time to establish relationships rather than focusing on getting people immediately into services. This may require extending the engagement phase and delaying movement into service planning to avoid the risk of premature termination—an outcome that may be more frequent for blacks, Chicanos, Asian Americans, and Native Americans than for Anglo clients (Sue & Sue, 1990).

Depending on the cultural circumstances, case managers should be prepared to begin an exploratory discussion to help clients understand that there is time to get to know one another before moving into more uncomfortable concerns (Thomason, 1991). Staff should provide brief explanations of why they are looking forward to being involved, and messages should be framed in conversational styles (e.g., friendly versus formal) that reflect the client's cultural preference.

Expert case managers will often rely on community referral agents and other natural gatekeepers for case finding and outreach. Because these populations often have large unmet service needs, many programs rely on natural supports such as family members, friends and relatives, and other indigenous resources including church and voluntary memberships, to help fill the considerable gap between what is needed and what the program can provide. To build these partnerships, staff should be familiar with how the (sub)culture defines well-being, health, and illness; diagnostic and treatment procedures; the agency's reputation; and personal relationship to authority. One can learn this by reading and by seeking cultural informants and linguistic representatives (Wilson, 1982).

Cultural expectations about personal growth and development, the family network's structure and authority, and the norms of help-seeking and caregiving are also important. Often the definition of family is inclusive and accepts persons who are other than relatives. Case managers should exert themselves to identify and engage these traditional and nontraditional helping agents as resources for the client. Field-based staff have an advantage in being able conduct on-site observation (e.g., who eats with the family, prepares meals, baby-sits, provides transportation and short-term loans). Who does the family confer with in times of crisis?

Good practice questions how the family and other caregivers view their own case management activity: When do they define their behavior as caring or protective in face of perceived environmental dangers? It is also important that one not impose middle-class stereotypes about how certain life-style or family interactions "ought to be." Both the client's and the family's readiness for program involvement should be reviewed, particularly in cultures where strong kin ties are paramount. Family and friends may either support or obstruct the help-giving process. This may be more common in protective families, which keep members dependent in an attempt to avoid situations that generate pain or risk (Castro, nd). In some cultures, requesting formal help is viewed as an abdication of family responsibility. In other groups, such as certain Asian American subsets, strong ethnic identification may emphasize the importance of preserving family reputation over an individual's needs. This can prevent seeking help to the point where initial contact occurs only after a considerable period of stress and acute crisis. Such individuals are likely be much more severely ill at initial contact than other groups (Tsai & Uemura, 1988), making it harder for staff to coordinate resources, avoid the more restrictive interventions, or to involve family members as colleagues. Finally, case managers should know that cultures are permeable and that even ethnically attached families are occasionally willing to suspend distrust to gain access to highly needed or essential services. Table 3.1 summarizes many of this section's points.

RAISING CULTURAL DIVERSITY CONCERNS IN PRACTICE

Hesitation about facing the effects of racism and ethnocentrism on one's practice can stem from many causes, including awareness that minority and mainstream cultures are similar as well as different, discomfort with one's own ethnicity, and avoidance of challenging one's self-image as a helpful, unbiased person (Bazron, 1989). Good practice starts with awareness of one's own attitudes and feelings toward a client's culture and with an accurate knowledge of the client's background and experiences (Romero, 1983).

The program's context also affects individual practice. Programs that unintentionally stratify clients and staff by race or culture or have been designed without consultative input from its cultural constituencies are more apt to have developed institutionalized barriers to service. These can be assessed by comparing noninvolvement and drop-out rates of minority persons to others in the service constituency. Differences between minority members and other groups in waiting lists for case management services and different patterns of service referral are also highly suggestive.

A finely tuned sense of relationship is extremely important in knowing when and how to raise diversity concerns. Not all miscommunication or lack of client progress can be attributed to cultural differences. A rule-out option is that cultural misunderstandings should be queried when there are no other obvious explanations. Sensitizing indicators can include unanticipated failure to follow-through or unexpected client "over-reaction" to service-seeking steps that staff take for granted,

TABLE 3.1 Examples of Culturally Competent Case Management Practice

- Concentrate on what the client sees as "real life" problems.
- Do a complete current environmental analysis; assess financial and social needs; back this with action.
- Prepare clients for services by offering role rehearsal and information; help clients complete forms; provide information on neighborhood resources using materials (e.g., graphics, translated materials) the client can understand.
- Call clients by their correct name and with the degree of formality expected in their culture; if in doubt, ask the client about pronunciation and cultural protocols related to first- and last-name and other honorifics.
- Be prepared to disclose about yourself, your home, your family, and your ideas so that the client can get to know you as a person.
- Be prepared to involve the family.
- Accompany clients and family members to client's appointments.
- Do not stand in the way of clients and family members who want to use indigenous healers/helpers.
- Be alert to clues about intergenerational conflict.
- Be sensitive to indirect issues that are raised.
- Make advance calls to service providers to confirm they are ready to receive the family.
- Coordinate service appointments and location.
- Provide transportation and coaching in use of mass transit.
- Explore reimbursement mechanisms for neighbors or other supports who could provide transportation or other short-term assistance.
- Be available after hours, evenings and weekends, at places where community members congregate; attend cultural immersion activities (e.g., festivals, ceremonies).
- Develop relationships with the community's most trusted helpers and gatekeepers.
- Develop relationships with cultural informants.
- Teach/encourage self-advocacy.
- Link to the community's emergency supports and volunteer assistance.
- Be patient.

SOURCES: Adapted from Bazron, 1989; Christensen, 1979; Cross et al., 1989; and Sue and Sue, 1990.

such as not telephoning for an appointment or refusing to see a school principal. Cultural issues should also be considered when a knowledgeable background or direct client statement suggests that the issue is suffused with subcultural meaning, when certain world views are expressed (especially about the presenting problems, its causes, or a preferred treatment) that are unfamiliar, or when verbal statements, dress, or other artifacts indicate a personal cultural identification.

TABLE 3.2 Personal Style in Engaging Black Clients

1. Initial contact
   - Use proper names, not nicknames.
   - Do not condescend.
   - Be sincere and genuine.
   - Avoid an authoritative posture.
   - Identify and acknowledge strengths.
   - Be direct and straightforward.
2. Building trust
   - Avoid game playing, reverse psychology.
   - Allow expressive thoughts and behaviors.
   - If you suspect that race is an issue, address it nondefensively.
   - Avoid presenting yourself as "the system;" express your professional concern.
   - Focus on the problem at hand.

SOURCE: Wright, 1991.

Case managers should avoid putting clients on the defensive if these situations arise. Good practice recommends a preference for a social conversation style rather than exploring these issues through direct questioning (see Table 3.2). The worker should begin by trying to clarify the client's expectations for program and personal responsibility and the values and activities the client considers important. Skilled staff will also weave knowledge of the history, political, economic, and social concerns into more generalized conversation, providing the individual with the opportunity to respond.

CULTURALLY COMPETENT CASE MANAGEMENT PRACTICE

Staff should be aware that case management modes of service delivery (e.g., nonclinical, problem-focused, action-oriented, and crisis-responsive) are often far more successful with minority clientele than traditional counseling and are possibly the intervention of first choice (Lefley & Bestman, 1984; Santa Clara County Mental Health, 1988). Culturally respectful case management requires that practice be adapted to the client's community and tempered by observations indicating the salient issues.

Case Finding

Culturally sensitive case finding requires innovative outreach in identifying the nontraditional referral agents who are gatekeepers to the client population. This can be especially difficult when connecting with those who lack knowledge of community resources or fear contact with formal authorities. When the targeted individual is an undocumented person or a recent emigre, contact with public representatives can be perceived as a threat to deport.

Case finding and assertive outreach is especially complicated when the individual is being served outside the system's ordinary referral channels. Some examples are black youth with mental illness, who are more often in the forensic system than in mental health care, and persons who are disengaged from mainstream systems of care—"street people," undocumented aliens, and the minority elderly. Case managers should develop routine connections with natural services (grocery stores, beauty parlors, herbalists and homeopathic practitioners, soup kitchens) existing in minority communities or adopt door-to-door procedures (Maguire, 1991).

Assessment

Routine service assessment should be modified to incorporate a specific assessment of the client's level of acculturation. People vary greatly in their ethnic group identification, and this is often situation-specific. For example, one set of meanings may be operative at home and others activated elsewhere. Assessment of the client's linguistic and cultural background, life-style and linguistic preferences, and situation-specific identification should coincide with more generic assessment.

Barriers to the assessment process should be considered and solutions developed. These barriers can include culturally biased assessment, testing, and recording techniques that can skew the historical record. Case managers should know that common diagnostic tools are limited or frequently misused when applied to nonmainstream cultures. Staff should also develop a network of local informants capable of providing technical assistance or specialized, culturally sensitive testing and assessment services.

The ordinary gathering of background information can be highly problematic in situations where the client's subculture teaches that strangers are to be distrusted or that official records are often used hostilely. The situation is exacerbated if the applicant is illiterate, afraid to disclose, or unfamiliar with the language or when staff have obvious social control functions, such as a protective service caseworker. Because of these factors, some clients may initially appear so emotionally distraught and functionally impaired that the case manager confuses a temporary and situational immobility with a more long-standing personal incapacity. Therefore baseline data should include not only information related to the individual's premorbid or precrisis functioning but also what the cultural context considers normal. It is good practice to check with collaterals about the individual's ordinary functioning before drawing conclusions. This should sometimes take precedence over specific formal assessment mechanisms (Horejsi et al., nd).

Certain intake protocols, especially standard social history queries, can also be experienced as irrelevant or as making unwarranted assumptions about the case manager's right to ask. Routine queries about school completion and job history, which are often statistically different for minority group members, illustrate cultural blindness. It is equally important that case managers not stereotype or assume that all minority clients will have failed in these accomplishments. It is better that all intake and social history questions be scrutinized for relevance and timing and that needed data be gotten by more indirect approaches.

Service Planning

Service planning can be impeded by mutual stereotyping, distrust, and lack of knowledge of the real factors that are certain to influence the plan's success. Both clients and case managers can be guilty of making prejudgments For example, clients sometimes view staff as prejudicially withholding desired resources, when in fact staff may have little control over access or the resources do not really exist. Conversely, workers often fail to recognize the extended family's role as a gatekeeper to service acceptance, and can set the plan up for failure by bypassing needed consultation.

The plan's trajectory can be seriously affected by sociocultural features in addition to those associated with compliance. Because minority individuals often have long histories of poverty-associated deprivation, they may be in poorer shape at system entry than others (Chatman & Turner-Friley, 1988). As a result, immediate needs often have to be responded to first, and service planning and treatment will occur conjointly within the assessment phase. Incredible amounts of time and effort and extraordinary persistence may also be required to coordinate paperwork and to establish resource eligibility when geographic mobility, homelessness, or language barriers exist.

Implementation of the Service Plan

Coordination of service recommendations can be difficult for culturally diverse clients. When there are language or other subcultural barriers, people may lack a clear understanding of the service plan or their own follow-up needs (Lee & Yee, 1988). Staff's ability to expedite service can often be restricted by the client's lack of access to transportation, good health care, or to respite caregivers. As a result, case managers may find themselves spending a disproportionate amount of time facilitating access before any targeted intervention can take place. Providing psychological support and administrative linking to services and entitlements can be far more difficult than expected. As advocates, case managers may have to engage in extended persuasion tactics to negotiate culturally appropriate (or any) services from schools, clinics, recreational programs, and churches.

The worker's goal as a broker is to persuade others to collaborate in the development of a system of care (Young, 1990). Role sharing, especially with natural helpers and other formal community agencies, is essential to relieve task overload. Engaging the natural support network presents a special challenge: "It is often the greatest resource available to the client and at the same time the least accessible to the formal helper . . .[however] sometimes the formal system only needs not to stand in the way of the natural system" (Cross et al., 1989, p. 50). The amount of effort spent in collateral contacts will be proportionally greater with these constituencies.

Case managers also need to know about recent economic and cultural changes that may have affected the subcultural community. Pervasive urban crime, violence, and substance abuse (Long, 1983) and the cultural dislocation associated with international migration have seriously affected access to traditional supports (Lee & Yee, 1988). Recent studies show that minority clients are often denied equal access to services because of outdated program assumptions about the vitality of the extended family and other traditional resources (Greene & Monahan, 1984). When this occurs, families who can least afford the burdens of caregiving are also more likely to be their member's case managers by default, rather than by choice.

Staff should develop interventions designed to help minority clients and their families negotiate the bureaucratic maze of services. Table 3.3 illustrates some of the most commonly recommended intervention strategies.

Advanced case managers working with these populations may want to move beyond everyday interventions to more system-level reform efforts. As advocates, they may seek to raise agency consciousness to unmet need, collect statistics, and experiment with programming to make the system more responsive. "A Model Program for Community-Based Health Services for Asian Americans: The Living At Home Project" (Table 3.4) illustrates one attempt at program adaptation.

TABLE 3.3 Quality Issues of Culturally Competent Practice

1. *Access*

   Are case managers assigned to programs in neighborhoods identified with people of color?

   Are these staff bicultural? Bilingual?

   Does the case manager "assume" that the applicant client or the caretaker is literate?

   Does the case manager know the culture's norms of respect and privacy? Has the case manager asked how the client wishes to be addressed in terms of honorary titles or relationships?

   If a translator is needed: Has the case manager extended planned visit/appointments to allow sufficient time for translation to occur? Has a translator been identified from a good source? Does this person have a track record and familiarity with service issues? Is the translator competent in the client's dialect?

   If a family member is used as translator: Has every effort been made to identify an indigenous speaker of age and status similar to that of the client? If an adult is the client, has every effort been taken *not* to use that person's child or a much younger family member?

2. *Assessment and service planning*

   Is the case manager aware of the cultural limitations and biases of the more common assessment techniques, social histories, intelligence tests?

   Is the case manager aware of any cultural explanations of illness or impediment, treatment, most favored treatment agents, or approaches that differ from those of mainstream culture?

   Is the case manager prepared to spend the time needed to establish a personal relationship and to share information about him/herself that may conform to that group's preferred interaction style?

3. *Service plan implementation*

   Is the case manager prepared to "start where the client is" and to deal with the requests for concrete and tangible services that often arise before the individual or caretaker is prepared to deal with the "referral" issue?

   Is the case manager prepared to spend the substantial time needed to broker services and to connect clients and programs?

   If visits are home- and community-based: Does the case manager know who the culture identifies as the family spokesperson or someone with a legitimate right to know? Does the case manager know whom that culture expects to speak to first?

   Does the case manager know if the client has access to transportation?

   Is the case manager prepared to facilitate or at least not stand in the way of the client's accessing natural helpers?

   Does the case manager know if the client or caretaker has a "most trusted" professional or cultural informant?

USE OF TRANSLATION SERVICES

Language barriers are one of the most serious limitations to a culturally competent practice. Case managers cannot provide effective services for

TABLE 3.4 A Model Program for Community-Based Health Services for Asian Americans: The Living At Home Project (Case Management in Aging)

In 1986, the South Cove Community Health Center (SCCHC) in Boston's Chinatown began a 3-year Living at Home (LAHP) Project, one of 20 national demonstrations funded by the Commonwealth Fund and the Pew Charitable Trust and co-sponsored by a broad coalition of 33 charitable foundations. These projects were intended to streamline access to care, to reduce duplication and identify service gaps, and to devise innovative responses.

The SCCHC project focused on providing care for ethnically isolated elderly and was one of six national "outreach/access" demonstrations. It proposed to introduce case management to Boston's elderly Chinese community by promoting bilingual and bicultural services.

The focal point was the project's bilingual, bicultural staff: a project administrator, two case managers, and two home-care nurses. They served as a bridge between East and West and attempted to improve communication among the medical and social service communities, residents and building management; among the generations; and between staff and clients.

The program used advocacy and brokerage. Case managers coordinated service delivery, helped clients complete Medicare and Medicaid application forms, and arranged for adult day care and home health aides. They were also a single point of contact for building managers who provided early alerts to need.

The LAHP acted as an advocate with hospitals and agencies to provide more comprehensive interpreter services and to fund a community-based pool of interpreters to provide ancillary functions, including escort. An intergenerational volunteer component recruited and trained bilingual high school and college students to visit homebound elderly.

This experience reinforced the complexity of providing bilingual staff. There was a very limited pool of trained professionals, and, although less experienced bilingual social workers were recruited, they needed longer training in case management techniques and community resources. Fund raising and difficulties with the Medicaid reimbursement schedule, make the program's continued future uncertain.

SOURCES: Adapted from Hughes and Weissert, 1988; and Lee and Yee, 1988.

people with whom they cannot communicate. Although greater use of indigenous staff has long been advocated, the reality is that in some geographic areas not only are such professionals scarce, but programs cannot realistically respond to the diversity of languages and dialects represented in the population.

As a result, case managers sometimes have to use interpreters, such as family members, neighbors, or paid staff. Good practice dictates the importance of selecting people who will respect confidentiality and the client's right to advocacy. Case managers should try to avoid using a child as a family interpreter wherever possible. Even though this may be regarded with pride by the youngster, it overturns the intergenerational structure and can create strain or prevent the adult member from participating fully. Children can also distort or fail to understand others' statements (Christensen, 1979). Using interpreters as partners in the case management process is difficult but not impossible. The strategy can be helpful to agencies because it can be a new source for reflective problem solving, it can raise the client's sense of comfort, and it can promote accurate exploration of ideas and values. The incorporation of translators as case management adjuncts can benefit both the program and the client (State of Hawaii, nd).

However, programs must be prepared to deal with translation service issues. Budget concerns to be negotiated up front by the program include the lack of third-party reimbursement, and the need to pay a translator. In addition, fewer clients can be served because of the longer time needed for translation (Speaks, 1990).

Many issues complicate the case manager-client relationship when an interpreter is inserted as a third presence (See Table 3.5). Extended contact may also be a double barrier for certain non-English-speaking, impaired populations (e.g., mentally ill immigrants or first-generation frail elderly). The worker may need extra time for planning and educating the translator about case management processes and the program's focus. A major payoff is, however, that program-literate interpreters can suggest lines of questioning, provide commentary on culturally important issues, and sensitize staff to client and community needs and perceptions.

CONSUMER EMPOWERMENT

The consumer empowerment movement represents a critical shift in federal policy. This emphasis is consonant with social work's historical emphasis on client self-determination (Biestek, 1957; Modrcin et al., 1985); nonetheless, it has only recently been institutionalized as mandated power sharing. Policy impetus has come from new views about service delivery, the extension of civil rights to captive client populations, and the process of "net-widening," which involves many private and nontraditional agents as service partners (Lewis et al., 1991). The movement has also been aided by the emergence of an increasingly powerful consumer/advocacy lobby, recognition that public dollars cannot possibly meet the level of unmet need, and policy models showing "backward" approaches to system design—starting from a needs assessment of the target population—as the most effective (Abel-Boone, Sandall, Loughry, & Frederick, 1990). Social support theory has

TABLE 3.5 Providing Case Management Services With an Interpreter

1. *Pre-contact telephone call*
   - Check if the interpreter will be available. Will this be on a one-time or on a continuing basis?
   - Explain what you are trying to accomplish.
   - Explore the client's and the interpreter's background: How good is the match (e.g., in terms of gender, age, rural-urban differences in experience, competence in dialects, whether the person is related to the family)?
   - Negotiate and schedule a pre-session face-to-face discussion. How much extra time is anticipated for interpretation and clarification, and for a short post-session debriefing.

2. *At the pre-session discussion*
   - Review confidentiality.
   - Explain and reinforce the meeting's goals.
   - Build a relationship with the interpreter.
   - Learn how to pronounce the client's name.
   - Request information about proxemics—norms of eye and physical contact—and culturally sensitive topics (e.g., personal finances).
   - Decide if the interpretation will be word for word or paraphrased.
   - Establish norms about timing and clarification: How long will each speak? When are interruptions permitted?
   - Discuss technical terms (e.g. medications, providers, entitlement programs) that are likely to be used in the upcoming contact.
   - Decide how each will be introduced to the client.
   - Establish ground rules for interpreter feedback: Will this be provided during or after the session? Will it include nonverbal cues, speech pattern observations, and volunteered cultural information?

3. *The client contact*
   - Introduce everyone present at the beginning.
   - Establish the client's agreement to the ground rules for communication.
   - Try to establish how much English the client knows; do not assume that the client does not understand what you and the interpreter are discussing.
   - Be sensitive to indications that the client is attempting to "split" your relationship with the interpreter.
   - Use simple English; avoid technical terms and slang.
   - Monitor nonverbal and process dynamics while the interpreter and the client are speaking.

4. *Post-session discussion*
   - Debrief issues that were not adequately discussed during the session.
   - Exchange impressions of the client.
   - Discuss problems or misunderstandings.
   - Schedule follow-up sessions, if needed.

SOURCE: State of Hawaii, nd.

also emphasized the in-kind contributions of the family and extended kin group (Biegel, Shore, & Gordon, 1984; Collins & Pancoast, 1976), the prophylactic role of natural supports as stress "buffers" (Caplan, 1974), and contributions of private individuals as their family member's long-term case manager (Backer & Richardson, 1989).

All these factors have encouraged policy support of consumers and family members, who are secondary consumers, as key stakeholders in the design, delivery, and evaluation of programs. Consumers are increasingly involved as agency board members, as administrative staff (Silva, 1990), as monitors and evaluators (Lorefice, Borus, & Keefe, 1982), and, in some cases, as providers of paid case management service (Mahler, Balze, & Risser, 1990; Sherman & Porter, 1991). The incorporation of consumers as an important constituency is backed by federal regulations such as P.L. 99-660, which requires an advisory role for mental health consumers, and P.L. 99-457, which promotes family involvement in early childhood education (Sheehan, 1988).

CONSUMER EMPOWERMENT:
BACKGROUND SKILLS AND STRATEGIES

Although the rhetoric of consumer-driven practice sometimes seems much greater than demonstrated know-how, there is a growing list of skills and attitudes for work with service consumers. Some feel that the foundation of empowerment lies in a clinical skill base that promotes self-definition and maximizes a client's case management. Social rehabilitation and strengths-based case management perspectives also highlight client capabilities (Trivette, Dunst, Deal, Hamer, & Propt, 1990) and include many specific recommendations for client-focused interventions.

Clinical skills for consumer empowerment include proficiency in relationship building, knowing when to sensitively confront behaviors that interfere with meeting goals, and helping clients become more skillful collaborators and negotiators. Staff can also advocate for their program to accept consumers as partners. Both consumers and like-minded staff need to network for mutual support (Unzicker, 1990). (See Table 3.6.)

THE FAMILY-PROFESSIONAL PARTNERSHIP

In the past decade, the service sector has increasingly explored how case management services are "alternatively" delivered by family members (e.g., Friesen, Griesbach, Jacobs, Katz-Leavy, & Olson, 1988; Friesen & Koroloff, 1990; Grosser & Vine, 1991; Hatfield & Lefley, 1987) and has described

TABLE 3.6 Questions for Consumers

At the time of admission to the case management program, or as soon as possible, consumers should be asked:

- Do they understand why they were referred to the case management program?
- If the client is an involuntary client or in a restrictive setting: Why do they feel this happened?
- What behavior(s)/situations are causing problems?
- What kinds of stress are they experiencing right now?
- What would they like to see happen?
- What do they feel they need?
- What would it take to have these needs met?

SOURCE: Brands, 1979.

the most effective interventions in strengthening the family-professional partnership (e.g., Ronnau, Rutter, & Donner, 1989; Simmons, Ivry, & Seltzer, 1985; Seltzer & Mayer, 1988). (See Table 3.7.)

The family's parallel case management practice has been far less studied (Seltzer, Ivry, & Litchfield, 1987) and appears to be less readily accepted by professionals than its role as a direct-care provider. Families have a longer understanding and contribute more support services than formal agents (Hatfield, 1981; Lamb & Oliphant, 1979). Families also provide the full complement of case management activities: they assess their member's comprehensive needs by knowing how their member is likely to act in different settings, they link by orchestrating and transporting to appointments, they provide feedback about client perception of services, and they monitor the client's changing status in the community. Also, families often routinely provide valuable short-term financial and crisis aid, and advocate for the client perspective. Finally, families provide early warnings about decompensation and impending need (Intagliata, Willer, & Egri, 1988).

The family's perception and relationship to the case manager also affects its orientation to the service community and their member's treatment compliance. Families appreciate staff who appear helpful and nonjudgmental, who contact them early in the service relationship, and who provide information and support (Grunebaum & Friedman, 1988; Ryglewicz, 1982). The family's perception of this relationship is a major determinant of its perception that their member's service package is satisfactory and of quality (Grella & Grusky, 1989). The family's view of the worker is also positively associated with the client's compliance with the service plan.

TABLE 3.7 Questions for Family Members

- Does the family want to be involved in service planning? Do all members agree that they want to be involved?
- Does the family feel that its involvement will be limited by other time, family, or work responsibilities? Can the case manager help with some of these issues?
- Is the family prepared to participate in the service plan process, or is coaching needed?
- How does the family assess its level of comfort in participating in service planning?
- Does the family see its previous planning efforts for the client as successful or unsuccessful or somewhere in between? Does the family see itself as having previously been a positive force for change?
- What does the family identify as the types of plans that have worked in the best interest of the client? How flexible and adaptable has the family been in terms of plans they have developed and seen through?
- How often does the family want to be involved?
- How does the family view co-case management? Does the family see itself or staff as the primary intervenor? Do they want the case manager to be a consultant or a doer?
- Does agency policy support the family's right to select and to "fire" the case manager? Do they know they have this right?
- What has to be worked out to reconcile differences in case management wishes among family members? Between family members and client?
- To what degree is the family's role supported by policy, regulation, or law?

SOURCES: Adapted from Able-Boone, Sandall, Loughry, and Frederic, 1990; Cophmer, 1983; Dunst, Trivette, and Deal, 1988.

Families endorse specific case manager behaviors. These are behaviors that are seen as altruistic and sensitive to their needs, that are conducted face-to-face in an unhurried atmosphere, and that are viewed as nonjudgmental and respectful of the range of expressed emotions. Timing is also an issue. The case manager should be sensitive to a family's readiness to take on additional case management functions and be aware of any need to renegotiate the partnership when situations change suddenly (Bailey, 1989; Bailey, 1991; Dunst, Trivette, & Deal, 1988; Dunst, Trivette, & Thompson, 1991; Summers et al., 1990; Winton & Bailey, 1990).

There are also behaviors that are rejected as unhelpful or as undermining the family's sense of worth. Case managers should avoid being patronizing or implying that the worker's help is something for which the family should be grateful. Interventions that are unsolicited or reinforce poor self-esteem, that do not provide what the family is requesting, or that address something it doesn't see as a need, are nonproductive.

Skills in promoting partnerships can be developed through participation in formal training (Vosler-Hunter, 1989). The core competency involves communication style and focus. Commitment to families is expressed by being proactive, nonintrusive, and positive and by being psychologically accessible. This is conveyed through an informal but respectful attitude. Case managers should take the time to view families as a unit, to consider possible family burdens and strengths, and to recognize that these can coexist (Beavers, 1989).

Differential assessment of a family's desired partnership should include assessment of family learning style and its current capabilities. Families learn and undergo developmental stages in their own case management skills and preferences (Olson, 1988). The assessment should reflect a family's strengths and needs and also how best to assist it. Depending on the family's record of accomplishment and repertoire of coping styles, case manager interventions can range from crisis stabilization to referral, task sharing, and emotional support. Where one family might require a crash course in accessing resources, another might need respite to reconnect with earlier helpful agents. The degree to which staff successfully engages families rests on the quality of the case management relationship. Families are more comfortable sharing their concerns with staff who take time to establish rapport and who pay attention to all levels of family communication, both what is overtly said and how things are expressed (Dunst & Trivette, 1988; Hobbs et al., 1984).

Interventions for empowerment include practices that support the family's efforts by increasing its likelihood of success. These help members gain new competencies or increase their control over life events, reinforce problem solving by providing information necessary to make informed decisions, help to anticipate things that can go wrong rather than waiting to intervene after the fact, and provide essential back-up and access to social supports. Interventions that build on family strengths rather than correcting deficits and that support family decisions and consciously attribute successful outcomes to the family's rather than to the case manager's efforts, are quality practices for consumer and family member empowerment (Table 3.8).

TRAINING FAMILY MEMBERS AS CASE MANAGEMENT EXTENDERS

Several innovative programs have offered formal training through agencies, advocacy organizations, or university settings to build case management partnerships. These programs intend to provide information and teach skills associated with knowledge of resources and negotiation. Under the aegis of the Research and Training Center to Improve

TABLE 3.8 Quality Case Management Behaviors for Consumer and Family Empowerment

1. *Introducing the process*
   - Describe co-case management as a shared function.
   - Ask the consumer and the family how much they would like to be involved, in general.
   - Ask how much they are able to be involved right now.
   - Periodically monitor to see if this position has changed.
2. *Assessment and service planning*
   - Continuously solicit consumer and family input.
   - Ask what is wanted, rather than just informing people about what has already been decided without input.
   - Discuss family/client rights in the service-planning process.
   - Provide coaching prior to the service-planning session and ask how you can help. Negotiate your degree of activity beforehand.
   - After assessment and planning sessions, explore family reactions, what might have been done differently, and what follow-up each of you will provide.
3. *Linking*
   - Ask consumers and family members how much they want to do in connecting to recommended services.
   - Support and assist the consumer/family's linking effort (e.g., provide phone numbers, identify some of the more approachable and knowledgeable resource persons)
   - Ask consumers and family members if they have relationships with other providers or community contacts. Ask if these relationships should be continued and how they can be enhanced.
4. *Monitoring*
   - Ask consumers and family members about their program impressions. Do they think that services are making a difference?
   - What would they would like the next steps to be?
   - Periodically check if family members feel overinvolved or burdened, and how you can help. Does the family want to be more or to be less involved at this time? Would they be interested in respite? Or would they like to participate in family-professional partnership training so they can work smarter, not harder?
   - Encourage individuals and family members to be informed consumers. Provide up-to-date information about resources and issues and encourage attendance at self-help and information forums.

Services for Seriously Emotionally Handicapped Children and their Families (Portland State University), workshops (Vosler-Hunter & Exo, 1987) and handbooks (Kelker, 1988) have been developed to celebrate a family's insights and to recognize concerns, to offer basic information about conditions, and to enhance the parent professional partnership. Different programs have also taught case management skills and provided

TABLE 3.9 The Family-Centered Community Care for the Elderly Project (Case Management in Aging)

Since 1982, the Jewish Family and Children's Service of Greater Boston has collaborated with the Boston University School of Social Work to develop programs to train relatives and friends of elderly persons to function as case managers with the support of their social workers.

The experimental intervention consisted of four components: the expectation that the family would assume some case management responsibility; partnership between family members and social workers in the development of the client's service plan; providing family members with informational manuals describing entitlements, programs, and community resources; and bi-weekly face-to-face meetings or telephone contacts with the social worker. During these encounters, the caseworker attempted to enhance family case management skills through individualized consultation while monitoring performance and providing supportive counseling and continued assessment of client needs.

The first of three studies trained families of 175 elderly clients to serve as case managers. Findings indicated that trained families were significantly more able to carry out case management functions compared to untrained families who only received the agency's regular services. The second study followed up 78 participating family members and found that the intervention effect persisted and that trained family members continued to provide case management functions two years later. A current replication study is exploring the effectiveness of this training program with a racially and ethnically diverse sample whose relatives have severe medical impairments.

SOURCES: Adapted from Simmons et al., 1985; Seltzer et al., 1987; and Seltzer and Mayer, 1988.

information about resources and entitlements to help families to be case management "extenders." These trials (See Table 3.9) have been modestly successful.

CLINICAL CASE MANAGEMENT

Clinical case management is one of the more controversial of the meta variables because it redirects interest from simple service coordination to a discussion of case management's potential for promoting intrapsychic client change (Bryan, 1990), that is, for changes in self-esteem, the development of trust, and the acquisition of new coping skills. Its advocates, many of whom work with mental health patients, assert that case management interventions cannot be divorced from awareness of traditional clinical issues (Anthony, Cohen, Farkas, & Cohen, 1988; Lamb, 1980) involving bonding and relationship building, transference and countertransference; and a client's ego and defensive processes, developmental stage, and unmet dependency needs.

Supporters of a clinically informed case management practice have also promoted it as a strategy of choice for providing outreach and engagement to clients who traditionally reject office-based clinical practice. Clinical approaches in which professionals aggressively case manage the client and pursue intervention recommendations based on their understanding of projected client life-styles and risk factors have been successfully transferred to different programs (Hoult, Reynolds, Charbonneau-Powis, Weekes, & Briggs, 1983; Stein & Test, 1980), illustrating how clinical knowledge of personality dynamics and diagnosis-related issues can be transformed into case management program policies and procedures. However, there is some concern that these program-driven models are likely to be setting-specific and cannot be easily transposed to other populations (Harris & Bergman, 1988c).

Staff may have a range of clinically infused roles, depending on their program's acceptance of the case manager's potential as an agent for personal change and program funding contingencies. Job titles can include that of counselor, consultant, therapeutic case advocate, or clinical case manager. Staff are more likely to assume clinically oriented responsibilities when other community resources are either lacking or are seen as nonaccepting of the case management program's population (Fiorentine & Grusky, 1990).

Many case-managed individuals have significant mental health or stress-related problems associated with their primary disability. In spite of this, clinical models are often restricted to programs serving persons presenting themselves for in-patient crisis admissions or who are heavy users of emergency and psychiatric hospitalization. Research also indicates that case managers value clinically informed interventions most in these specialized mental health settings, even if their program's model is that of assessment/linkage.

DEFINITION OF CLINICAL CASE MANAGEMENT

Clinical case management has a two-pronged thrust; it is more focused on the changes, options, and pacing of relationships than "broker" models, and it weaves clinical understandings throughout the process of disposition planning, service referral, advocacy, and follow-up. Some view this as an advanced, more expert modality. It builds on an infrastructure of the generic skills of assessment, planning, linking, monitoring, and advocacy and weds this to client engagement, consultation, and collaboration to other treating clinicians, individual psychotherapy, psychoeducation, and crisis intervention. A clinically informed practice is manifested through the conduct of skilled biopsychosocial assessments, demonstrated understanding of different personality types and their needs, skill in tailoring the client's physical and social environment, and being able to intervene appropriately as the client's need for support and structure changes (Harris & Bergman, 1987; Kanter, 1985a, 1985e, 1989).

Community Connections in Washington, DC, represents a paradigm of a clinical case management program providing enriched case management services (Table 3.10).

Kanter (1989, p. 361) defines clinical case management as "a modality of mental health practice" that "is not merely an administrative system for coordinating services." Defined as an intervention to address the overall maintenance of the client's physical and social environment, its goals include facilitating physical survival and personal growth, encouraging community participation, and assisting in recovery from or adaptation to a disabling condition. An extended personal relationship between a case manager, a most-in-need, long-term client, and (often) members of the client's family or caregivers is the core of the intervention and makes more expert, clinically informed judgments possible. The clinical approach is also distinguished by its emphasis on squarely facing those recurring circumstances that support the case manager's authority to assume a "quasi-parental" role in making decisions on behalf of individuals who may be in acutely impaired phases, while also considering those circumstances that warrant reduction of staff support. Harris and Bergman (1988c) understand the process of clinical case management to have three therapeutic tasks: forming a relationship between the case manager and the patient, whose very disabilities make interpersonal relating and intimacy difficult; the use of the case manager as a model for healthy behaviors and as a potential object for identification; and active intervention in the patient's daily life to structure a mutually tolerant environment. These definitions recognize the importance of collaboration and suggest, in Bachrach's (1989, p. 884) phrase, that clinical case management "closes a circle by positing a relationship between brokering and clinical functions."

THE PROCESS OF CLINICAL CASE MANAGEMENT

The core of clinical case management is forging a trusting relationship between case managers and their clients into a therapeutic alliance (Anthony et al., 1988; Harris & Bergman, 1988c). Without this, information that case managers collect may be insubstantial—vague at best, inaccurate at worst. A relationship involving the exchange of primary feelings and respect is essential if case managers are to develop plans

TABLE 3.10 Clinical Case Management: Community Connections, Washington, DC (Case Management in Mental Health)

Community Connections, a private, nonprofit agency, provides comprehensive services to psychiatrically disabled persons. Clients often have histories of multiple hospitalization and have failed in traditional treatment, may be at risk for "falling through the cracks" and becoming homeless, and have been labeled as treatment resistant or treatment failures.

The program has no exclusionary admission criterion and clients may not be ejected from the program. Instead, the program is expected to accommodate to the clients' needs and individual interpersonal styles.

The typical caseload is 15-20. Although the program is staffed by mental health professionals and includes masters-level social workers, psychologists, and psychiatric nurses, clients are assigned to a primary clinician who is fully responsible for an individual's treatment and who is expected to form a close relationship with the client and his or her family. This provides the client with someone to rely on and minimizes fragmentation. Staff also operate loosely as a team in information sharing.

The program provides assertive outreach such as taking workers to shelters or other places where people congregate, as well as home-based services. Food and other inducements may be used as incentives for participation.

Community Connection services include securing entitlements, accessing services and linkage, providing assistance in rehospitalization, aggressive monitoring of medication compliance, and establishing conservatorships. More than 90% of clients are provided direct help with money management. In addition, the program provides physical health care, counseling and psychotherapy, crisis intervention and crisis beds, and flexible supervised housing options.

SOURCE: Harris, 1986.

that truly represent the client's wishes. Superficial relationships, especially with the hardest to reach, are likely to result only in shallow compliance followed by drop-out.

Clinical case management requires time, skill, creativity, and flexibility in building and pacing the helping relationship. The required competencies are similar to those characterizing other advanced therapies: skills in developing trust and in furthering the relationship, respecting psychological defenses, building self-esteem, making judgments and being able to explore relevant issues, and considering what sort of reflective, clarifying, or interpretive comments are most appropriate to the needs of the situation.

Clinically informed assessment places more emphasis on "history, etiology, restorative potential, and professional judgments that summarize conclusions" (Gwyther, 1988, p. 15) than other forms of case management. As a consultant, the case manager alerts colleagues to the individual's emotional status, provides firsthand knowledge of the client's current and baseline community behaviors, and keeps staff informed about the client's exposure to environmental and interpersonal stressors. This information, along with suggestions about what has previously helped the client to divert crisis or manage stress or move to higher levels of self-maintenance, can result in a revised service plan or in alternative programming.

A case manager's clinical expertise can affect a program's perception of his/her authority and ability to monitor explicitly psychotherapeutic interventions. Case managers are less able to affect a program's treatment of clients when there is considerable organizational or professional distance between themselves and other staff, whether the setting is in mental health or in another practice area (Schwartz et al., 1982). Because of this, negotiation may be more effectively conducted when there is the perception of greater equivalence in each professional's knowledge base.

Clinical tactics focus on ego support, crisis intervention, psychoeducation, financial management, and environmental manipulation. Helping individuals with poor self-esteem to gain a better sense of competency and worth is a major objective. A second goal is to assist in community reintegration and to link with natural supports. Information sharing, structured problem solving, role modeling and role play, as well as the provision of highly reinforced positive support are among the favored psychoeducation approaches. Clinical case management programs encapsulated in a larger treatment system will mirror that program's dominant model of intervention. Settings that emphasize social skills training will highlight such competencies as establishing and maintaining friendships, holding conversations, self-managing medications and symptoms, and self-care. Clinical programs that are grounded in psychosocial education will feature reinforcement of affective skills and expressive communication (Vaccaro, Liberman, Wallace, & Blackwell, 1992).

Clinical case managers should also know how to create a therapeutic environmental milieu tailored to the client's needs and wishes, a function some link as most historically connected to Mary Richmond's social casework (Kanter, 1990). Interventions can include environmental enrichment activities, such as connecting consumers to landlords, neighbors, or community "buddies" to provide for previously missing supports, or may require environmental transfer (e.g., shifting individuals to different situations such as arranging for a new roommate or for a less stressful job). Finally, because even modest environmental changes can profoundly affect a most-impaired client, clinically prepared staff can better monitor if changes are experienced as stressful or supportive.

Clinically informed practice is most appropriate when working with special populations. The need appears highest for "deep end" clients: individuals with serious psychiatric, cognitive, or affect impairment; involuntary clients; clients with long histories of unsuccessful treatment or recidivism; clients manifesting loss of skills associated with long-term institutionalization; and seriously impaired persons who cannot tolerate relationships.

Clinical skills are also situationally required and are needed to make determinations of dangerousness, risk, or the capacity for informed consent. Short-term crisis-focused interventions involving posttraumatic stress or violence prevention and de-escalation are also better conducted from an informed clinical understanding.

STAFFING ISSUES

Clinical case management often requires senior staff with programmatic experience and a background that includes advanced training in psychopathology and interpersonal relationships (Altshuler & Forward, 1978). Master's- or doctoral-level staff are preferred (Holloway, 1991). Job-entry guidelines may include in-depth knowledge of the service environment, prior experience in allied settings, and recent training in the newest career techniques and treatment approaches. Programs with a case management career ladder may assign these senior case managers to the most clinically difficult cases. Senior case managers may also carry small caseloads that they are expected to see almost daily, or they may manage much larger caseloads with finesse. This staff may also function in a "blended role of administrator-clinician" (Marlowe, Marlowe, & Willetts, 1983). As such, they provide triage at the client's entry for diagnosis, referral, and case assignment; assist in program design; and offer supervision to less-experienced case aides or paraprofessionals who provide community liaison.

Clinical case management must be supported at the highest levels of program administration to be viable. To work properly, senior administrators should develop staffing and salary guidelines that recruit and retain individuals with the necessary preparation and field-based expertise. The program design should be amenable to clinical practice and incorporate structural supports for staff's contributions as gatekeepers, team members, or team leaders. Another option is to offer *titrated* levels of service, which permit staff who work with the most difficult cases to have smaller caseloads. In addition, there should be sufficient budget dollars and scheduling of psychiatric or other consultation to ensure high-quality clinical interventions. Structuring the milieu to allow bonds to develop (e.g., providing an office space for privacy, or establishing a client-linked fund to be used for recreational and other conjoint community activities) is another example of administrative support.

MULTIDISCIPLINARY PRACTICE: NEW MODELS

The proliferation of helping specialties in the past 25 years has created a new barrier to accessing services: the existence of professionally fragmented, pluralistic theories of individual behavior and how to best meet needs. For many providers, the requirement of having to combine these eclectic approaches into a single product—a coherent service plan—has been resolved through institutionalized support of the multidisciplinary perspective. This has become the "gold standard" of quality care. Case managers are commonly assigned lead responsibility for initiating and coordinating multidisciplinary approaches for clients throughout all phases of the assessment-monitoring-evaluation cycle (National Association of Social Workers, 1984). While this has sometimes been accompanied by sharpening of individual skills, on a systems level new kinds of team building have also been tried.

Although multidisciplinary programming is a well-justified path to service planning, its real life implementation can be perfunctory rather than synergistic. Service plans are often disjointed rather than comprehensive, or include incongruous recommendations based on counsel that is unclear or not accepted by other professionals. This situation creates hybrid plans that satisfy no one and are essentially ignored in program follow-through. Consumers and families also suffer when faced with conflicting advice or partial and discontinuous service recommendations that further muddy an already fragmented program environment.

Many agencies have adopted a multidisciplinary team (MDT) model to reduce professional chaos. These units, composed of selectively recruited knowledge experts who meet periodically, often have serious problems in structure and process. MDTs become even more complex when a case manager is inserted as a new team player with major gatekeeping responsibilities. Both the case manager's professional and MDT role can be unclear to others or resented, and this can worsen preexisting group tensions involving power sharing and trust.

STRUCTURAL AND PROCESS ISSUES

Although the MDT is often promoted as a doable and necessary approach to assembling professional knowledge, the concept can deteriorate in practice. The most common pathologies involve teams that convene superficially rather than work as an integrated body. Symptoms include unhealthy amounts of tension, arguments over whose perspective should predominate in service planning, confrontation about oversight responsibility, and discomfort with including family members and consumers as consultees in planning and review.

A more benign MDT failure occurs when naive team units are convened that work in parallel rather than synergistically. Factors that stunt team growth include disparate levels of professional participation resulting in skewed effort, absence of comprehensive discussion about needs and issues, recommendations that are not mindful of resource availability nor sensitive to the burdens the plan imposes on the family's or client's life-style, and lack of training in team building (Bailey, 1984).

Team conflict can be endemic in some settings (Lowe & Herranen, 1978, 1982; Mailick & Ashley, 1981; Sands, Stafford, & McClelland, 1990). This can reflect tensions arising from status inequality or suspicion of outside experts or represent insularity and a different professional vocabulary and views of service priorities. Territoriality and fear of being outnumbered or having a low impact on decision making can also be contributory (McAfee, 1987).

The case manager's position in the MDT is often precarious and may involve a difficult period of testing and conditional acceptance. As a new team member and the appointed guardian of the service package, case managers are at risk for being the target of group dissension. The situation can worsen when case managers use their authority to deny requests for consultants or service recommendations on the grounds they are too expensive.

Staff sometimes add to their marginal status by going against the group's decisions. Bypassing referrals to programs the case manager feels have poor reputations or telling the group that its recommendations are for services that do not exist locally can be resented by the others as defiant. Asking administrators to release specialists from crowded and billable work schedules in order to attend team meetings is also highly unpopular. As a result, the case manager's front-end effort is indispensable. It is good practice to take the time and effort to work out such preliminaries as how roles and alliances will be developed and the nature of the meeting's agenda and dynamics.

Consumer Involvement

Including consumers and family members in the MDT has created substantial professional concern about this strategy's appropriateness, clinical implications, and pacing. This includes the fear of needlessly placing additional expectations on already overburdened families. Exposing lay persons to the spectacle of staff disagreement is also seen as counterproductive, especially if a team's visible lack of know-how causes family members to relinquish hope. It has been suggested that lay attendance will inhibit the vigorous professional arguments needed to promote superior problem solving. Finally, people do not agree about whether family members should attend meetings continuously during their member's involvement, or intermittently; under what circumstances the family could appropriately assume officially recognized lead responsibilities; and whether a family member could be a team leader.

The history of including family members as key stakeholders in the case management team is redundant with examples of well-intended but shortsighted tactics. Initial efforts, especially in early intervention, sometimes tried to involve family members at all costs and penalized child consumers by refusing to serve those whose parents were unable or unwilling to participate (McGonigel & Garland, 1988). Other programs misused a family's presence as a sign of agreement with professionally driven and often unrealistic service plans ultimately disruptive of family needs and resources. More recently, recommended practice has been to expand a family's decision for involvement: moving from issues of nonparticipation versus participation to empowering families to make knowledgeable choices about immediate and future levels of activity.

MDT CASE MANAGEMENT PITFALLS

MDT case management is a difficult activity. When an MDT is in arrears, clients and their families may find themselves increasingly confused and faced by more, rather than less, disparate or partial service recommendations. Symptoms of poorly functioning MDT activity include inability to develop coherent service plans, chronic disagreement over diagnoses and service recommendations, and endless and inconclusive discussion about terminology or the reliability of testing or other assessment procedures.

Other indicators of professional disagreement include failure to develop conjoint assessments and an unwillingness to change initial positions or to reconcile strategies. Service plans that are ritualistically developed, that repeatedly defer a coherent plan of action, or that recommend services unresponsive to a consumer's requests for specific help suggest limited multidisciplinary respect. There may also be a generalized downplaying of the case manager's contributions. At their worst, dysfunctioning teams bear the stigma of an unhappy organizational climate: interprofessional blaming and name calling and a pervasive absence of a shared language, group norms, or ways of perceiving.

ALTERNATIVE MDT APPROACHES

In the past ten years, there has been extensive debate about how to revitalize MDTs to encourage more coherent service planning and better programming. Although innovations have been reported in aging (Gaitz, 1987), education (James, Smith, & Mann, 1991), health (Mailick & Jordan, 1977; Nason, 1983), and mental retardation/developmental disabilities (Sands et al., 1990), the most intellectual ferment has occurred in early intervention and special education (Campbell, 1987; Garland, Woodruff, & Buck, 1988; Spencer & Coye, 1988; Woody, Woody, & Greenberg, 1991). This is primarily a function of the landmark Public Law (P.L.) 99-457, Part H: the Education for the Handicapped Amendments of 1986. This act mandated family-centered services and a "family service plan," and established parental participation as consultants to the service planning team as a standard of practice.

Three innovative model approaches with strong case management elements have emerged: *multidisciplinary, interdisciplinary/intraprofessional,* and *transdisciplinary.* Although no one model is considered adequate (Bailey, 1984), all attend to team learning issues (Campbell, 1987).

The Multidisciplinary Approach

The more traditional, multidisciplinary approach is typically characterized by separate discipline-specific assessments, followed by isolated plan development and implementation. Peterson (cited in McGonigel & Garland, 1988, p. 12) compares interaction among MDT members to parallel play in young children—"side by side, but separate." In these settings, recognized expertise is treated as confined to one's own profession. Should lay input be provided, it ordinarily occurs between families and *individual* staff. From there, any second-hand information provided to the team runs the risk of being devalued, dismissed, or ignored. Staff development also occurs independently, with little cross-sharing.

This prototype has proven to be the most troublesome for case management. Service recommendations are often isolated and goals are often not coordinated but consist of menus of options. These units are most prone to providing discontinuous and occasionally contradictory plans of action. They shift the burden of integrating recommendations onto consumers.

The Interdisciplinary/Intraprofessional Model

The interdisciplinary/intraprofessional model is a more advanced approach that formalizes internal communication to create a more coordinated service plan. The model assumes that independent, discipline-specific assessments continue to occur. However, more time is devoted to staff development and to informed service planning.

Intraprofessional teams are characterized by greater attention to routine and consensus building. Regular meetings are generally scheduled to discuss cases. In addition, consumers or family members are expected to meet with the team or one of its representatives. Each team member is expected to provide collaborative consultation (West & Idol, 1990) so more informed consensus can emerge.

Although this approach represents a second-stage development, its case management activity is limited to generating the service plan. This can lead to plans that go nowhere. For example, the team itself may not provide any interventions, may not have considered actual resource availability while making recommendations, or may create referrals without a transitional model, falling somewhere along a continuum between the more simplistic MDT and the more fully integrated transdisciplinary approach. Although direct services are often delivered in isolation, select members may "stretch" role performance by assuming additional responsibilities where possible (Campbell, 1987). The team may also extend its life beyond brief meetings by identifying some focal agent to provide direct services and continuing consultation to the others. This facilitates information exchange and encourages similarity of purpose. The case manager can be this focal agent (Table 3.11).

The Transdisciplinary Model

The transdisciplinary model, borrowed from the field of early education, is the most recent MDT arrangement (McGonigel & Garland, 1988; Woodruff & McGonigel, 1987). While this approach is not for every program, it has encouraged widespread discussion of the volitional and situational nature of case management, role ownership, and how service delivery can be better coordinated using structured team learning and internal consultation as resource enhancement activities.

TABLE 3.11 KOOL-IS: Interprofessional Case Management With Homeless Children (Case Management With Children and Youth)

The number of American homeless families is epidemic. Between 500,000 and 750,000 school age children are homeless; 57% do not attending school regularly. Barriers include lack of medical care; child refusing, too tired or hungry to attend school; lack of school records for transfer; and many others.

In 1989, the Seattle Washington School District developed the Kids Organized on Learning in School (KOOL-IS) to coordinate health, social, and education services for this population and their families. The program used a school-based transition classroom, where children could immediately take a nap or get a snack, school supplies, clothing, or academic remediation or enrichment.

The program included a case manager, an interprofessional case management team, and a community service network. The case manager maintained sustained contact with the student and family and provided ongoing consultation to other team members.

The interprofessional case management team included the school principal, case manager, family support worker, coordinator of volunteer services, volunteer worker/tutor, and evaluator. The school nurse, and volunteer nursing and teaching staff, participated as required. The team trained school personnel to recognize children's needs and to make team referrals, helped children and families to access services, and coordinated individual and group tutoring in the transition room. A network of community-based services also provided access to specialized resources.

Seventy-one children were served during the first year. Primary presenting problems included housing, academic, and multiple emergency needs; family unemployment and crisis; domestic violence; substance abuse; and diagnosed mental illness.

SOURCE: James et al., 1991.

This approach is associated with many innovations related to intake, assessment, and service planning (Table 3.12).

For our purposes, two concepts are critical: role release and the expanded role of team members as consultants. *Role release* refers to the exchange of skills and information across disciplines so that interventions can be integrated, rather than fragmented. This is accomplished by planned sharing and by staff development during which professionals learn basic terminology and simple interventions from one another. This expands the resources available to the client through the team's lead agent.

The process works as follows: One person is generally designated to work with the consumer, thereby reducing the number of staff involved in direct client contact and relieving the consumer from some of the need to relate to multiple persons. Within the team all members, including the focal agent, are expected to continuously acquire new learning

TABLE 3.12 Project Optimums: A Transdisciplinary Approach in Early Intervention Intake, Assessment, and Service Planning (Case Management With Children and Youth)

Project Optimus, an outreach program funded from 1978 to 1986 to provide transdisciplinary (TD) training in early intervention, developed a unique approach to assessment and service planning based on the position that responsibility could be rotated among team members. To avoid traditional labels, this lead person was referred to as the primary service provider (PSP). This project's TD approach used a multistage intake and assessment process, which included a preassessment intake and an elaborately prepared "arena assessment."

The intake was intended to engage the family, to acquire background data, and to provide the family with information about their partnership in the TD process. Intake information included previous use of services and diagnostic data. Other family-centered information collected was: its view of the child's level of functioning, learning style, condition, and needs; data related to its support systems, stresses, and coping behaviors; and the family's program expectations.

The intake helped family members to anticipate the arena and service options. Parents were encouraged to identify the best time for their child's assessment and to bring others to the assessment for moral support.

The team selected its roles prior to the arena assessment. An assessment facilitator was selected, and other team members provided consultation about appropriate developmental tools, areas of concern, and how to involve the family and child. The assessment facilitator was either the person who conducted the intake or another team member.

During the arena assessment, the facilitator worked with the child and parents. Other team members observed and recorded the child's behavior and the parent-child interactions. Parents had the option of being either participants or observers. They were encouraged to interpret their child's responses or to make suggestions about approaches that the facilitator might find useful.

The TD protocol called for postsession meetings for continued family input and debriefing, and for internal team development. The first session was conducted immediately after the arena assessment with the family and other team members. Here ideas were exchanged, the child's strengths and needs established, and the family's goals and priorities discussed.

A second postsession TD meeting was held for staff development and critique without the family present. Here the final PSP (case manager) assignment was made, and the team evaluated the assessment process. Finally, one team member, usually the PSP, developed a written report summarizing the team's finding and recommendations. This authorized the PSP to carry out the service plan with the family. All team members continued to provide the family and PSP with formal and informal support and backup services when complicated situations arose.

SOURCES: McGonigel and Garland, 1988, and Woodruff and McGonigel, 1987.

through internal consultation provided under the supervision of others deemed appropriate (Hart, 1977).

Transdisciplinary consultation expands its consultative efforts to include families as direct care providers and as team resources. The twin concepts of role release and role sharing mean that members can assume different active roles during service delivery: as providers, as agents of limited services, or as consultants. Any participant, including the family, is given limited license to assume responsibility for a number of staff functions, including case management. Professionals are still held accountable for the specific tutorial, the surrogate's performance, and for the client's progress.

The transdisciplinary model is the most intellectually and organizationally provocative of all three approaches; it proposes that the primary case manager be identified case-by-case and includes a method for ensuring that competency is maintained. Although it permits a number of program adaptations (Lyon & Lyon, 1980), all permutations highlight the case manager's role as a team facilitator and as a practice specialist.

This model opens case management as a role to be negotiated with involved specialists. One individual, generally referred to as the *primary service provider* or *case manager*, is authorized to carry out the plan with the family. Under P.L. 99-457, this should be a representative from the profession most immediately relevant to the child's or family's needs, a position that some families reject as restricting their choice and as substituting academic credentials for consumer preferences.

The transdisciplinary approach raises significant service planning and monitoring issues that other case management models have ignored: How can case managers determine specialty needs and assess the quality, sufficiency, and intervention schedule for services outside their own professional training? The transdisciplinary solution highlights a process for teaching core competencies to increase the designated case manager's knowledge base.

This model is not easily transferable to programs outside of early education, and even here it requires administrative sanction and tremendous staff time commitment for planning, service, training, and ongoing evaluation (Woodruff & McGonigel, 1987). Its broadest use seems to be as a way of encouraging programs to rethink routine assignment of case management responsibility and how staffing patterns can be stretched to individually respond to client needs.

STRATEGIES FOR MDT DEVELOPMENT

Recommended practices to improve MDT performance range from the least costly to those requiring major provider commitment in time,

TABLE 3.13 An Exercise for Assessing MDT Effectiveness

This exercise is used to encourage discussion among MDT members about their team's effectiveness.

Each member should rate the items privately, briefly noting his or her reasons. Scores on an item-by-item basis should be collected and a group score should be established for each item. Members are asked to discuss their ratings in voluntary, open discussion. The group should focus on items that were perceived as most troublesome or as most successful, and/or those that show the greatest range in responses.

For case managers, additional discussion should occur about they can do to help resolve issues: Is it something that is central or tangential to their role? Should it be conducted by the case manager, by the program supervisor, or by someone higher?

In the following scale:

    1 = Team does not meet task requirements

    2 = Team meets most task requirements

    3 = Team meets the major task requirements

    4 = Team meets all task requirements

    5 = Team consistently exceeds expectations

1. *Goals and objectives:*

   How well does the team meet the objectives of providing MDT input and review?

   How respectful are the members of each other's professional perspective?

   How respectful are the members of the case manager's perspective?

   How respectful are the members of the consumer's/family member's perspective?

2. *Planning and organizing:*

   Does the team have access to the information and records needed to make informed decisions?

   How well does the MDT review and share information in an orderly fashion?

   How routinely are the case manager's assessments, notes, and summaries included as part of the case presentation?

   How well is the consumer/family member prepared to particapate in the MDT?

   How adequately does the case manager alert other MDT members to probable consumer/family member concerns?

3. *Problem definitions and solutions:*

   How well does the MDT encourage differences in professional and family opinion to be voiced?

   How well do members modify recommendations to corporate each other's suggestions?

   How well does the team resolve differences by working toward a consensus, rather than delaying decisions or allowing a few members to dominate?

4. *Control:*

   How well has the team established controls to ensure that recommendations are followed through? What are these controls?

   How well does the team validate the different provider service plans are "in synch" with the case management plan? How does the team do this?

TABLE 3.13 Continued

---

5. *Follow-up:*
   How well does the MDT follow up with family and providers to verify that team recommendations have achieved their anticipated purpose?
   How well does the MDT modify its plan and take corrective action when needed?
6. *Commitment:*
   How committed are members to the MDT? (What does the team consider evidence of commitment?)

SOURCE: Kaczmarek, Gold0stein, and Pennington, 1992.

the conduct of needs assessments, and the purchase of outside technical assistance. One or more of these tactics may be simultaneously implemented to help a team "work smarter not harder."

Team Self-Analysis of MDT Functioning

Needs assessments to analyze an organization's cultural supports for consultative MDTs are available. These instruments commonly focus on a program's workstyle, its goals and objectives, its ability to plan and to organize, its degree of intellectual openness and problem-solving capability, its capacity to monitor and to provide follow-up, and the strengths of its commitment to teamwork (Kaczmarek, Goldstein, & Pennington, 1992). (See Table 3.13.)

Standards of practice for a truly collaborative MDT include shared respect and a knowledge of limitations, consensus about preferred work styles for making group decisions, sensitivity to the members' comfort with consumer-centeredness, awareness of the importance of group process, and a commitment to lifelong learning through formal and informal idea exchanges. Howard (1982, quoted in Woodruff & McGonigel, 1987, p. 167) suggests that a baseline for MDT success is member recognition and acceptance of differences in skills and approaches; a recognition of practice limitations and a willingness to ask others for help and information; and the creation of a nonthreatening atmosphere that encourages discussion.

The case management literature describes several innovations related to MDT enhancement. These include weekend camp experiences designed to build bridges between children's protective service workers and client families (Berger, 1981), supplementary training to link academics and field-based practitioners (Lefley, Berhnheim, & Goldman, 1989), and multi-agency support programs that encourage staff to share case management-related problems about feeling "victimized" by the system and difficulties in requesting collegial support (Krell, Richardson, LaManna, & Kairys, 1983).

Although conflict can be a reality of MDT life, it can be a source of collective growth (Margolis & Fiorelli, 1984). Conflict, especially controlled versions, can sharpen awareness of substantive service issues, produce innovative problem resolution, heighten a sense of team identity, and provide opportunities to address latent and overt tensions.

The case manager's ability to control MDT conflict is partly dependent on the worker's skills and knowledge, structural position on the team, background relationships with other members, and program policy. Nonetheless, conflict can be a powerful tool for client advocacy. It is sometimes good practice to exploit dissension by helping members to appreciate how their own struggles with system barriers, regulations and service gaps replicate consumers' efforts in trying to "make it through the maze" (Nason, 1981, 1983). Case managers can also try to negotiate informal agreements among the major team players prior to the formal MDT session. (See Table 3.14.)

Use of Consultants

An immediate and useful way for organizations to become more competent is to employ a mentor consultant with extensive knowledge of MDT issues. This can be done on a trial basis to evaluate the consultant, to explore if an extended contract would be beneficial, and to set the terms for subsequent meetings.

MDT consultants can be invited to assist case management programs on either an ongoing or a retrospective basis (Krupinski & Lippman, 1984). Consultants can be asked to assist in specific case conferences (*clinical consultation*), to review policies and procedures to promote team building and service delivery (*administrative consultation*), to provide needs assessments and recommendations for follow-up, or to undertake didactic training.

Ideally, consultation should be group-initiated rather than management-imposed. It will also require administrative support for release time and training-related expenses. This can be a touchy issue for financially pinched programs with high productivity expectations that have difficulty responding to requests for staff to be out of the office. If greatly needed, MDT training should be presented as a priority and not merely as a need.

Programs can also recruit in-house experts as consultants. This can be a good strategy for more unique programs who might be concerned that staff will reject external consultants as not appreciating program

TABLE 3.14 Suggested Case Manager Intervention in Enhancing the MDT

Define key issues that are stumbling blocks to teamwork. Are they widespread issues or do they indicate limited failure (e.g., is the issue primarily confined to some aspect of assessment, planning, linkage, or re-evaluation?)

Compile evidence of MDT procedures that interfere with reaching intended goals.

Identify innovative community programs that can provide MDT or related program consultation.

Verify that others share your perceptions of problems: Is it as important to them as to the consumer and/or yourself?

Plan a remediation strategy:

Consider how you can learn more as a team about case management and direct service interventions for hard to reach and special populations.

Discuss if a family/consumer advocate should be included in the MDT to regularly provide informed lay input.

Consider what an advocate's job description should be and how the position could be funded.

In the meeting:

Trade information; link your insights to other's expertise.

Make it easy to compromise; admit your own knowledge deficits.

Overtly link the team's perceptions to the needs expressed by consumers/family members.

Suggest credible alternatives, if possible. Promise to provide MDT with feedback about how well suggestions work.

Judiciously remind the team if there are areas where compromise cannot be permitted (e.g., by regulation or judicial code).

Commit yourself to seeing that the MDT plan is implemented as written.

realities. At other times, external consultants may be preferred as a source of fresh ideas. This need not cost additional money, since many local planning councils, universities, or foundations may be willing to support a time-limited request for capacity building. In addition, requests can be made to public state and regional technical assistance and training resources (Commonwealth of Pennsylvania, Office of Mental Health, 1991; South Carolina Department of Mental Health, 1991; Texas Office of Mental Health and Mental Retardation, 1985).

Finally, case managers and other team members may decide on a course of shared cross-training. This has been found to be a highly effective means of engaging different providers and encouraging new relationships. When the case management program is being introduced, other service programs and allied case management agencies can be invited to participate in orientation and other training sessions as a way to publicize the new service, to encourage networking, and to upgrade the community providers' knowledge base.

Chapter 4

ADVANCED STAFFING PATTERNS AND SUPERVISION

As practitioners of an emerging service trying to intercede in complex situations, case management providers are often faced with choices about what are the most desired and most effective staffing patterns. Ongoing controversy pits those who see case management as a direct intervention requiring well-educated staff who are highly experienced and skilled in establishing primary relationships (Dill, 1987; Lamb, 1980), against those who believe case management calls for organizational and community skills that can be provided by "alternative" employees (Emlet & Hall, 1991). Amid heated discussion of professional and academic preparation, preliminary research suggests that masters- and nonmasters-level workers provide different patterns of service activity (Pulice, Huz, & Taber, 1991). It is clear that the occupation is changing and that images of staff excellence are grounded in the program's model and resource structure, salaries and other "perks," the job market, and the service population's attractiveness (Caragonne, 1980; Johnson & Rubin, 1983). These factors make hiring choices problematic.

This chapter reviews advanced programs through the lens of human resources development (HRD) or personnel issues: What are the recommended qualifications for staff, for recruitment and retention, for training and supervision? How can providers prepare new workers for positions when the staff's previous training may have been discontinuous or nonexistent (Mandeville & Maholick, 1969)? Practice does not exist in an organizational vacuum but reflects a program's supervisory structure, staffing constellation, and education and training requirements—the "bones" of the work setting.

STAFFING/PERSONNEL

STAFF QUALIFICATIONS

As client-serving organizations (Rosengren & Litwak, 1970), case management providers depend on their staff's ability to form relationships, to intervene effectively, and to accomplish the organization's mandate. The ideal staff size is still unknown, and answers reflect different opinions about what case managers accomplish, how their work is conducted, what educational preparation is essential, and whether case management is defined as an ancillary or as a clinically informed intervention.

Support for greater use of a community's natural resources, linkage people, and gatekeepers as effective intervenors is associated historically with HRD guidelines enunciated in the 1978 report of the President's Commission on Mental Health and by the earlier War on Poverty (Grosser, Henry, & Kelly, 1969). This strategy was defended as a naturalistic intervention, an innovative response to a huge personnel-resource gap, and a way to enhance effectiveness by diminishing the social distance between helpers and consumers. These policies can also promote staff diversity, including its racial and cultural composition, while helping to control program costs.

Supporters of a minimalist case management model often champion looser hiring guidelines. In their view, case management's brokering and counseling functions require common sense, persistence, a grasp of the ecological community, and good organization skills. Some advanced settings have also found that interpersonal competence and experience can override formal educational requirements (Kurtz et al., 1984). In Witheridge's (1989, p. 623) experience, it is more important to focus on the person, not the academic degree. While academic accomplishment conveys information about the applicant, one should consider "personality factors first, and credentials second, in the hiring process." Similar arguments have been adopted by those favoring the employment of case management consumers and indigenous community members as being more sensitive to needed system change.

Advocates of case management as more than mere "brokering of services" (Anthony, Cohen, Farkas, & Cohen, 1988; Lamb, 1980) favor advanced academic requirements. Based on their interpretation of the co-mingling of case management and clinical functions in intervening with the most needy, they claim that a good therapist is also a good case manager. To them, a discrete case management entity is bad programming. It ignores the case management services commonly provided by skilled clinicians, adds an unnecessary expensive layer to the program, dilutes the therapeutic alliance between clinician and clients, and weakens staff's effectiveness in advocating in the professional systems of care (Kanter, 1988). Finally, some argue that the more educationally qualified staff are better prepared to work autonomously and to deal with complex issues related to finding and allocating scarce resources and providing differential support.

Arguments favoring the primary professional-as-resource manager have been justified by physicians (Like, 1988), nurses (DelTogno-Armansco, Olivas, & Hartner, 1989), school home visitors (Aaranson, 1989), and other professionals who can legitimately claim expertise. These claims are more just turf protection; they represent thoughtful concern with the complexity of the issues.

Discipline and Experiential Background Features

The varied educational preparation of case management staff makes discussion of professional requirements somewhat immaterial. In reality, entry-level staff are hired from many different backgrounds, with social work, sociology, psychology, and nursing predominating (Goldstrum & Mandersheid, 1983). No one profession can claim to an educational monopoly, especially since the field's rapid change is likely to outpace the development and adoption of formal curriculum in the professional graduate schools (Applebaum, 1988a).

As a result, there is consensus that prior experience, rather than educational background, is a major hiring consideration. Many advanced programs prefer to recruit seasoned staff who are experienced in working with professionals and in community or institutional settings where the case managed population is found (Miller & Miller, 1989). Larger units with many staff positions available or units that cannot find job applicants with the desired combination of credentials have sometimes resolved the issue by creating staff combinations—hybrid "super case managers'—who are recruited from the most-desired professions. The strategy of pairing or balancing new hires (e.g., a nurse and a community organizer or social worker) appears to be widespread. This practice helps programs to upgrade knowledge through interdisciplinary sharing and promotes the use of informed peer support and peer supervision (Walden, Hammer, & Kurland, 1990).

Levels of Academic Preparation

Curriculum developers and employers continue to debate whether post-graduate or baccalaureate education should be the standard of entry practice in advanced settings. Proponents of a graduate degree as a baseline have argued that it provides a better knowledge base (Weil et al., 1985), an ethical basis of practice (Weick, Rapp, Sullivan, & Kisthardt, 1989), and an ability to synthesize disparate case management activities into an integrated whole (Johnson & Rubin, 1983). According to Rapp & Chamberlain (1985, p. 418), graduate preparation equips staff for the complex tasks of facing the "problems of fragmented services and the treatment of clients who need more support and assistance than traditional outpatient services can provide." Preliminary research shows, however, that those with very different levels of background education can effectively acquire job related competencies through in-service, agency-based, or postemployment training (Bromberg et al., 1991; Intagliata, 1982; Wasylenki et al., 1985).

Although evidence is limited, there is some indication that educational qualifications for case managers have been generally set at lower levels in the public sector than in the private sector (Secord, 1987). Nonetheless, when asked, supervisors and administrators frequently prefer to hire staff with at least a bachelor's degree rather than paraprofessionals because the former are thought to have better writing and verbal skills and a more developed ability to work independently (Intagliata & Baker, 1983). There is also a suggestion from the child abuse field (Berkeley Planning Associates, 1977) of a positive relationship between years of formal education and case manager effectiveness.

The MSW Model of Advanced Generalist Practice

Social work's claim to a special affinity for preparing advanced case managers rests more on a theoretically defended than on a pragmatically demonstrated ground. The most common argument is that case management and the undergraduate social work curriculum's *generalist* are conceptually compatible and include parallel emphasis on core coordinating and problem-solving activities (Minahan, 1976). Rapp and his associates (Modrcin et al., 1985; Sullivan, 1992) have also done a masterful job in linking "strengths based" case management to social work's core values. This includes a mutual focus on the individual's strengths, the primacy of the helping relationship, respect for self-determination and client-driven interventions, the use of assertive outreach, and the importance of understanding the person in the context of the ecological community.

As case management services continue to expand to the most hard-to-reach populations, there is growing recognition that staff are being asked to stretch in unforeseen ways. Case managers are continually being faced with a diversity of new services and program regulations that limit practice and impose new role expectations (Rapp & Poertner, 1980). As a result, more sophisticated programs are aware of the need to create a diversified personnel base with more heterogeneity and skill levels (Bachrach, 1992). An MSW *advanced generalist practice* is one suggested academic solution to this staffing quandary (Brieland & Korr, 1990).

Curriculum guidelines for an advanced generalist MSW are in their infancy. Greene & Lewis's (1991) Delphi analysis of curriculum requirements for case management practice in aging found a conservative bent among field practitioners, coupled with support for learning objectives reflecting traditional social work values, knowledge, and skill. The top-rated objectives included knowledge and skill related to the use of community resources, the ability to identify and to mobilize the client's informal support systems, and functional assessment. Certain skills associated with the "newer dimensions" (Greene & Lewis, 1991, p. 44) of social work case management, which had been anticipated (e.g., systems accountability, fiscal authority, and contract negotiation), were surprisingly ignored. The authors hypothesize that their respondents were assuming that work settings are better equipped to provide more specifically job-related, specialized training.

The advanced generalist MSW has been conceptualized as a multi-track curriculum, capable of preparing graduate students for either direct practice or for program supervision and administration. An advanced degree for practice should address the micro competencies needed for interventions with the more difficult, complex cases. Knowing how to help "families and primary groups to reach their full potential and . . . [how to facilitate] more effective interaction with the larger social environment" are additional goals (Moore, 1990, p. 444). In contrast, an administrative and supervision track would highlight case management policy development and implementation, program operations, job analysis and design, work monitoring, and staff training.

A final educational debate concerns the locus of future thrusts and whether BSW programs have the programmatic and field-based capacity to prepare students for advanced practice. Because most graduate faculty now are neither interested nor prepared to develop a graduate sequence, BSW programs continue to bear the primary responsibility for preparing employees. Job market factors are also important. Hiring, salary, and civil service restrictions often limit a program's ability to afford masters-prepared individuals. As result, trained BSWs represent a pragmatic compromise between marketplace and academic factors.

A few graduate schools are already offering bridge programs that combine service delivery with student training (Billig & Levinson, 1989; Rapp & Chamberlain, 1985). These programs have been described as both cost-effective and as a return to social work's roots. They typically include a practicum experience where students serve several active clients intensively. Students may also conduct support groups or monitor a small number of clients whose active goals have been met but who need periodic contact to maintain stability. While such programs can be a good way to recruit masters-level staff to case management, they have been criticized as violating long-term continuity-of-care needs (Kanter, 1987a) and not displaying sufficient commitment to field staff training and academic follow-through.

Role of Paraprofessional Staff

The role of paraprofessionals in advanced service settings is still uncertain. Some authors suggest that nonprofessional case managers who work in advanced settings are more prone to higher levels of stress and burnout, as contrasted with those with a professional education. This is seen as potentially compromising the quality of service and as burdening clients with the need to cope with high staff turnover (Kanter, 1987a). Rebuttal arguments favor a more diversified staffing continuum as a means to cost-effectiveness and to support a more flexible administrative capability for staff deployment. More sophisticated appreciation for the range of case management functions has also stimulated revised staffing patterns. This can include the introduction of case management aides as adjunct providers of time-intensive activities such as transportation and accompaniment, as group co-facilitators, and as liaison to neighborhood and local resources.

Functional Job Analysis

Rigid hiring requirements can be a serious impediment to responsive practice. The reality is that the job is being accomplished by persons with different educational and experiential qualifications. A more appropriate question would be how better to match staff's preparation and the job description, or how the organization can better recruit and prepare a more generically or partially prepared staff to accomplish the work at hand. Table 4.1, "Questions About Staff Preparation and Background," proposes a number of functional items for undertaking a job analysis.

STAFF DEVELOPMENT

Program access to a sequential plan of training that is compatible with the setting's philosophy (Bromberg et al., 1991) and case management mission (Pulice, Huz, & Taber, 1991) is a well-recognized HRD concern.

TABLE 4.1 Questions About Staff Preparation and Background

Does the position require extensive formal knowledge? Should directly applicable experience be considered in lieu of this? Should related experience be a supplementary requirement?

Is the case manager usually required to work independently and autonomously or routinely?

How extensive is (are) the service system(s) to which case managers are expected to relate? Are there many or few programs and services?

How large is the repertoire of functions? Is the work primarily confined to resource and services acquisition and coordination, or does it include the expectation of an intimate, change-producing relationship?

Is it anticipated that the clients may have some impairment in their ability to communicate? If so, how impaired? Is it anticipated that the clients may have difficulty in their ability to develop and/or to sustain relationships? What factors interfere with the client's ability to communicate and/or relate?

How much time is the case manager expected to spend in time-consuming but low skill activities, such as providing transportation or everyday companionship?

Does the job description call for the case manager to direct or coordinate others activities? Does it include supervising aides or others, or being a team leader?

How often is the case manager expected to interact with others of mid management or higher level status?

Because of the profession's changing nature, staff development activities are important to orienting workers, providing a baseline competence, and for upgrading skills.

Case management training has come to be popularly seen as an HRD intervention that promises programs many benefits at relatively little cost. Proponents support it as a way to recruit, retain, and promote efficiency by teaching staff how to work "smarter not harder." This is an issue of immeasurable importance in some programs where the costs of case management have been calculated to meet or to even exceed more traditional approaches (Bush, Langford, Rosen, & Gott, 1990; Franklin, Solovitz, Mason, Clemons, & Miller, 1987; Goering, Wasylenki, Farkas, Lancee, & Ballantyne, 1988; Wright, Heiman, Shupe, & Olvera, 1989). In geographic areas where professional resources are scarce, training has also been used to qualify workers with good interpersonal skills but limited formal credentials. Finally, training has also been widely accepted as a way to help case managers to cope with widespread burnout issues.

Nonetheless, in spite of a growing consensus about the elements of good curriculum, this is little analysis of specific training programs' developmental contents. How does one systematically build a case management learning pyramid, for example. Even less attention has been paid to the continuum of learning needs that discriminate between the educational objectives of "first time" case manager and the objectives of experienced staff and their supervisors.

Training approaches for the new case management are often innovative. A large-scale HRD survey of mental health case management training in twelve southern states shows that four strategies are most common: off-site, brief training conducted in conference-type settings; self-instructional learning overseen by program supervisors; in-house staff development; and practicum-type experiences in which new staff rotate through model programs (Raiff & Ostrosky, 1992).

Despite these efforts, issues related to the continuum of preservice and in-service training have been left to individual providers or to public sector planners. There has been some input from academic institutions but often little extended resource backing. Such programs are intended to provide workers with a greater readiness for the task and to reinvigorate the more experienced "veterans" (Bromberg et al., 1991). These efforts typically consist of brief introductory workshops that sometimes cannot be sustained through public funding. Neither can they possibly provide case managers with the complex set of skills required nor support long-term growth in competency (Ridgeway et al., 1986).

Best practices for case management training are based on the principles of adult learning: training must be individualized, experiential, display respect for the ability of the learner to solve problems, and be competency based (Raiff, 1990). This means that participants should be encouraged to discuss their previous experiences and prior images of case management services, and they should be provided with planned opportunities to learn problem-solving skills from each other rather than from an authoritative instructor. Exemplary programs have included statewide efforts to certify case management supervisors as on-site trainers (Texas Department of Mental Health and Mental Retardation, 1985; Kentucky IMPACT, 1991), the development of parallel "basic" and "accelerated" learning tracks to respond to the needs of entry workers with different preemployment skill levels, and the incorporation of ongoing "alumni" group sessions to continue the educational process and to fill in the gaps in a limited training calendar (Hunter College School of Social Work, 1990).

Newly developed case management programs frequently borrow, adapt, or buy prepackaged material when they cannot afford, or lack access to, qualified curriculum specialists. Participants generally do not like this approach because it cannot address local and regional case management priorities and resource concerns. To compensate, many

programs supplement "canned" instructional packages or rely wholly
on the use of local experts who are respected by their peers (Levine &
Fleming, 1985). These local experts commonly include persons identified as respected direct line or supervisory staff, senior administrators
who have displayed strong commitments to the program, or individuals
with recognized expertise in the allied systems that case managers are
expected to impact.

Case management consumers, family members, and advocates are
important and underutilized complements to any training activity. As
co-trainers and as members of the training audience, their comments
provide valuable "insider" information and help to keep the program's
mission in focus. Good practice dictates that it is important to recruit
individuals who are comfortable and effective representatives of the
consumer constituency. Consumers who have been in a case management relationship of the type the program is addressing, experienced
advocates, and persons who have been involved with the most salient
systems of care in both a professional and a personal capacity are
excellent candidates (Stern, Serra, Borden, Williams, & Raiff, 1990).

Good curriculum design requires that task-focused content, mutual
problem-solving, and an overview of values and philosophy be paramount. An emphasis on competency-based training is essential. Lessons
from the Channeling Demonstration indicate that staff consistently
need additional training in core case management activities despite any
previous related experience or training (Applebaum, 1988a). Many
current training programs have also been criticized as emphasizing
"front-end" assessment/service planning functions to the neglect of
process and clinically informed practice. An outline of frequently identified training modules is provided in Table 4.2.

In addition to formal training, the newer case management HRD
activities have generated many innovative development practices. *Shad-
owing,* the practice of having new staff accompany highly experienced
case managers, is a tremendously effective technique and a capstone
learning experience. Other development resources include: "update"
seminars that spotlight the best local, regional, or statewide practices;
in-service consultation; networking at professional meetings; and newsletter exchanges. "Distance education," such as teleconferences, is
increasingly being used, especially in rural areas. The newly formed
National Association of Case Managers represents one coalition of case
managers from many different fields and is prepared to offer multisett-
ing training on a biannual basis.

ALTERNATIVE PERSONNEL:
CONSUMER CASE MANAGERS

The employment of consumers as case managers is grounded in the premise that people with extended experience as users of health and other human services have gained useful first-hand expertise that should be integrated into the service-delivery structure (Sherman & Porter, 1991). Arguments in favor of consumer case managers proliferate and often echo earlier rationales used to hire *new careerists* during the War on Poverty (Grosser, Henry, & Kelly, 1969; Haskell, 1969) and used by self-help movement advocates (Gartner & Reissman, 1977). These arguments favor the consumer staff's potential for establishing rapport with the hardest-to-reach clients, their role-modeling capability, and their first-hand pragmatic experiences with the systems of care. These contributions can greatly enhance the organization's knowledge base. (See Table 4.3.)

In addition to client-focused justifications, consumer case management programs can be seen as being in a provider's best interest. As one vehicle for crossing the boundaries between the helper and the helped, a consumer case management program may help to convince service constituencies of the provider's altruistic commitment to helping others (Mahler, Blaze, & Risser, 1990). Alternative staff may also be bridges into the community when there is considerable educational, social, or demographic disparity between the regular staff and the program's service population.

Although in their infancy, consumer case manager programs include risks for the provider that must be strategically addressed before program implementation. A common risk is overselling the program to such an extent that early false starts are interpreted as a breaking of faith and catastrophic. Supporters also disagree about how much time is needed to recruit, screen, and train qualified participants. However, realistic time lines for program start-up are paramount. Sherman & Porter (1991) recommend that providers admit risks up front and not jeopardize their programs by making unfounded claims.

Issues related to consumer case management programs are myriad. There are still many unknowns about their effectiveness as well as the most promising job and program design features. An early decision point is whether or not the program should be philosophically defended as a general program enhancement or as a type of compassionate "supported employment." With the latter approach comes the risk of unintentionally "ghettoizing" the position even as it opens access to certain funding streams.

TABLE 4.2 A Proposed Matrix of Training Modules to Prepare Advanced Case
Managers

---

1. *Philosophy of Service, Value Base of Practice*
   Orientation to philosophy and values, historical foundations and recent models of case
   management in social work, current debates and topics related to the specific field of
   case management practice (e.g., child abuse, mental health, aging).

2. *Learning About the Client Population*
   Common patterns (e.g., not "causes") of the problem/disability, symptoms and symptom
   management.

   Current philosophies and approaches to treatment; technical terms used to refer to the
   problem/disability in allied treatment settings.

   Triage: recognizing priority situations that require professional evaluation and consultation by treatment specialists.

   What the client can/cannot be expected to do in terms of independence of functioning
   within the community, identification of the most common service needs.

   Specialized skills needed to communicate with clients: How to work with clients with
   communication or cognitive impairments, how to work with involuntary clients, how
   to overcome client resistance.

   Risk factors associated with clients: What are the most common, worst case scenarios?
   Projected rates of morbidity, mortality, and/or recidivism.

   Culturally relevant case management.

3. *The Ecology of the Service Environment*
   Required paperwork and documentation: Establishing eligibility, record of service
   provision, client status reports unique to the case management program.

   Other service providers: Eligibility criteria, knowledge of funding streams and service
   unit costs, required paperwork needed to access entitlements or needed services and
   programs, information about local community-based resources.

   Third party payment: The limitations of insurance and the Medicare and Medicaid
   systems.

   Building partnerships with the formal sector: Negotiation skills and strategies for
   dealing with caregivers and professionals in the allied sectors.

   Building partnerships with the informal sector: Official policies, how to provide
   support to informal caregivers, educating and assisting informal caregivers for co-case
   management.

   Helping clients and caregivers deal with feelings and issues regarding placement
   and/or movement into less restrictive or more restrictive settings, providing emotional
   support.

   Techniques for home visiting and other nonoffice-based methods.

4. *Case Management Functions*
   Assessment: Development of comprehensive assessments, specialized assessments,
   how to solicit information from other providers and collaterals in the individual's
   support network. Interviews and observation as ancillary assessment techniques.

   Service planning and goal development: How to write goal-focused, comprehensive
   service plans. How to write progress notes that show how the case manager's ongoing
   activities are related to the care/service plan.

TABLE 4.2 Continued

Monitoring and review of service plan implementation, techniques of monitoring. Techniques of supportive counseling.

5. Program Evaluation
   The most commonly used evaluation strategies.
   Using income indicators to change individual practice.

6. Job Management
   Time management: How to balance the conflicting demand to keep records, to meet with clients frequently, and to simultaneously cope with several providers.

   Stress management techniques associated with coping on a day-by-day basis with very frail or highly at-risk populations.

SOURCES: Adapted from Applebaum, 1988a; Applebaum and Wilson, 1988; Pittsburgh Program for Affordable Health Care, 1989; Commonwealth of Pennsylvania, Office of Mental Health, 1991; Walden et al., 1990.

From the perspective of new programming, best practice calls for an extensive, front-end, needs-assessment process. This should be done in several phases, including internally (Zgonc & Jones-Smith, 1990) and with the community's provider systems (Sherman & Porter, 1991). Recommendations include solicitation of staff, community and program input, and provision for follow-up orientation. This approach can help to solve problems, to secure commitments to free up scarce resources, and to prepare a receptive environmental climate once the program is actually started. In addition, early public relations done as part of the needs assessment process helps to lay the foundation in preparing other providers to be more receptive to hiring a consumer training program's graduates.

Community-wide needs assessment should include: discussion of quality assurance issues and related monitoring strategies, the criteria for screening and assessing job applicants, and the development of measurable standards of performance. Persons with authority to make administrative decisions and representatives of consumer or advocacy groups should be partners in plan development from the beginning. Job redesign and accommodation are common features of consumer case management programs. Good practice suggests that hiring should be accompanied by specialized training and provision for remedial training activities. Other accommodations, such as the tailoring of job responsibilities and stress relief arrangements, are also important to program success. Modified job descriptions that allow for respite, time out, shortened work hours, job and caseload sharing, and flexible

TABLE 4.3 Families Helping Families: A Consumer Case Management Program for Homeless Families (Case Management With Children and Youth)

Families Helping Families (FHF) provides specialist foster family services, including case management, to homeless families. Established in 1989, FHF differed from more conventional programs primarily concerned with providing affordable housing. FHF's unique premise was that families who have been survivors of poverty, homelessness, and domestic violence could be successful mentors to others currently experiencing these problems.

The program included community outreach and training and supervision for host families. At start-up, mentor families underwent a state licensure process that included background checks for possible criminal records, home studies, and verification of insurance coverage. Host and participant families were carefully matched. A formal orientation included skill building in adult communication and goal setting as well as training in case management topics such as accessing housing, services, and low-income family entitlements.

Professional staff offered information, coaching, and support to the host families and facilitated a monthly support group. Paired participant and host families also met together with professional staff to problem solve and to review goals.

The project's experience with the first 14 families was that successful host families are racially, culturally, and economically diverse; are open and flexible about privacy; may have been homeless themselves, yet have sufficient distance to teach survival skills; have stability within their own families and communities; are flexible and nonjudgmental, yet retain a strong sense of self and personal boundaries.

The mentor family program promises to be an alternative model for specialized foster care with potentially much broader applications in the field of child welfare.

SOURCE: Cornish and Nelson, 1991.

scheduling, have been proposed as responsive accommodations to the consumer constituency's likely residual risk factors. These strategies are also salient to the needs of regular staff. Finally, it is important that any job descriptions be flexible (while matching the program's expectations) and be realistic in what the program promises.

The recruitment and integration of consumer staff into the organization must be approached planfully. Innovative recruiting must be balanced by a well-thought-out recruitment and screening strategy. Prospective staff should also be provided with trials and options to test out the match between their initial interest and the ultimate hiring decision. Programs that reach into the consumer community should also develop alternative choices for candidates who do not pass pre-screening or who voluntarily drop-out. This is important to retain program legitimacy as an altruistically concerned provider. Providing college credits for remedial or job-related training undertaken is one means of helping probationary candidates to become more employable in the general marketplace, not merely in the hiring agency.

Consumer case managers can be important program resources but they may create many staff uncertainties. Planning should include decisions about how consumer case managers will be introduced to staff and how the latter's concerns about practice standards, job security, and fears that the others will be given "unfair" training and work advantages will be dealt with.

Agencies that anticipate employing consumer case managers should provide staff with opportunities to express their concerns and to ventilate. It is also important that the program's administration have developed a well-thought-out philosophical position that is proactive rather than defensive. Management should be prepared to deal with fears that consumer staff will be used as cheap substitutes or used to deprofessionalize existing positions. While no assurances can completely lay this issue to rest, developing standardized job descriptions and performance expectations can help allay fears that alternative hiring will be quixotic.

Both consumer staff and regular staff can benefit from training that includes team building, sensitivity raising, and discussion of more general staff concerns. Recent anecdotal material and the allied experiences of the War on Poverty report that hostile reactions and unfamiliarity with alternative staffing concepts are often prevalent and result in failure to use new careerists to their fullest potential (Ryndes, 1989). In fact, the least successful consumer case management programs seem to be those that unilaterally downgrade their job functions to more menial tasks (Sherman & Porter, 1991).

Consumer case managers have been effectively used as direct providers and as extenders of the regular case management service (Cornish & Nelson, 1991; Sonsel, Paradise, & Stroup, 1988). To reap the benefits of alternative staffing practices, it is recommended that consumer staff have access to a menu of options that supplement training. This can include confidentiality training, more extended orientation, and any needed remediation in mathematics and writing. Support meetings, both scheduled and impromptu, are essential. These are especially recommended in the aftermath of client or colleague decompensation or set-back to help the others cope with personal feelings of loss and grief. Support meetings are also advised during a program's early phases when staff hostility is likely to be at its greatest, or following critical incidents that may involve role boundaries.

SUPERVISION

It is widely felt that the supervisory relationship is a critical HRD factor that is important to staff retention, job satisfaction, and performance. When work parameters are unclear and the constituency very needy, the multifaceted contributions of the supervisor as broker, staff advocate, primary social support, consultant, empowerer, and resource manager are critical. Many supervisors feel that a parallel process (Kahn, 1979) exists between their own interventions and the work of front line staff, that they are "their case managers' case manager." Points of similarity include individualizing assessment, offering creative problem solving, facilitating access to resources, and devising personal growth supporting opportunities.

THE SUPERVISOR'S ROLE

Case management supervisors provide administrative and staff support resembling the consultative relationship. Practice wisdom holds that supervisors are best recruited from a background that includes either substantial experience and training in advanced generalist practice (O'Connor, 1988) or a graduate degree and experience in advanced case management (Grisham, White, & Miller, 1983). These qualifying experiences help individuals to be informed consultants to their immediate staff and to any senior administrators requesting assistance in setting policy and establishing staffing guidelines.

Since advanced systems are often in a beginning stage, supervisory responsibility for developing functional protocols, for providing staff oversight, and for detailing the program's accountabilities is likely to be more intense than in well-established service systems.

> How well staff perform their functions and how committed they are depends largely on their training, their motivation, the support they receive from their supervisor and team members, and the resources they have available to them. How a supervisor sets the stage for staff to operate at this type of capacity is complex and challenging (Texas Department of Mental Health and Mental Retardation, 1985, p. 3s).

In brief, a supervisor's role in new case management systems is to coordinate administratively and to integrate staff's work to help achieve the unit's objectives. This can include a continuous cycle of program improvement, restructuring and maintenance, especially as the unit's knowledge base of program capacities and pitfalls expands over time. Supervisors in more organizationally developed programs are responsible for overall program well-being and for establishing quality assurance practices that help to guarantee that services are provided to the targeted population.

Newer programs often expect supervisors to play a role in program formation. *Policy setting* responsibilities include creating client-focused performance standards. In addition, policies and procedures must be developed to ensure that the most-in-need are targeted for services and to monitor that services are delivered in a timely and responsible fashion. Other duties include communicating admission criterion to referral resources and to clients and developing clear mission statements about the priority population(s). Policies are also needed for dealing with "system resistant" clients and forms of assertive outreach and to create procedures to determine the need for transfer or closure. External relationships are a condition for developing continuity of care arrangements with other service programs and building and maintaining a positive network with the community and service providers. Establishing trusting relationships with program administrators and policy teams that will advocate for the program and the clients, and evaluating program processes, impact, information needs and client satisfaction round out policy-related responsibilities.

Staff-centered responsibilities include writing accurate position descriptions that link skill and pay, and making case assignments that balance the caseload mix and match the client's level of need to the case manager's ability. Supervisors should also provide staff with opportunities for peer support for feedback and assistance and should conduct individual performance appraisals (Texas Department of Mental Health and Mental Retardation, 1985). Expert supervisors weigh role sharing or other forms of back-up to build program flexibility and design a work flow that outlines the process of case assignment, registration, and review.

A case management supervisor must also create an integrated working unit. This can be especially challenging when line staff have dissimilar work and educational backgrounds. All new staff need to be oriented to program mission, procedures and standards of service, plan development and implementation, the program's interpretation of advocacy, and local resources and services. Some staff may also need intensive reorientation, especially if their current employer does not fully adopt cost containment or client advocacy approaches supported in earlier work settings (Schwartz et al., 1982).

Recurring staff tensions associated with the newer aspects of case management is a major supervisory concern. Anxieties can arise from the work's often public nature or from role ambiguity. Policies, especially those that cap service or restrict programming or that mandate termination of services, may be resented as short-sighted or inhumane. Other common staff concerns include fear of being physically harmed while in homes or in the community and distress about the consequences of case management decisions, especially those that a involve allocation of needed, very scarce resources. Being angry at clients, feeling oppressed and unappreciated by the system, seeing oneself as "totally responsible" for another's actions, being unable to separate oneself from the job, ambivalence about clients and the job itself, and having a need to "be in control" of client and family behaviors (Krell, et al., 1983) are recurring staff dilemmas.

SUPERVISION STYLES

Although there are many different styles of leadership and no single style seems to meet the needs of all workers (Bolton & Bolton, 1984), good human service supervision includes general management approaches that support quality improvement and staff empowerment. These models are most highly developed in the private sector (Hodge, 1989, p. 51). Best practice behaviors include a commitment to quality, being people-oriented, and conducting oneself so as to be viewed as open to new ideas—"zealous" and "invested in helping the people they serve get what they need and want."

Good supervisors are "competent, caring, and committed" (Klein & Posey, 1986) to staff and see their work as important. They view themselves as colleagues rather than as authoritarian experts or as disciplinarians. Good supervisors also mentor their staff and provide coaching and structured, planned growth opportunities. Support is provided by being available and approachable for problem solving, expressing confidence and allowing mistakes, and backing up workers when difficult decisions are necessary (Texas Department of Mental Health and Mental Retardation, 1985, p. 43s). *Being available* may mean that consultative supervision is available as-needed because staff cannot wait for a scheduled appointment to discuss a situation that occurred after-hours. *Expressing confidence* implies that the supervisor provides praise, and creates opportunities to witness praiseworthy behaviors. This may mean accompanying case managers on home visits or rotating the on-call. *Backing up staff* even when their actions prove to be inappropriate or unpopular with administration is thought to be "the chief determinant of how they view the supervisor." This means supporting staff when they act in good faith and exercise reasonable discretion and helping them to learn through mistakes rather than blaming them (Texas Department of Mental Health and Mental Retardation, 1985).

Effective supervisors are essential to program success, especially during unit start-up. Successful programs help to "sell" case management services to superiors who control needed internal resources. These marketing activities should also be extended to the community's network of providers who provide referral and control needed services or assets (Zgonc & Jones-Smith, 1990). The dimensions of personal reputation include being viewed as able to attract, to develop, and to keep talented people; being known as innovative and responsible to the community; and having one's program enjoy a reputation as a quality service that is both fiscally accountable and makes good use of corporate resources (Ballen, 1992).

Frederick Herzberg's (1959) theory of organizational motivation identifies six *satisfiers:* work-related motivators whose relationship to job perception have been confirmed in over 25 years of testing. Each motivation has implications for good supervisory practice (Quick, 1986).

Achievement

Achievement is defined as the successful completion of a job or a task: in Hodge's (1989) use it involves providing positive reinforcement and helping staff respect themselves as "winners" when their clients make gains.

Helping staff to have a sense of progress is often very difficult with the newer case management populations. Workers should be advised to "go slow and grow," and to spotlight even small, incremental evidence of client progress or service plan achievement. Staff could be helped to recognize the validity of community maintenance, or longer periods between crises, or less use of emergency or expensive community resources as signs of successful intervention. Mastery of service plan development, especially plans that disaggregate interventions into several accomplishable steps, can also help sensitize staff to their own and their clients' successes.

Recognition of Achievement

As case management supervisors often have limited ability to reinforce their staff's accomplishments though salaries and other monetary incentives, they must recognize achievement through alternative reward structures. Although adequate compensation is important for recruiting qualified individuals and signaling administrative program support, supervisory recognition can be as important as salary in staff retention. Good practice includes several morale-building interventions. These can include the use of celebratory occasions, such as festive once-a-month staff luncheons, sending informal, written thank-you notes, conveying letters of appreciation from other programs and clients or families through interoffice channels so that individual accomplishments are brought to a superior's attention, writing an article or open letter in the agency's paper, and making public statements about how useful the case manager has been to the program.

Good supervision practice includes the development of clear performance appraisal guidelines. Because newer case management programs are often evolving, staff's understanding of their roles and permissible activities cannot be taken for granted. It is important for staff to know when they have met program expectations and to receive recognition for milestone achievements. Depending on the setting, quality performance standards may include managing an expected case size, achieving the expected percentage of time spent in face to face contact, or capping costs so that caseload averages meet program standards. The case manager's ability to move the client through the program at a normatively expected rate provides other achievement benchmarks. These can include meeting corporate expectations about the time elapsed between the request for help and first seeing the client or successfully expediting a refund. Other yardsticks include submission of reports, the degree to which chart audits find service plans to be current and comprehensive, the match between the progress notes and the plan's stated goals, the correspondence between the service plan and the treatment plan in the more clinically oriented case management programs, and how well external efforts are successfully "pooled" in the master plan.

It also important to establish achievement criteria that are within a person's control. Inexperienced case managers sometimes set themselves up for disappointment by equating personal achievement with program outcomes that partly lie outside of their jurisdiction. Supervisors should help staff to test their perceptions of reality, clarify their work assignments, and help set role boundaries. Supervisors should also be prepared to run interference when staff are expected to accomplish the unachievable: for example, when staff are asked to manage a service continuum that does not really exist or when staff lacks authority to remediate policy deficiencies.

Other reinforcers will depend on specific program policies and guidelines. Bonuses or one-time-only salary upgrades, judicious allowance of sabbaticals and flex-time, and use of formal and informal titles to designate a staff member's special competencies and interests (the homeless case manager), are possibilities. Providing opportunities to participate in training, either as part of the training audience or as a co-presenter, and asking the case manager to return to the agency in a *train-the-trainer* role are also ways to demonstrate appreciation.

Finally, for supervisory feedback to be perceived as more than superficial comments, it must be balanced. That is, it should not be unremittingly positive when this is not earned. Negative feedback should be provided in a caring manner when necessary. Hodge (1989) recommends heavy use of positive feedback in the early stages of trying to change staff behaviors and intermittent or unpredictable positive reinforcement once new behaviors have become customary.

Work-Related Factors

The extent to which the case manager views the job and its responsibilities as inherently rewarding and personally growth-producing is a major source of job satisfaction. Supervisors can be facilitative by repeatedly reinforcing the job's worthiness and the program's importance as an intervention.

Communicating the program's altruistic and ideological components can also help link professional identity to the work setting. Staff should be helped to see how their efforts fit into larger, even national, policy thrusts, or how their interventions make a difference. Programs that provide student field settings, or that are associated with major research endeavors, or that others view as state-of-the-art can also help to create a sense of professional pride.

Creating a desirable work environment and providing commonly needed equipment (e.g., beepers, personal computers, and cars that are equipped with cellular telephones and that are large enough to transport clients, significant others, and household belongings) can also signal recognition of a program's importance while making the job easier. Supervisors can help by developing budgets and flexible spending accounts that facilitate their staff's everyday efforts.

Responsibility

Growth in the scope of work-related responsibilities provides positive feedback for work accomplishment; similarly, skillful use of case and work assignment can be used to signal supervisory confidence and employer appreciation. Caseload assignment can be transformed into a motivator when the more expert staff are asked to assume responsibility for cases that are inherently interesting or challenging or that require very complex coordination. Supervisors can also delegate some of their own administrative responsibility, starting from a modest basis (e.g., representing the supervisor at an interagency coordinating meeting). These tactics have to be used with care to avoid the appearance of "dumping."

Good practice for assigning increased responsibility starts with determining the case manager's preference and interests. Added work or case assignments should be framed as positive recognition of a job well done rather than as a punishment. Frequent checking to see if the case manager is feeling overwhelmed by the enhanced assignments and offering to intervene periodically if needed are also helpful.

Advancement and Agency Growth Options

Pay increments and promotion are the most commonly identified forms of work reinforcement, yet many providers have salary and staffing ceilings that can limit supervisory control of salaries and staff advancement. In these situations, it is even more important that supervisors develop alternative staff options for professional growth.

Occupational research supports the use of alternative reinforcers. Research shows that salary generally ranks only third or fourth as a job-related motivation. It is true that people pay attention to earnings, especially if the job is grossly underpaid; however, once baseline standards have been met and salary increases meted, increased earnings often do not motivate for better performance. In addition, because salary increments are often associated with across-the-board cost-of-living raises, they often lose their symbolic value as a recognition of individual achievement.

Advanced supervisory practice, therefore, includes review of alternative ways to "vertically stretch" staff's growth as competent professionals. Opportunities to gain more knowledge, responsibility, and earned reputation are important pathways to tapping these motivators. Table 4.4 offers a checklist of common rewards that can be used for supervisees.

GROUP SUPERVISION FOR CASE MANAGERS: AN ADVANCED MODEL

Group supervision is a highly recommended but poorly discussed strategy for helping case managers to grow as professionals (Getzel, Goldberg, & Solmon, 1971; Kruger, Cherniss, Maher, & Leichtman, 1988). It involves regularly scheduled meetings between program supervisors and their staff for mutual problem-solving and caseload updates. This provides a forum for practice socialization and allows

TABLE 4.4 10 Steps for Making the Job More Rewarding for Supervisees

1. Ask the case manager to assume additional duties that are compatible with the job classification (job enlargement), such as developing new forms of outreach.

2. Add responsibility from a higher level: for instance, ask the worker to orient other professionals, students, or interns on the multidisciplinary team.

3. In consultation, rotate case managers among tasks and situations to increase staff skills and to provide job variety. Conversely, structure caseloads so that workers are not overwhelmed with an excess of the most difficult cases.

4. Ask staff to take on committee or task force assignments that interest them. Ask the worker to chair a meeting or to represent you at meetings.

5. Be accessible. Provide training, coaching, and ready access to supervision, both planned and on an as-needed basis. Let staff know you care about their concerns. Diminish distance between yourself and staff by sharing case loads, office space, or the emergency on-call rotation.

6. To the extent possible, help staff to have more choices in selecting assignments, setting office hours and scheduling vacations, and doing work at home (e.g., while on call), if feasible.

7. Support the staff in every way possible. Provide consistent positive feedback, and offer at least three times as much praise as criticism. If discipline is called for, discipline in private and praise in public.

8. Establish and review the supervision schedule so as to reflect the individual's actual need for close supervision or monitoring; maintain as-needed availability but decrease individual sessions with more expert case managers.

9. When a situation is seen as most difficult or unrewarding: Compensate for those times when case managers are asked to take on unpleasant or high-risk situations with a good potential for failure; assign a time limit, provide extra attention and understanding, or make a special personal plea for help. Reinforce your commitment to making program resources available to do the best job possible. Count yourself in as a resource.

10. Treat your subordinates fairly and don't play favorites. Remember to say, "Thank you."

SOURCE: Quick, 1986.

case managers to share their "difficulties, problems and disappointments" while permitting an exchange of the "richness of different styles and creative interventions" (Marks & Hixon, 1986, p. 419) the service population sometimes requires.

As a vehicle for new professionals, group supervision is often recommended as a preferred strategy for solidifying staff identity and as a quality assurance practice. One of its major functions is as a monitoring device. Because "newer" case management practice often occurs in the community or involves quasi-independent decision making, scheduled supervision groups are important to monitor that services are being provided with uniformity. It is also one way to confirm that the case managers' professional identity and client advocacy are not being co-opted by providers involved in direct-service delivery.

Case management supervision groups can develop distinctive routines and organizational climates. In some settings, the norm may be to bring problematic cases up for group brainstorming; in others, the case manager may also be required to regularly hold milestone reviews (Berkeley Planning Associates, 1978). Case review may be conducted using random selection criteria either identified by other staff or by the supervisor (Hare & Frankena, 1972). Discussion can emphasize generic case management issues or can incorporate clinically-oriented supervision (Friedman, 1992). It is also recommended that the meetings be treated as "protected time," having mandated attendance and occurring without interruptions.

Despite differences in supervision styles, these groups can be expected to follow the general trajectories of small group formation. Best practice suggests that supervisors anticipate these processes to maximize the group's development potential.

A widely accepted didactic model divides the stages of group development into forming, storming, norming, and performing. In the initial or *forming* phase, considerable uncertainty exists about the group's roles, tasks, and routines, especially if the supervisor or the program are new. Extended questioning about the group's protocols often echo the case managers' personal doubts about work load management and discomfort with program ambiguities. Discussion may also focus on safe, task-centered items, such as eligibility requirements or forms and procedures, thereby deflecting group review of individual practice. Other start-up groups may skew the conversation by focusing on abstract philosophy rather than concentrating on down-to-earth service planning, coordinating, and linking issues.

Good practice suggests that movement can be facilitated through this awkward stage by establishing the group's operating guidelines and by reinforcing that this is a place for mutual learning. Although giving "I need help" examples is a good form of supervisory modeling, at this stage it is unrealistic to expect staff to talk about risk taking or instances where they felt they had performed on a less-than-acceptable basis. The staff's need for a sense of structure can be met by setting time guidelines or standards of case presentation, instead of letting the group flounder by itself.

As groups move into the *storming* stage, the euphoria and tentativeness associated with phase one may be replaced by heightened tension. One symptom is general wavering between being highly exhilarated or being very negative about the service, especially if the program is in an early phase and promised staff, space, or supports have not arrived on schedule. Criticism and hostility toward the program's designers or senior administrators may be blatant. Because most newer case management programs require measurable evidence of client gains, case managers often react at this point by setting unrealistic goals for themselves or for their clients. They may complain that cases are not being assigned rapidly enough (or its converse, too rapidly) and may see outcomes in absolutes, rather than in partial gains.

Staff discomfort can also be expressed by unusually high levels of disagreement and rigidity. Intolerance for different approaches can be masked by authoritative (if inexact) declarations of what the regulations will and will not allow. Although discussion can appear overtly task-focused, staff interactions often reveal biases, stereotypes, and preexisting attitudes related to their clients and to the work at hand. Some will insist on applying solutions that have worked for them in other settings, while some will take a wait-and-see or an experimental attitude.

Extensive conversation about different causes or reasons for a client's situation can be common at this stage. This can represent an avoidance mechanism: by focusing on historical issues rather than what interventions are currently needed, staff can avoid exposing skill deficiencies. Extended, debated theoretical discussion is also symbolic of the taking sides that is occurring. Another manifestation of group disharmony is that individuals will often focus on "their" cases' specifics, rather than permitting more general, issues-focused discussion. This can also be a time of invidious comparison rather than camaraderie ("I get all the cases that live under the bridge.").

Although the storming stage does include movement to more role-centered discussion, it is more common to find elements of secrecy. Staff may resist the legitimacy of peer or supervisory review by making autonomous decisions without the group's input or prior discussion. A curious mixture of premature autonomy and excessive feelings of inadequacy can co-exist. Expressions of guilt about failing can commingle with a belief that one can be omnipotent in controlling client's situations. While expressions of support can help the group bond, a skewed emphasis on hand-holding can unintentionally divert the members from upgrading their repertoire of intervention behaviors.

Group coalescence is attained during the third or *norming* stage. Benchmarks include the establishment of a group culture, a shared orientation, and a degree of mutual comfort. Indicators can include expressions of camaraderie and the absence of hostility; the establishment of formal and informal routines, especially those related to case sharing; and the ability to get things done and to find solutions to issues

TABLE 4.5 Outline for Case Conference Presentation of Case Manager Client Information (Case Management in Mental Health)

I. *Description of the client:*

  A. The opening statement should provide the following client background information:

   1. Name (first name only), age, and gender.
   2. Marital status, religious and ethnic background.
   3. Occupation and current living situation.
   4. Most dependable social support contacts.
   5. Date of first appearance for case management services, and the chief problem and its duration.

  B. Brief description of distinguishing client characteristics:

   1. General physical appearance, e.g., typical dress, posture, grooming.
   2. Ability to relate to case manager and others.
   3. Predominant moods and attitudes.
   4. Description of strengths.

II. *Description of major challenges for client requiring case management services:*

  A. Identification of case management eligibility criteria:

   1. Diagnosis (when and where it was last made).
   2. Treatment history within past two years.
   3. Functional level at time of admission and at present.

  B. Brief overview of client functioning in following community life domains:

   1. Health care maintenance.
   2. Housing/independence of living.
   3. Vocational/educational activities.
   4. Income/entitlement status.
   5. Socialization and informal supports.
   6. Activities of daily living.

---

involving scarce resources and complex service coordination. Groups in this stage are highly productive, in that time is spent in more creative problem solving. Action plans are made that almost every one understands, rather than members leaving each session with individual ideas of what has been decided.

This phase is characterized by more open communication. Some of the "hot shot" behaviors of the earlier stages will have been modified to become more truly consultative. As a unit, the members have a clearer and more realistic understanding of what their functions are, and what should and should not be appropriately asked of them as case

TABLE 4.5 Continued

III. *Description of current problem area:*

  A. Background of current case manager/client problem:

    1. What is it (in concise terms)?

    2. How long has it existed?

    3. Where/how does it occur and who is affected?

  B. Case manager's current assessment of the problem area:

    1. Thoughts on how problem developed.

    2. Observations of factors that worsen problem.

    3. Description of usual counter actions taken.

IV. *Description of desired outcome(s):*

  A. Background of what has been done to date:

    1. What have you done to resolve or remedy the problem?

    2. What have others (colleagues, family, other professionals) done?

    3. What have been the most successful approaches? The least successful?

  B. Case manager's proposed plan of action:

    1. What type of input are you hoping to get from colleagues?

    2. What type of resolution would be most satisfying to you?

    3. What type of resolution would be most satisfying to your client?

SOURCE: Eastern Pennsylvania Psychiatric Institute/Medical College of Pennsylvania, nd.

managers. There is also a greater willingness to disclose preferences as well as mistakes and to evaluate professional actions more dispassionately. Finally, the members' affiliative sensibility may be expressed through spontaneous offers to assist in carrying heavy case loads, to take an on-call out of turn, and to introduce clients to one another. Table 4.5 presents one such working outline used for case presentation in group supervision.

In the fourth or *performing* stage, the group comes into its own as a valuable professional and organizational resource. As a group, staff can better evaluate their practice and share a collective sense of interventions that either work or are less effective. The program's identity will have progressed from being defensive or overly patronizing to a more collegial approach in corporate relationships. Some groups will now be able to act effectively as system change initiators, pinpointing needed program modifications and previously unrecognized community needs.

There may be increased momentum to link community-based case management interventions to innovative program-based services, for example, new forms of program follow-up and joint technical assistance. Finally, the most expert units are likely to enjoy greater community prestige and find their work easier because the program is viewed as able to deliver. These successes will continue to reinforce the staff's commitment to the service and to their fellow workers.

Chapter 5

CASE MANAGEMENT SYSTEMS OF CARE
Organization and Intersystem Innovations

As a planned endeavor to coordinate and monitor service usage, client pathways, and system costs, the new case management is associated with many remarkable innovations in program design, operations, and financing (Borenstein; 1990; Dorwart, 1990; Lehman, 1988; Weisman, 1988). Many of these innovations have been systematically researched, and although the findings are sometimes contradictory (Borland, McRae, & Lycan, 1989; Boydell, Trainor, & Intagliata, 1986; Callahan, 1989; Rubin, 1990), they have spotlighted the need for strategic planning, more information about the interactive provider-environment relationship, better knowledge of "best design" features for organizational sponsorship, and greater awareness of barriers and opportunities in service initiation and implementation.

This chapter moves to the macro perspective, adopting O'Connor's distinction between case management as a "practice" and a "system." On the macro level, case management is a "complex . . . of interrelated functions performed by personnel at various occupational levels in the service delivery system" (O'Connor, 1988, p. 97). Systems issues include policy decisions related to the selection of program goals and models (Bachrach, 1989; Korr & Cloninger, 1991; Merrill, 1985), the packaging of services and service prototypes, the use of specialized or generic community resources, and interfaces with local, state, or federal entities. Some advanced programs have developed information systems to support client tracking and quality control, which make midstream program review more feasible (Applebaum, 1988a; Holloway, 1991; Netting, 1992).

This chapter reviews recent macro thrusts in three areas: (a) innovations in internal program structures, (b) new forms of interagency or interprogram relationships, and (c) advanced mechanisms for resource allocation and monitoring. Although there is categorical overlap, internal structural issues include decisions related to staffing and size, location and internal accountabilities, and the organization of the case management unit. Community collaboration, intersystem agreements, and formulas for collective participation and conflict resolution are "meso" level or "interprogram" factors (Walden, Hammer, & Kurland, 1990). Because a program's financing structure profoundly affects the kind of care planning provided, the last section incorporates a discussion of recent case management programs with strong fiduciary control elements (e.g., managed-care approaches).

INNOVATIONS IN INTERNAL STRUCTURE

A spate of literature describing the relationship between a provider's internal structure and its quality and scope of services has tried to link organization capacity and setting characteristics to desired program outcomes (Capitman, Haskins, & Bernstein, 1986; Carcagno & Kemper, 1988; Clark et al., 1990). Program sponsorship and size (Abrahams & Leutz, 1983), whether the program is free-standing or part of a larger agency (Applebaum, 1988a), the effects of market competitiveness (Jerrell & Hu, 1989), and decisions to contract direct services with one or more providers (Christianson, 1988) have been studied as independent variables. While spotlighting various decision points, as yet this research has often been too limited or flawed in design and execution to unequivocally recommend future program directions.

A program's model of service, table of organization, state or local regulations, or leadership vision are major shapers of direct practice. Rothman (1992) has summarized five factors that influence practice: (a) whether the program is freestanding or is housed elsewhere, (b) the program's authority and control over funding and contracts, (c) staff's dominant professional reference group, (d) characteristics of the target population that may affect caseload size and practice specialization, and (e) whether staff provide direct services along with case management activity.

The position of the staff in the larger organization also affects a program's ability to obtain needed internal resources and to have its agendas supported. Altshuler and Forward (1978) have called for a general restructuring, recommending an "inverted hierarchy" that vests more prestige, greater salary rewards, and additional administrative authority in case management staff. The range of case management services offered by a program is a second structural issue. Providers lie along a continuum from minimal programs limited to information and referral to more comprehensive "full service" programs, which may even include capitated purchase of services (Grisham, White, & Miller, 1983). Programs vested with greater authority may also expect staff to be responsible for a broadened repertoire that may include quality assurance, system change, authority to prescreen and to control funds, and the right to certify purchase of services.

Policies and procedures that govern the organization are also limiting factors. Common restrictions include mandated consultation to families or other professionals, client contact expectations, and related recording and reporting requirements (Callahan, 1989). Others policies that circumscribe practice include regulations that control eligibility determination or case assignment, or encourage or disallow commingling of direct and case management services. Limits on transferring or exchanging case management responsibilities, or limits on defining service purchase and allocation restrict staff autonomy (Austin, 1983). Because of these complexities, no single best program model exists; instead, a variety of approaches work and should be appreciated for their internal logic.

TEAM CASE MANAGEMENT

Few alternative organizational arrangements have excited as much interest in structural options as *team case management.* A case management team shares responsibilities for a caseload with many possible variations in size, backup, and extensiveness of sharing.

Team case management has been conceptually defended as a humanistic and necessary adjunct to case management as a guarantor of continuity of care. For practical reasons, implementation is often considered when program descriptions mandate 24-hour, on-call availability (Test, 1979). Anticipated staff turnover, the need to provide coverage for sick leave and vacation leave, or the expectation that the program will have to manage simultaneous emergencies, may suggest teams as a pragmatic solution. Teams are also vehicles for supportive consultation, shared problem solving, and mutual respite.

Although team management is considered an effective option, not all agree that it offers optimal services or that it is necessary throughout a client's service history. Teams can potentially overwhelm consumers by introducing a confusing cast of staff members (Bond, Pensec et al., 1991). They may also interrupt those intense therapeutic alliances some see as essential for interpersonal change and self-growth (Harris &

Bergman, 1987; Kanter, 1989). The escalating costs and unproven contributions of added salaried professionals must be factored into budgeting decisions. Finally, there is some evidence (Steinberg and Carter, 1983) that, regardless of program description, true team case management only rarely occurs.

Research suggests that neither individual nor team case management is automatically superior; each has certain trade-offs. No matter how they are initially structured, many teams are highly dynamic and often modify staffing practices and delivery options over time and in response to changing circumstances (Asper, Groenhout, & Snowden, 1990). Leadership teams composed of individuals with access to resources to make things happen, or other types of administrative support, are recommended practice for evolutionary transitions (Zgonc & Jones-Smith, 1990).

Team approaches range from partnerships and simple teams to much more complicated structures, such as continuous care teams and their earlier variants (Thompson, Griffith, & Leaf, 1990). Case management partnerships best describe the relatively loose affiliations often found in case management units. These nominal partnerships are often restricted to group supervision designed to familiarize the work unit with client intake and status movement and with the most immediately pressing situations. *Buddy arrangements,* in which paired case managers provide mutual backup, is another option. Buddy arrangements commonly include two or more internal staff but can involve several provider programs. One instance (Bond, Pensec et al., 1991) has been reported of a city-wide arrangement that traded-off after-hours coverage and provided peer support.

Simple case management teams consist of organized subunits in a case management or a clinical setting that share responsibility for providing services to a set of clients. Transitional hybrid programs also exist that incorporate certain aspects of the more complex Continuous Care Team model (described below) without being fully comprehensive or full-service team interventions (Bush et al., 1990; Jerrell & Hu, 1989).

Simple case management teams are often multidisciplinary and include representatives of the most-allied professions plus one or more aides or other part-time specialists with clearly defined but limited functions. These nominal teams are distinguished by the work unit's sense of collective identity. For example, staff may refer to themselves as integrated (Paradis, 1987) or call themselves a case management team (Bush et al., 1990). Because the team's case management function is paramount, sometimes those hired as case managers are more often used as consultants to the rest of the team rather than as direct practitioners.

Research indicates that teams provide different intensities and profiles of services than individual case managers, are better equipped to respond to crisis, and have more knowledge of community-based resources (Cohen, 1983; Zimmer, Eggert & Chiverton, 1990). Several demonstrations report that teams excel in the quality and accuracy of their assessments, and in their ability to provide realistic treatment goals and comprehensive services (Downing, 1985).

Practice wisdom holds that teams are preferred to individual case management, and they are widely seen as a way to ensure quality service. Teams have also been pragmatically recommended as the model of choice when sufficient funds and trained personnel are available. Nonetheless, a team's leading edge is far from established. Although substantial research has been conducted, these studies have often been methodologically flawed and many have been characterized by limited time lines, inappropriate or poorly specified contrast groups, and incomparable definitions of case management (Goering et al., 1988). A team's hidden costs, such as administrative overhead and nonbillable time spent in coordinating meetings, have not yet been rigorously factored into team versus individual comparisons.

The *continuous care team* (CCT) represents one of the more highly sophisticated, theoretically well-developed team case management models. Its core rests on access to significant internal resources and its decision-making authority. CCTs are found primarily in advanced mental health case management settings, especially those that have adopted a psychosocial rehabilitation approach to treatment (Bachrach, 1986; Stein, 1987; Test, 1979).

CCTs have undergone several permutations in name and in scope of effort (Olfson, 1990; Stein, 1990). Evolving versions of the original CCT concept have been successfully carried out in several American cities (e.g., Bedell & Ward, 1989; Borland et al., 1989; Dincin, 1981; Witheridge & Dincin, 1985) and around the world (Hoult et al., 1984).

As initially conceived, a CCT "implies that the same mental health team will be responsible indefinitely for a given consumer no matter where the consumer is—hospital, residential placement, shelter, family, own apartment—and no matter what the client's need" (Torrey, 1986). The team is expected take responsibility for seeing that needs are met but does not necessarily meet all the individual's needs itself. "This fixed point of responsibility means that the client always has a consistent resource" (Test, 1979). Preliminary findings indicate that a client's relationship to the team can be successfully maintained even though individual staff migrate to other positions or to other providers. CCT design issues are myriad. The prototype is for a multidisciplinary staff whose expertise generally encompasses the targeted population's full spectrum of major service needs. The CCT is held collectively responsible for a client's case management. It prototypically merges clinical and case management roles, monitors clients' physical health, administers medication, facilitates job placement or placement in a volunteer job, and arranges for housing. The varying CCT models are characterized by different service philosophies. Other differences are whether or not the program provides direct services along with brokerage and whether any add-on service package includes family psychoeducation, mobile crisis, or vocational services. The CCT's relative embrace of assertive outreach or highly aggressive monitoring, its alliance to psychosocial rehabilitation models, and its ability to control financial monitoring and gatekeeping to inpatient hospitalization are other distinguishing variables.

Because CCTs are administratively expensive, they are generally reserved for the most highly at-risk clients. Daily contact with clients and weekly contact with the family or support structure is common (Taube, Morlock, Burns, & Santos, 1990). Caseload size varies greatly, ranging from 1 to 10 for those who work with the most difficult clients to as high as 1 to 50 for more stable patients (Stein, 1990). In some CCTs, staff have no assigned caseload and all are responsible for providing services to clients; in others, specific staff are designated as a client's "lead case manager" to ensure accountability for charting progress and service plans. When a team shares the total caseload, individual staff obligations are much larger than a proportionate client ratio would suggest. This can be an unanticipated factor in burnout.

The concept of continuous treatment also implies around-the-clock availability. CCTs generally rotate on-call responsibility and provide emergency case management and community-based clinical care. Teams may have shifts to provide for daily, weekend, and on night call, or may provide weekday-only coverage with a limited time "stretch" factor for emergencies. Other programs use emergency backup services as designated after-hours contacts, with CCT telephone and on-call consultation available as needed.

Program start-up has had mixed results, with some programs reporting early effectiveness (Bond, Miller, Krumwied, & Ward, 1988) and others describing this as a struggle (Bond, Mcdonel, Miller, & Pensec, 1991). A suggested rule of thumb is that CCTs may need a 1- to 2-year period to become fully operational.

Team building, planning and coordination, and the development of a group culture are operating priorities. Frequent unit meetings, reportedly as high as daily or twice a day, can be held to address treatment planning, client and system issues, and to decide on team admissions (Arana et al., 1991; Degan et al., 1990). There is also widespread provision for supplementary just-in-time meetings called in response to client crisis. Joint home visits and cofacilitation of therapy groups are other strategies used to provide client support and to diminish staff's sense of isolation.

There has been little discussion of a CCT's administrative pay-offs. Torrey (1986) suggests that, because clients are more likely to remain continuously active, staff is relieved of the paper work associated with formal case re-opening and termination. The administrative downside is that staff may be unwilling to rotate shifts or to share responsibility or supervision with individuals outside their own profession. Job descriptions can also conflict with union rules.

Because CCTs generally do not control all needed client services, interagency conflict arises with "frustrating regularity" (Witheridge, 1989), especially with other providers who share a strong stake in the client's programming. Dispute mediation meetings between CCT and other service representatives is often required; good practice suggests this is best dealt with at the supervisory or even higher administrative levels.

Team case management is an exciting attempt at innovative programming rather than a well-demonstrated generalist intervention. Administrators interested in adapting team-based models to their own programs and communities must consider the benefits and potential staffing and philosophical issues (see Table 5.1). Choices will reflect decisions related to staff and resource allocation and many factors outside of a program's immediate control. These can include state and local priorities, the size and heterogeneity of the service population, the availability of community alternatives, the program's ability to control or influence other providers, and access to start up and to continued funding.

SYSTEM INTERFACE

Relationships to a community's other programs and generic resources are affected by many variables including the provider's reputation, size, funding sources, gatekeeping responsibility, reimbursement authority, and informal clout. There are many reasons why service providers may

TABLE 5.1 Pros and Cons of CCTS (Case Management in Mental Health)

Pros	Cons
Allows for a long-term relationship with the client.	Administratively expensive and programmatically difficult to implement. Not practical for larger service systems
Increases consumer choice about who is to be primary case manager.	Confounds the case manager role; requires additional training and scheduling.
Team input promotes in-depth knowledge of client. Team can better recognize early signs of decompensation.	Staff can suffer from oversaturation of meetings and have less time for direct service.
Can respond more immediately to the client's change in status and need for altered pattern of service because of in-depth knowledge of client's customary level of functioning.	Can result in more costly service usage (e.g., increase in use of expensive programs). Programs that match up with what the team feels is optimal may not be available.
Encourages synergistic problem solving and superior team decision making.	Can create communication overload. Decision making may not be improved.
Can provide internally most of the support elements necessary to promote community tenure.	Requires waiver of traditional union and program boundaries.
Continuous availability of staff over time in spite of personnel changes.	Fosters dependence. Not program efficient. Research indicates gains not sustained over long haul.
Does not create intrusive one-to-one relationships that some clients cannot handle.	Dilutes the therapeutic alliance. Adds additional, costly layers of personnel.
Is able to help program-resistant clients remain in the community.	Does not have a consistently demonstrated impact on use of community programming. Is most successful only with subsets of populations.
Encourages optimism and hope among team members who are provided with team supports.	Alternative modalities include good supervision, advanced training, other supports.

look askance or resist collaboration. Typical organizational barriers include interagency competition, feared loss of organizational autonomy, ideological and status conflict, and interprofessional rivalries and other turf issues involving scarce funding dollars (Street & Friedman, 1984a, 1984b; Stroul, 1983). These issues can have grave repercussions when service to joint clients, pooling of scarce resources, and essential program referrals are involved.

This section spotlights extraordinary private and public intersystem endeavors. The first illustrates a philanthropically supported, private-sector initiative in the field of aging that was designed to encourage voluntary networking between case management providers. The second illustrates the systems-building approach promoted by the federal government under its CASSP (Child and Adolescent Service System Program) initiative. It introduces the notion of a centralized authority and other forms of organizational criss-cross designed to manage services to multiprogram youth and to bring about highly needed system change.

VOLUNTARY NETWORKING FOR CASE MANAGEMENT

The idea of a case management consortium to pool resources and to provide centralized intake, assessment, and referral, represents one collective response to service system fragmentation. Networking agreements can develop single points of access for needed limited resources, decrease the off-putting wait between referral and program acceptance, raise consciousness about specialty area-wide needs, assist weaker programs, and otherwise help to maximize coordinated service delivery

The national Living-at-Home Program (LAHP) was a private initiative funded by a wide spectrum of philanthropies to develop new outreach, referral, service coordination, and staffing models (Bogdonoff, 1991; Hughes & Weissert, 1988; Lee & Yee, 1988). Its broad goal was to develop networks to promote case management and to facilitate service access so the frail elderly could continue to live at home. The program's rationale was that increased interprovider coordination would result in economies of scale that would enable agencies to meet needs more efficiently.

The LAHP was funded in 20 sites; networks ranged from 1 to as many as 75 agencies. A large variety of approaches were implemented that served areas ranging from well-defined geographical and ethnic neighborhoods to city- and county-wide regions. Outcome research confirmed that such voluntary arrangements could successfully provide integrated case management as well as substantial amounts of needed aging services. (See Table 5.2; see also Table 3.4)

Recommended practices derived from the LAHP experience include the following: First, networked programs have a better chance of success when priorities are shared and initial high agreement about goals is sustained. A variety of communication channels is essential. Face-to-face communication among network members should be high at baseline; however, more formal communication arrangements must evolve. Scheduled group problem solving, written reports, and regularly scheduled staff

TABLE 5.2 United by Technology: Cincinnati Ohio, Living-at-Home Program (LAHP) (Case Management in Aging)

The Cincinnati, Ohio, LAHP was a county-based project that eventually networked 23 affiliates. The lead agent was the Council on Aging, the local area agency on aging. From the beginning, it was determined that the major product would be a computerized uniform assessment that could be used for information and referral, to track clients, and to coordinate volunteer effort.

The program's major accomplishment was the development of a joint assessment and a set of working procedures to overcome possible objections related to client confidentiality. Both shared and protected client files were created. Demographic and service information was entered on most but not all clients. In this way, the social worker could discover the extensiveness of a client's services and avoid duplication or make referrals if additional services were needed. However, under certain circumstances, records remained "private" (e.g., those who refused to sign a consent or who were receiving adult protective services or alcoholism counseling). This solution was seen as a breakthrough in developing multi-agency trust.

The LAHP assessment was a three-page form that reflected the best features of forms used at other model programs. Participating agencies were also required to report services requested and those actually provided. The system was evaluated as useful for information management and sharing client-related data; for learning about other programs; for training new case managers; and for referral follow-through. It could be used by both large and smaller agencies.

System utility was demonstrated in many ways: as a source of descriptive client and service information exceeding many smaller program's previous capacities; as a help for referral; and as a means of scheduling and coordinating numerous appointments. It was also widely supported as a management tool that could provide detailed reports helpful in planning, publicity, and leveraging dollars. Specific uses included monitoring case manager caseloads; understanding neighborhood services; and helping to prioritize clients with the greatest need.

SOURCE: Bogdonoff et al., 1991.

meetings help to institutionalize communication. Universal assessment instruments, or shared computerized information systems or other networked instrumentation, are also helpful once turf and proprietary concerns have been addressed. Shared budgeting and staffing are much more difficult to achieve and need long periods of planning and trust-building. Finally, relationships must be consciously developed and encouraged to grow in a positive direction (Hughes et al., 1991).

Attempts to create corporate mechanisms for joint case management are more likely to succeed when the parties have committed substantial effort to front-end planning. This allows corporate realities to be explored and enriches interprogram knowledge. Development plans should include opportunities for informal networking and taking the time to identify shared interests and priorities. The construction of formal intersystem agreements and procedures is immediate and vital.

A case study of a Medicaid case management program (Walden, Hammer, & Kurland, 1990) details a set of good practices for program start-up that correlates well with the LAHP's coalition-building experiences. Planning effort at the macro level was again identified as critical to success. System-building recommendations include early involvement of respected individuals whose counsel is taken seriously and obtaining unequivocal administrative commitment for program start-up. Planned on-site visits and needs assessments are important to collect accurate information and perceptions. Formal policies should be created to encourage equitable distribution of service referrals. These help to prevent future conflicts of interest and signal respect for the programs' growth and survival concerns.

FEDERAL AND STATE INITIATIVES: CASSP

The idea of a continuum of services with case management as a centerpiece program is most associated with the "modestly funded but highly effective" Child and Adolescent Service System Program (CASSP) (England & Cole, 1992, p. 630). Funded in 1984 in response to the Children's Defense Fund's documentation of the plight of mentally ill youth, unclaimed and neglected by numerous government and community agencies responsible for their care (Knitzer, 1982), CASSP has supported many interagency and statewide collaborations. Its prime goal is to build a system of care: to improve the systems under which our nation's most troubled youngsters receive services, to prevent inappropriate restrictive placements, and to provide for transition into the adult service sector.

CASSP is a philosophically driven approach to integrated service delivery that calls for program coordination and balance. Its basic values include the principles of individualized service, family empowerment, innovative financing, and normalization of care. These translate into a focus on the individual child and family, and a belief that services should be provided within the most normalized environment. Other CASSP values call for partnerships with families, the importance of a strengths-based ecological orientation, cultural competence, and unconditional care. The child's right to case management has been a central CASSP value from the program's inception. These guiding principles have been recently enlarged to include support for rethinking traditional financing mechanisms so that service dollars will follow the child (Burchard & Clarke, 1990; Duchnowski & Friedman, 1990; Friesen & Koroloff, 1990).

CASSP represents a structuralist's mecca. The development of mechanisms to prioritize clients, provide oversight responsibilities, and coordinate a multi-system service plan is at its heart. There should be "mechanisms, arrangements, structures or processes to ensure that the services are provided in a coordinated, cohesive manner" (Stroul & Friedman, 1986, p. iv). Within this approach, case management is seen as the glue that holds the system together. According to Behar (1985),

Case management is perhaps the most essential unifying factor in service delivery. . . . [It] has emerged as: (a) the element of planning and coordinating that has combined the workings of all agencies concerned with the child, (b) the energizing factor that has propelled the service plan into the reality of service delivery, and (c) the case advocacy strength that has sustained a commitment to each child and an optimism about each child's capacity to change. (p. 194)

Three superordinate, coordinating mechanisms have been identified for community-based systems of care: management by a *consolidated agency,* management by a *lead agency,* or management by *multiple* (cluster) agencies. A consolidated state agency provides all children's services, either directly or through contract. In this arrangement the individual case manager's authority to organize a service plan typically derives from working under the auspices of the community unit of that agency.

The lead agency approach uses legal mandate or voluntary interagency agreement to designate a single agency for the management of the system of care. Good practice holds that this agreement must be accompanied by a clear specification of the role and duties of each provider system, and by a willingness to cooperate. In CASSP's experience, the designation of a lead agency has varied regionally, and its placement can be in other systems (e.g., education) than just mental health. Experience has also shown that states using a lead agency approach often start with a narrowly restrictive definition of youngsters served in order to maximize limited use of resources.

The management of the system by multiple agencies requires that these constituent structures clearly define their role, duties, and resource contributions. Joint funding and joint supervision of case management staff are permitted under a so-called *cluster* arrangement. Here, the corporate entity consists of representatives of all key child-serving agencies (e.g., mental health, mental retardation, education/special education, juvenile justice, public welfare) that meet locally and at the state level to review high need cases and to develop plans that are subsequently coordinated by the case management staff. Skills in strategic planning, problem solving, conflict resolution, and conveying mutual respect are essential for professional practice at the individual level (Stroul & Friedman, 1986).

Cluster systems have produced many practical recommendations for lead agency development that have been widely disseminated since CASSP's inception. Emerging standards of good practice include the development of a single interagency entity with a formal schedule that meets at a fixed time and date, mandated attendance and participation by senior agency executives who can immediately commit resources to carry out the agreed-to plan of services, development of a community-based "map of the future" to identify and to prioritize service needs, and moving from a case focus to a systems focus (Stroul, 1992a, 1992b).

CASSP has also encouraged the development of many other middle- and local-level coordinating bodies designed to provide discrete input yet also offer a system of checks and opportunities. A two-tiered system is one example. A first tier can be represented by a Case Review Committee (CRC) that reviews the more complex cases, approves unusual service requests or funding arrangements, and focuses on service system and interagency relationship issues. The second tier can consist of a parallel state-level interagency team that assumes responsibility for system and policy overview and is also empowered to review and make findings for cases that cannot be locally resolved (Katz-Leavy, Lourie, Stroul, & Zeigler-Dendy, 1992).

Practice recommendations for staffing CRCs are for agency delegates with different perspectives and training, with provision for representation by family and child advocates. CRCs assist local case managers by identifying, accessing, and developing less restrictive resources. When less restrictive approaches are not available or appropriate, CRCs also work to assure the best possible match between child and program ("Procedures for the Bennington local interagency team," nd).

Although CRCs can exist at either the state or local level, it is considered important that at least the initial review be conducted at the community level. This helps to ensure local input from informants who know the child best and encourages greater community awareness of needs and acceptance of its responsibility to serve its youngsters.

Recommended procedures to build local and the other interagency networks essential to the collective case management vision include a needs assessment that supports the creation of a formal community-based body with specified functions. Preplanning should target the identification of formal and informal provider representatives, local staff who can be trained in "system of care" issues, and consumers and representatives of formal and informal planning bodies. Direct service providers with strong links in the exiting community structure should be recruited as potential team members. The most preferred providers are those with good track records, in harmony with the program mission, and having expertise to lend to planning. Agencies that are recruited into the partnership should also have institutional coordination/collaboration capabilities, enjoy public and private visibility, share the CASSP vision, and have some financial resources to lend to the enterprise. Once initiated, the body should be provided with training and consultation. The group should explore implementation models, evaluate their goodness of fit against the needs and services of the local community, and identify local training and technical assistance resources. Arrangements should be formalized in an interagency structure with lead responsibility for program development. This group should be granted the authority to obtain needed resources and to guide service development. It should also have the authority to support the program supervisor and to develop procedures for joint planning and staffing for collaboration and monitoring. This committee's oversight functions should include development of consumer-driven policies and procedures; it should also be accountable for ongoing provision of community education on service-related issues (Family Resource Council of North Carolina, 1992).

The CASSP initiative has also generated a stunning array of case management approaches for immediate direct practice. A common arrangement is for case management oversight responsibility to be assumed by the standing interagency team that serves as a portal of entry to children's services. This team is empowered to conduct needs assessments, provide county-level planning, and to offer case planning and follow-along. The typical standing interagency committee will consist of a core group representing the most relevant child-serving systems; it is commonly supplemented by individuals specific to any youth under consideration.

Other communities have developed two-tiered case management entities. In these arrangements, a youth-specific team is responsible for a child's service planning and implementation, while the higher-level standing team is responsible for prioritizing children and offering oversight.

Standards of practice for youth-specific teams call for a composition that includes: the parent and/or surrogate parent, social worker or probation officer if the child is in custody, a lead teacher and/or vocational counselor, a case manager, a child and/or parent advocate, other persons influential in the child's or family's life who may in instrumental in developing effective services (e.g., neighbor, friend, relative, or physician), and the child, unless to do so would be detrimental to the child's development (VanDenBerg, in press).

Regardless of format, the interagency approach has been cited as an indispensable component of care. It encourages complete information sharing and helps to pool multiple agencies' staff and service resources so that there is shared responsibility for time-consuming and complex cases. These group processes also release creativity and energy on behalf of planning for the child.

Building a system of care around children has its own life cycle. There is often a need for more frequent team meetings during the early phases of planning, with decreased, or on-the-spot, or subgroup meetings called to respond to emerging problems. It is estimated that a child and family's passage through initial intake, maintenance, and discharge may take at least 2 to 3 years (Katz-Leavy, Lourie, Stroul, & Zeigler-Dendy, 1992). (See Table 5.3.)

Other state-of-the-art coordinating mechanisms have included the development of three-tiered systems and centralized intake procedures. Time-limited case conferences are efficient formats for productive use of staff time and help to keep committee members focused. "Expert" mini-teams that share a specialized rather than a mixed caseload (e.g., who have only child welfare, juvenile court, or special education cases), that work collaboratively, and are available for agency consultation are a recent practice spin-off (Goldman, 1992).

CASSP case managers have been variously described as brokers, advocates, and clinical or therapeutic case managers, depending on state and program preference. It should be noted that the term *therapeutic case manager* is very different in child practice and reflects the notion that children are best served when their everyday environments are saturated with mental-health-promoting meaning (Knitzer, Steinberg, & Fleisch, 1990; Mason, Young, & Yoakum, nd; Young, 1990). Caseloads are generally small, reportedly ranging from 5 to 12.

Empowering case managers and providing needed resources and direction are essential elements of good programming. Personnel descriptions should ideally assign staff so that there is accountability to a community coordinating body or CRC, or other gatekeeper to services. On the individual level, case managers are expected to exercise brokerage functions and to have access to flexible funds to "wrap" individualized services around children and families. Programmatic support for staff should include policies and practices that advance family-centeredness and cultural competence.

On the day-to-day level, the case manager is responsible for conducting the ecological assessment, bringing it to the interagency team's initial meeting, and for facilitating the interagency service planning process. Other functions include gathering diagnostic information from

TABLE 5.3 Bluegrass IMPACT, Kentucky: A Robert Wood Johnson Foundation Mental Health Services Program for Youth Initiative (Case Management for Children and Youth)

Bluegrass IMPACT, a service delivery system designed to serve the needs of Kentucky's children with severe emotional problems, represents one of eight state programs selected in 1990 for an implementation grant for $2.4 million over a 4-year period.

The project's goals include improving interagency coordination, ensuring financing for a comprehensive system of care through creative interagency collaboration and public-private partnerships; and developing a full continuum of community and family-based services.

Over 65 agencies were involved in program design and development. The core of the system is service coordination (case management), which is regionally provided by Local Admissions and Review Committee (LARCs). The mandated members of LARCs include local representatives from the Department for Social Services, the community health center, the schools, and the courts. Optional representation is sought from consumer and parent groups, health departments, and private child-care and other agencies whose involvement is necessary and appropriate to a given region. These committees are responsible for admission decisions, services reviews, and facilitations of local effort.

LARCs are staffed by Local Resource Coordinators (LRCs) who oversee the service coordination efforts within the catchment areas, supervise teams of eight service coordinators, assign cases and monitor progress. Case managers broker services and are a single point of accountability for all agencies working with the child.

For each child, there is a Child's Interagency Planning and Implementation Team consisting of agency workers with primary responsibility for the child. Although agency participation is mandated by interagency agreement for all the major agencies involved, the service coordinator is expected to enlist cooperation from other agencies, private practitioners, and volunteers.

Each catchment also has a Flexible Response Team (FRT) to provide wraparound services. These teams provide crisis stabilization, special in- and after-school support, specialized skill building such as behavior management, temporary shelter, in-home respite, and transportation. Other locally available services include school support, intensive in-home services, therapeutic foster care, residential support services, and summer programming.

Movement into the program is accomplished in stages; starting with a referral meeting with a child's parents or guardian, proceeding to Nominations before the LRC and presentation to the LARC. After a case is selected, a service coordinator is assigned, meets with a family and child, and convenes a child's team for case planning. The subsequent treatment plan is submitted to the LARC for acceptance and periodic review. Case managers continue to coordinate and to determine need throughout the child's program involvement.

SOURCE: Kentucky Impact, 1990.

case records and through personal direct contacts, developing a summary of all major diagnostic and treatment issues (including a review of all strengths and deficits), and making recommendations for needed additional evaluations and the next steps (see Table 5.4).

TABLE 5.4 Guidelines for Interagency Case Planning Conference (Case Management for Children and Youth)

Prior to meeting: The service coordinator notifies the referral source and core team members of meeting time, place, location • Invites appropriate family members, the child/youth, and other auxiliary personnel whose experience or expertise may help the decision making process • Provides referral source, family members or auxiliary personnel with a brief summary of the type of information the team is requesting

During the meeting: Team roles should be established. • One member should be selected to facilitate the meeting • One member should be selected to chart the "issues" and "service plan" part of the meeting • One member should be selected to cue support and encouragement of family/child throughout the meeting and facilitated process

The agency requesting the conference designates a person to present an overview • Content overview should include current status of the case and its essential history, a brief portrait of family dynamics, and a statement of options that the agency has explored

The opening presentation is limited to 10 uninterrupted minutes • Other presenters follow the overview, each focusing on their aspect of the case • Each follow-up presentation is limited to 5 minutes • 3 minutes are allocated for follow-up questions and clarification after each presentation

All presentations should draw from available documentation, focus on the problem's behavioral dimensions, and aim to report known previous interventions and outcomes

A 10 minute "brainstorming" session follows • Predominant issues are succinctly identified and listed in some visible form (e.g., poster board) • The team should verify these are "issues," however, there is no discussion at this point

The conferees formulate an interagency service plan focusing on tasks to be accomplished, taking one issue at a time • Consideration should be given first to immediate need issues • The range of potential interventions should be "brainstormed" • Solutions include changing Setting Variables, the Behavior, and/or the Response Variables • Discussion of interventions should not be agency specific • Options which have been identified should be discussed in terms of potential providers, funding sources

Discussion should consider whether a service might be "built" for this particular case that might create a broader "pool" of children/youth with similar needs and thus warrant additional consideration, planning, and advocacy

The 2-3 most workable/feasible possibilities should be discussed • The case plan should be divided into tasks • A team member may be assigned the task of further exploration • The case conference facilitator designates a multi-agency case manager to coordinate the service plan

The designated case manager collects and controls all case materials distributed at the conference, and keeps the issues list for follow-up purposes • Records and later distributes copies of the service plan to conference participants and others with task assignments (ideally, within 24 hours) • Monitors implementation of the plan • Is a contact for information about significant developments, changes in child's status, need for revision of case plan

---

SOURCE: Raiff, N. R. (1992). The SED Network-Florida. *Curriculum for community based child and adolescent case management training.* Pittsburgh, PA: Western Psychiatric Institute and Clinic. Reprinted with permission.

A rich, community-based knowledge is essential. Children's case managers should be able to identify the least restrictive setting currently

relevant for the client's needs. Other duties include scheduling community conferences to which representatives of current and potentially
involved agencies and other appropriate individuals (e.g., parents, parent substitutes, and the child) are invited. In conjunction with others,
the children's case manager should help to brainstorm and develop a
service plan that reflects interagency input and that clearly states each
agency's role in the plan. Depending on the child's age, it is almost
always essential that the service plan be coordinated with the child
education's plan. CASSP case managers are also expected to provide
periodic and more comprehensive reviews of the service plan, act as the
child's and the family's advocate, and help design services when none
are available through existing programs. Educating parents and community members about the integration of children with serious emotional or mental disorders into the community are important outreach
activities (Behar, 1985; Santarcangelo, 1990).

MANAGED CARE

Few issues have excited as much heated debate as the place, propri-
ety, and payment issues involved with case management approaches
that emphasize a financial control, managed-care function. Embraced
by many policymakers as a much needed mechanism to control the
escalating costs of public service, especially health services to the poor
(Humphreys et al., 1988), this strategy is being disseminated to other
human service settings as a responsible form of quality assurance and
as a way to balance budgets while leveraging new programs.

Managed care encompasses a series of strategies for assuring quality
care while controlling rising costs of service. This is accomplished by
a variety of tactics, either singly or in tandem, that try to either limit
service utilization (e.g., restricting access or capping services) (Tischler,
1990) and/or to contain costs (e.g., offering providers incentives for cost
control or cost-sharing) (Saue, 1988). Individuals who make these
important access decisions, monitor progress, suggest alternatives, or
recommend termination are called case managers.

Many social workers are uncomfortable with managed care, believ-
ing that it is very different from more traditional case management. A
major concern is that managed care is client unfriendly, reflecting the
interests of corporate sponsors rather than service recipients (Edinburg
& Cottler, 1990). This is not a universal position. Advocates, especially
administrators interested in system change, have argued that accountabilities and organization survival require revisiting how the business

of the health and human services is conducted. According to its proponents, fiduciary control promises sweeping positive changes: new forms of provider collaboration, "bundling" monies from different funding streams to meet clients' individualized needs, forcing the service environment to develop alternatives to costly institutional treatment, and offering highly needed program coordination (Abrahams et al., 1988; Richardson & Austad, 1991; White, 1988).

In the terminology of managed care, case management is "a systematic approach to identifying high-cost patients, assessing potential opportunities to coordinate their care, developing treatment plans that improve quality and control costs, and managing patients' total care to ensure optimum outcomes" (quoted in Fisher, 1987, p. 287). Although this concept was initially developed to contain total health care costs, it has come to be more broadly interpreted to include management of related areas such as price, quality, and accessibility of services (Curtiss, 1989).

Advanced managed-care approaches are found most often in the health care industry where medical case management for high-cost illness is often afforded to patients likely to incur catastrophic expenses (Henderson & Collard, 1988; McCormick, 1988). It is a targeted intervention that focuses on a minority of patients who account for a majority of expenditures. Commonly targeted patients include high-risk infants, AIDS patients, patients with end-stage cancer, head injury victims, organ transplant candidates, and patients with chronic psychiatric or substance abuse problems (Miller & Miller, 1989). Managed-care approaches typically attempt to identify, monitor, and manage high-cost cases early in the course of an episode before catastrophic costs are incurred.

Although interest in medical case management has burgeoned in the past decade, its historical roots are traced to the rehabilitation-based models of case management used for workers' compensation programs since the 1940s and even earlier (DeLeon, VandenBos, & Bulatao, 1991). Its strongest recent advocates have been primarily employers, major insurers, and health management firms ("Blues' Case Management," 1987; "Case Management Could Open," 1988; McCormick, 1988). The Federal government expressed interest in managed care for Medicare and Medicaid patients as early as 1982. By 1987, 1.1 million of the 22.5 million Medicaid recipients, and by 1990, 1.3 million of the 33.2 million Medicare recipients were enrolled in health maintenance organizations (HMOs), the predominant vehicle for managed care. These programs differ in whether beneficiaries are able to choose voluntary enrollment in case management or whether enrollment is mandatory. Although these represent the largest public ventures into managed care, some states have also begun to experiment with statewide capitated health funding proposals (Mechanic & Aiken, 1987; Hurley & Freund, 1988)

Among the most common methods used for cost containment are: preadmission or preauthorization certification requiring initial service review that uses formula guidelines or clinical understanding to authorize procedures and number of units of service; concurrent utilization review, to ensure that continued care is justified; second opinion programs; incentives or constraints to receive care from a select number of providers nominated in the expectation that they will be efficient providers; and insurance benefit packages that require the employer or user to share in a greater percentage of the costs of care. These approaches try to reduce either the overall rates of utilization or the average unit price of service.

Managed care also shifts responsibility for expense control to providers so that they are encouraged to be more frugal. This involves financial incentives and control strategies that affect the payment timing and the levels at which service units are defined or bundled (Lehman 1988, p. 68). Payment may occur either retrospectively, that is, after a service is rendered, according to an established fee for service and often with a predetermined limited or "cap," or prospectively, such as through capitation payment, which prospectively pays the provider to guarantee all of a client's service needs for a delimited period, most typically for a year. Harris and Bergman (1988a) have argued that capitation financing is preferred because it defines reimbursement schedules in terms of individuals rather than services.

The introduction of these financial elements has dramatically changed many features of the service environment. A primary difference is that the case management program is introduced as a third-party player with significant power to authorize funding approval and eligibility determination. This endows the model with tremendous potential to change existing delivery patterns in favor of promoting greater services integration and/or a general shift in emphasis and alternative program development. In addition to shifting the ecology of services and their systematic relationships, case management providers can force major internal changes within direct service organizations by affecting hiring standards and policies and procedures related to program entry and discharge planning. Finally, the case manager can have very different authority within the system of care. The capability of payment authorization empowers staff to authorize or to deny services, to shift services to less expensive or less restrictive options, and to determine what additional services and amount of services are or are not necessary. This has led some to conclude that the financial control elements of service management are essential components of advanced practice, without which the service's potential is irretrievably diluted. "If case managers do not control the funding for services, they have little authority other than persuasion with which to coordinate services effectively among multiple service providers" (Loomis, 1988, p. 222). At the same time, ". . . [it] has added to the growth of the case management concept by making the case manager an integral part of the financial planning process and . . . [permitted] the case manager a great deal of latitude in the allocation of services" (Humphreys et al., 1988).

The long-term effects of managed services are still uncertain. They may lead to more expensive costs nationally and on an individual basis. It is also near certain that competition among case management providers will increase as managed-care approaches supersede or supplement more traditional "broker of service" approaches (Applebaum & Austin, 1990), and that this will affect the costs of case management and program staffing and inventiveness.

Managed care differs from other types of case management, but the two are not necessarily mutually exclusive. Managed care/case management has these unique macro features: It (a) imposes limits on choice of provider, (b) attempts to modify utilization patterns through coordination of service delivery, (c) shares risks with providers to alter provider behavior or to encourage new service formation, (d) shifts the incentive for structural changes and cost containment to the primary provider rather than leaving it to the individual consumer (Hurley & Freund, 1988).

The practitioner's role in managed-care systems has been variously referred to as a " 'watchdog' for each person's funds and effectiveness of service" (Morgenlander, 1990), or more politely, as a gatekeeper who provides active, boundary-spanning, ongoing consultation to one or more providers (Broskowski & Marks, 1992). Program and practice try to influence the client's use of certain providers, or to limit the number and types of procedures employed in intervention. Case management providers will differ in certain approaches and levels of staffing according to populations served.

Primary care case management programs (Merrill, 1985) are most often found in HMOs and various Medicaid managed-care demonstrations, such as those that have required mandatory enrollment for Aid to Families with Dependent Children (AFDC) recipients (Hurley & Fruend, 1988). In these programs, a physician or a registered nurse with physician consultation is commonly the case manager.

Medical-social case management models that focus on clients already at risk are a second prototype (Merrill, 1985). These programs are often designed to prevent, delay, or divert institutionalization, most often through utilization of home-based and community-based services. In these settings, the case management agent often has access to monies from grants or the authority to waive normal client eligibility criteria for needed services.

The National Channeling Demonstration, a 10-state research project conducted by the federal government between 1981 and 1985 to test the effects of an expanded array of case-managed, community-based, long-term-care services to prevent institutionalization illustrates this thrust. Here, a major question was the differences in outcomes between a Basic Case Management Model, which afforded case managers only limited dollars outside of traditional funding sources to purchase services, and a Financial Control Model, where case managers had extensive authority over community-based health and social services and spent almost 10 times as much each month per capita. Basic model programs were more likely to develop plans involving access to entitlements and supports; whereas financial control programs identified more problems with personal care and problems associated with health and emotional problems and paid greater attention to quality controls and the development of formal methods of monitoring. The project also failed to demonstrate cost effectiveness (Applebaum, 1988a, 1988b; Applebaum & Christianson, 1988; Carcagno & Kemper, 1988; Humphreys et al., 1988).

The Social/Health Maintenance Organization (S/HMO), is a congressionally mandated demonstration with a strong medical/social case management component. Sponsored by the Health Care Finance Administration (1985-1992) to provide needed and authorized acute, ambulatory, and long-term-care services to enrolled Medicare-eligible persons over age 65, each program sponsor receives a fixed capitated amount from Medicare and a monthly premium from the enrollee and is at risk for any losses incurred outside this fixed budget (Abrahams et al., 1988). Other recent demonstrations that incorporate capitated funding include the prestigious Robert Wood Johnson initiatives in long-term care (Applebaum & Austin, 1990; Capitman, MacAdam, & Yee, 1988), chronic mental illness (Shore & Cohen, 1990; Goldman, Lehman et al., 1990; Goldman, Morrissey, & Ridgely, 1990), and mental health services for youth (England & Cole, 1992) (See Table 5.5).

These programs generally prohibit expenditures greater than those required for institutional care but do fund services that would not otherwise be available. Models differ in their scope of authority. In some so-called "service management" approaches, case managers develop service plans within predetermined cost caps, usually a specified percentage of the cost of institutional care. The newer, managed-care

TABLE 5.5 Philadelphia's Capitation Plan for Mental Health Services

In July 1988, under the auspices of Philadelphia's Office of Mental Health/Mental Retardation (OMH/MR), the city began to implement a capitation demonstration project. This is one of nine projects supported by the Robert Wood Johnson (RWJ) Foundation Program on Chronic Mental Illness. All RWJ programs are expected to develop a central authority combining fiscal, administrative, and clinical responsibility for care and four other features: continuity of care, a full range of services, a housing plan, and new sources of financing.

The Philadelphia grant is intended to cover the administrative costs of changing the city's system for financing and managing mental health services to its Medicaid clients.

The city's Office of Mental Health has created a central authority which is organized as a not-for-profit 501(c)3 corporation. This body is expected to function as a health insurance organization with responsibility for overseeing the entire range of psychiatric services to Medicaid clients.

The Philadelphia experiment calls for three major changes in the funding and delivery of services. First, divergent funding streams are consolidated under the central authority using State and city-county dollars ("single stream funding") based on a formula derived from the previous year's Medicaid dollars. This is accomplished by a plan to close Philadelphia State Hospital and to reallocate resources.

Second, services are managed by the central authority using such strategies as the introduction of intensive case management for high users, selection of preferred providers of inpatient care, preauthorization of inpatient admissions, concurrent review of the length of hospitalization, selection of preferred hospital providers, development of program alternatives, use of performance contracts with community mental health centers, and the addition of new residential beds.

Third, the program targets about 2,000 high users of inpatient and emergency services who receive Medicaid-reimbursed psychiatric services at the cost of more than $6,000 annually.

The authority's payment system is a hybrid of capitation, fee-for-service, performance contracting, and program funding.

High-user Medicaid clients received capitated services that are calculated on an analysis of current costs and utilization rates. These will be risk-adjusted, so that they will increase with a higher likelihood of hospitalization and longer hospital stay.

It is anticipated that the use of single-stream funding will substitute increased community-based services for inpatient care. However, a variety of other financial outcomes are anticipated with a "mixed" financial outlook. Predictions include that: per capita costs of mental health care may decrease, total costs of Medicaid psychiatric care may increase overall, and costs may be shifted from programs funded by Medicaid to city dollars.

The emergent nature of this program calls for evaluation research that will study the overall impact and unanswered quality of care issues. The Philadelphia capitation financing scheme will help to clarify the fiscal relationship between authority and service providers in terms of such methods as competitive bidding, incentive contracts, or direct provision of service; and other economic issues associated with public mental health such as ability to avoid the rigidities of civil service systems and the effects of regulation authority.

SOURCES: Goldman, Morrissey, and Ridgely, 1990; Rothbard et al., 1989; Schinnar and Rothbard, 1989; and Shore and Cohen, 1990.

model uses prospective financing as an initiative. This shifts financial responsibility and liability for expenditures to provider agencies, which are then at risk for costs that exceed the prepaid amount but that can create a surplus if costs are kept below the capitated payments the agency receives. The risks of managed-care approaches have been widely discussed, along with incentives for system-level responses. It is widely acknowledged that suspicion concerning program impact will always be endemic, at least in the initial stages. The disadvantages at the macro level include expression of widespread negative effect on individual treatment, more global service system concerns, and the added costs of doing business.

Managed care can be potentially disruptive of the type of services received and the relationship between clients and direct service providers. The most frequently voiced concerns include: anticipated fragmentation of care resulting from communication barriers between clinicians and anonymous utilization reviewers, disruption of treatment due to frequent and intrusive review processes, and protection of confidentiality.

On the systems level, there is some anxiety that managed care will restrict choices or cause the field to "dry up" so that certain services, especially those that are innovative or risk-taking, will no longer be available. Programs could be forced to offer a less expensive unit cost of service without having the authority to ensure that adequate staffing patterns and staff quality are maintained. Managed-care proposals can also seriously alienate providers. There are also many hidden costs to be factored into the service equation: the need to develop and pay for a managed-care staff and the attendant bureaucratic expenses associated with utilization review, productivity monitoring and quality assurances, and instability in relationships due to yearly renegotiation of contracts (Borenstein, 1990; Callahan, 1989). Assurances that managed-care approaches can effectively halt the rise in health care and allied costs, and that they do not harm some clients is as yet insufficient (Newman & Bricklin, 1991; Rodriguez, 1989; Weisman, 1988).

Not all cases are appropriate for managed care. A fully comprehensive managed-care approach should be restricted to only the most complex and expensive cases. Although diagnosis or other categorical conditions have been mainly used as predictors of targeting patients for managed care, contingency factors such as age, treatment setting, or geographic region should be considered (Goldstein et al., 1988). Programs also need to anticipate shifts in the financial landscape and should know how to create sufficient surpluses so that future incurred costs associated with increases in fixed costs or service costs can be accommodated.

When managed care is appropriate, it should begin early. Service plans should also be tailored to accommodate regional differences in resources and the area's practices. Standards of high-quality care should be developed to assist in decision making and carrying out the other phases of case management. And, last, it is essential that the program must maintain a focus on the client's well-being.

Many good practices have been identified to nurture the growth of high quality managed care. Suggestions include the development of provider credentialing standards and practices, quality assurance and utilization review procedures, and medical records review. Facility and staff reputation and staff turnover rates can be treated as indicators of provider reliability. Written grievance procedures and a schedule and method for determining enrollee satisfaction imply a program's commitment to quality and should be factors in provider selection. Finally, on-site monitoring is essential to review operations and to assess how well a program is working.

Recommendations for better managed care systems include rational assignment of staff function. Training in outcome measures and outcome-based decision making and fiscal and data based management is important. Staff should be able to assess a provider's likelihood of financial and administrative survival and know how to apply clinical and field-based judgements about other care options. The case manager should also be skilled in persuasion and other interpersonal tactics, which encourage clients to use endorsed services. Finally, staff should have the authority to recommend services. When making decisions, case managers should consider the effect of service costs on their program's budget and know how to assess the impact of less costly interventions on the recipient's quality of life (Fisher, 1987; Patterson, 1990; Weiner, 1990). Finally, staff should continue to develop options and to research alternatives to the existing menu.

CONCLUDING STATEMENT

This overview of advances in case management illustrates some of the most exciting developments in a vehemently debated, empirically flexible, and emerging field of service. While dialectical discussion continues about social work's professional relationship to case management as an enterprise, there can be little doubt that these programs have arrived and will shortly affect most social work practitioners either as a practice of choice or as a constraining influence.

Advanced case management is a complex approach to many intricate and complicated problems. It is likely that the service environment will continue to grow in scope and diversity, reflecting the changes in the world in which we live. New needs and service populations will emerge as advocacy challenges and breakthroughs in treatment and service systems become institutionalized. Competition for the right to be a provider of case management services will also increase as direct providers facing increasingly lean times try to exercise control over their corporate destinies or to gain access to new, potentially profitable programs. Competition is likely to be spread among a much larger field of players: advocacy organizations, direct public service providers, for-profit management corporations, and combinations of self-employed consultants. More rigorous standards of case management practice, licensing, and credentialing are plausible.

Social workers have an obligation to ensure that broad policy efforts to contain expenses, to limit care to the most-in-need, and to create ambitious schema for forging community-wide relationships do not lose sight of the importance of the individual, the much larger scope of unfunded need, and the obligation to integrate case management with actual support for direct service delivery. The profession should assume leadership to see that a coherent and tested system of accountability is developed and that institutionalization of measures of effectiveness remains a public and an occupational priority. Recommendations for new systems of resource allocation and control should be carefully scrutinized and the profession should work to support those deemed in the public's best interest. Alliance-building efforts between social workers, case managers, and consumers are likely, along with new knowledge about effective strategic partnerships.

A critical issue facing the profession is the still-to-come contributions of social work's values and knowledge base, educational resources, and research expertise. Much more is needed for developing elements of good practice, quality assurances, and assisting the transformation of state-of-the-art knowledge into everyday practice. The role and obligations of graduate programs in supporting public practice have not been recent curricula priorities, yet pressures are increasing to build stronger connections between academia and field-based manpower needs.

This book provides broad guidelines for the pursuit of such knowledge and raises questions that are not yet answered and still need to be asked. Johnson and Rubin's (1983, p. 54) challenge remains as salient today as it did a decade ago: "The history and commitments of social work give social work every reason to assert a leadership role in this area. It remains to be seen whether social work practitioners will make such a claim."

REFERENCES

Aaranson, M. (1989). The case manager-home visitor. *Child Welfare, 68*(3), 339-334.

Abel-Boone, H., Sandall, S. R., Loughry, A., & Frederick, L. (1990). An informed, family-centered approach to Public Law 99-457: Parental views. *Topics in Early Childhood Special Education, 10*(1), 100-111.

Abrahams, R., & Lamb, S. (1988). Developing reliable assessment in case-managed geriatric long term care programs. *Quality Review Bulletin, 14,* 179-186.

Abrahams, R., & Leutz, W. (1983). The consolidated model of case management and service provision to the elderly. *Pride Institute Journal of Long Term Home Health Care, 2*(Fall), 29-34.

Abrahams, R., Nonnenkamp, L., Dunn, S., Mehta, S., & Woodard, P. (1988). Case management in the social health maintenance organization. *Generations, 12*(5), 39-43.

Abramczyk, L. W. (1989, April). *Social work education for working with seriously emotionally disturbed children and adolescents.* Paper from a symposium on social work education and child mental health, sponsored by the National Association of Deans and Directors of Schools of Social Work (NADDSSW). Charleston, SC: National Association of Deans and Directors of Schools of Social Work.

Abramson, J. C. (1990). Enhancing patient participation: Clinical strategies in the discharge planning process. *Social Work in Health Care, 14*(4), 53-68.

Adams, A. C., & Schlesinger, E. G. (1988). Group approach to training ethnic-sensitive practitioners. In C. Jacobs & D. Bowles (Eds.), *Ethnicity and race* (pp. 204-216). Silver Springs, MD: National Association of Social Workers.

Altshuler, S. C., & Forward, J. (1978). The inverted hierarchy: A case manager approach to mental health services. *Administration in Mental Health, 6*(1), 57-68.

American Hospital Association. (1988). Discharge planner or case manager? *Discharge Planning Update, 8*(1), 10.

American Psychiatric Association. (1987). *Diagnostic and statistical manual of mental disorders.* Washington, DC: Author.

Anthony, W. A., Cohen, M., Farkas, M., & Cohen, B. F. (1988). Clinical care update: The chronically mentally ill: Case management—More than a response to a dysfunctional system. *Community Mental Health Journal, 24*(3), 219-228.

Applebaum, R. (1988a). Lessons from the National Channeling Demonstration. *Generations, 12*(5), 58-61.

Applebaum, R. (1988b). Evaluation of the National Long Term Care Demonstration: Recruitment and characteristics of channeling clients [Special issue]. *Health Services Research, 231.*

Applebaum, R., & Austin, C. D. (1990). *Long-term care case management: Design and evaluation.* New York: Springer.

Applebaum, R., & Christianson, J. (1988). Using case management to monitor community-based long term care. *Quality Review Bulletin, 14,* 227-231.

Applebaum, R. A., & Wilson, N. L. (1988). Training needs of case managers serving long-term care clients: Lessons from the National Long-Term Care Channeling Demonstration. *Gerontologist, 28*(2), 172-176.

Arana, J. D., Hastings, B., & Herron, E. (1991). Continuous care teams in intensive outpatient treatment of chronic mentally ill patients. *Hospital and Community Psychiatry, 42*(5), 503-507.

Ashley, A. (1988). Case management: The need to define goals. *Hospital and Community Psychiatry, 39*(5), 499-500.

Asper, R. D., Groenhout, J., & Snowden. P. (Speakers). (1990, September). *Spotlight: Kent County, Michigan: Program evaluation—Moving from a brokerage model to an assertive treatment team model.* (Cassette Recording No. T039). Paper presented at Foundations for Success: A Blueprint for the Future. The First National Case Management Conference, Cincinnati, Ohio. Richmond, VA: Visual Aids Electronics.

Atchley, S. J. (1989). The Ohio quality assurance project. *Generations 13*(1), 57-59.

Austin, C. D. (1983). Case management in long-term care: Options and opportunities. *Health and Social Work, 8*(1), 16-30.

Austin, C. D. (1988, November). Case management: Myths and realities. Paper presented at the National Association of Social Work Professional Symposium, Philadelphia, PA.

Axelrod, S., & Wetzler, S. (1989). Factors associated with better compliance with psychiatric aftercare. *Hospital and Community Psychiatry, 40,* 397-401.

Bachrach, L. L. (1979). Planning mental health services for chronic patients. *Hospital and Community Psychiatry, 30,* 387-393.

Bachrach, L. L. (1986). The challenge of service planning for chronic mental patients. Community Mental Health Journal, 27, 170-174.

Bachrach, L. L. (1989). Case management: Toward a shared definition. *Hospital and Community Psychiatry, 40,* 883-884.

Bachrach, L. L. (1991). The thirteenth principle. *Hospital and Community Psychiatry, 42,* 1205-1206.

Bachrach, L. L. (1992). Case management revisited. *Hospital and Community Psychiatry, 43,* 209-210.

Bachrach, L. L., Talbott, J. A., & Meyerson, A. T. (1987). The chronic psychiatric patient as a "difficult" patient: A conceptual analysis. In A. T. Meyerson (Ed.), *Barriers to treating the chronic mentally ill. New Directions for Mental Health Services, 33,* 35-49.

Backer, T. E., & Richardson, D. (1989). Building bridges: Psychologists and families of the mentally ill. *American Psychologist, 44,* 546-560.

Bailey, D. (1984). A triaxial model of the interdisciplinary team and group process. *Exceptional Children, 51*(1), 17-25.

Bailey, D. B. (1989). Case management in early intervention. *Journal of Early Intervention, 13*(2), 120-134.

Bailey, D. B. (1991). Issues and perspectives on family assessment. *Infants and Young Children, 4*(1), 26-34.

Baker, F., Intagliata, J., & Kirchstein, R. (1980). *Case management evaluation: Second interim report.* Buffalo, NY: Tefco Services, Inc.

Baker, F., & Weiss, R. S. (1984). The nature of case management support. *Hospital and Community Psychiatry, 35*, 925-928.

Ballen, K. (1992, February 10), America's most admired corporations. *Fortune*, pp. 40-46.

Ballew, J. R., & Mink, G. (1986). *Case management in the human services*. Springfield, IL: Charles C Thomas.

Bazron, B. (1989). *The minority severely emotionally disturbed child: Considerations for special education and mental health services: A task force report*. Washington, DC: Georgetown University Child Development Center.

Beavers, J. (1989). Physical and cognitive handicaps. In L. Combrinck-Graham (Ed.), *Children in family contexts: Perspectives on Treatment* (pp. 193-212). New York: Guilford.

Bedell, J., & Ward, J. C. (1989). An intensive community-based treatment alternative to state hospitalization. *Hospital and Community Psychiatry, 40*, 533-535.

Behar, L. (1985). Changing patterns of state responsibility: A case study of North Carolina. *Journal of Clinical Child Psychology, 14*, 188-195.

Beinecke, R. H. (1986). New frameworks for understanding oversight practices. *Evaluation and Program Planning, 9*, 121-126.

Berger, V. (1981). Residential weekends for client families as an aid to case management. Child Abuse and Neglect, 5, 309-315.

Berkeley Planning Associates. (1978). *Evaluation of child abuse and neglect demonstration projects, 1974-1977*. Hyattsville, MD: Department of Health, Education, and Welfare.

Bernheim, K. F. (1989). Psychologists and families of the severely mentally ill: The role of family consultation. *American Psychologist, 44*, 561-564.

Biegel, D. E., Shore, B. K., & Gordon, E. (1984). *Building support networks for the elderly: Theory and applications*. Beverly Hills, CA: Sage.

Biestek, F. P. (1957). *The casework relationship*. Chicago: Loyola University Press.

Bigelow, D. A., & Young, D. J. (1983). *Effectiveness of a case management program*. Unpublished manuscript, University of Washington, Graduate School of Nursing, Seattle.

Billig, N., & Levinson, C. (1989). Social work students as case managers: A model of service delivery and training. *Hospital and Community Psychiatry, 40*, 411-413.

Blakely, T. J. (1991). *Advocacy in the social work curriculum*. Paper presented at the meeting of the Council on Social Work Education, New Orleans, LA.

Blazyk, S., Crawford C., & Wimberly, E. T. (1987). The ombudsman and the case manager. *Social Work, 32*, 451-453.

Blues' case management programs win support. (1987, September 20). *Hospitals*, p. 28.

Bogdonoff, M. D. (1991). An overview of the living-at-home program. In M. D. Bogdonoff, S. L. Hughes, W. G. Weissert, & E. Paulsen (Eds.), *The Living-at-Home program: Innovations in service access and case management* (pp. 9-21). New York: Springer.

Bolton, R., & Bolton, D. G. (1984). *Social style/management style*. New York: AMACON.

Bond, G. R., Mcdonel, E. C., Miller, L. D., & Pensec, M. (1991). Assertive community treatment and reference groups: An evaluation of their effectiveness for young adults with serious mental illness and substance abuse problems. *Psychosocial Rehabilitation Journal, 15*(2), 31-43.

Bond, G. R., Miller, L. D., Krumwied, R. D., & Ward, R. S. (1988). Assertive case management in three CMHC's: A controlled study. *Hospital and Community Psychiatry, 39*, 411-418.

Bond, G. R., Pensec, M., Dietzen, L., McCafferty, D., Giemza, R., & Sipple, H. W. (1991). Intensive case management for frequent users of psychiatric hospitals in a large city: A comparison of team and individual caseloads. *Psychosocial Rehabilitation Journal, 15*(1), 90-98.

Bond, G. R., Witheridge, T. F., Dincin, J., & Wasmer, D. (1991). Assertive community treatment: Correcting some misconceptions. *American Journal of Community Psychology, 19,* 41-51.

Bond, G. R., Witheridge, T. F., Dincin, J., Wasmer, D., Webb, J., & De Graaf-Kaser, R. (1990). Assertive community treatment for frequent users of psychiatric hospitals in a large city: A controlled study. *American Journal of Community Psychology, 18,* 865-891.

Borenstein, D. B. (1990). Managed care: A means of rationing psychiatric treatment. *Hospital and Community Psychiatry, 41,* 1095-1098.

Borland, A., McRae, J., & Lycan, C. (1989). Outcomes of five years of continuous intensive case management. *Hospital and Community Psychiatry, 40,* 369-376.

Boydell, K., Trainor, J., & Intagliata, J. (1986). A participatory approach to the evaluation design of a case management program for the long-term mentally ill. *Canada's Mental Health, 34,* 11-13.

Brager, G. A. (1968). Advocacy and political behavior. *Social Work, 13,* 5-15.

Brands, A. B. (Ed.). (1979). *Planning for discharge and follow-up services for mentally ill patients.* Rockville, MD: Department of Health and Human Services.

Brekke, J. S. (1988). What do we really know about community support programs? Strategies for better monitoring. *Hospital and Community Psychiatry, 39,* 946-952.

Brieland, D., & Korr, W. S. (1989, April). Education and training for social workers serving mentally ill children. In L. W. Abramczyk (Ed.), *Social work education for working with seriously emotionally disturbed children and adolescents* (pp. 85-99). Paper submitted at symposium on social work education and child mental health, sponsored by the National Association of Deans and Directors of Schools of Social Work (NADDSSW). Charleston, South Carolina: National Association of Deans and Directors of Schools of Social Work.

Brindis, C., Barth, R. P., & Loomis, A. (1987). Continuous counseling: Case management with teenage parents. *Social Casework, 68,* 164-172.

Bromberg, E. M., Starr, R., Donovan, R., Carney, J., Pernell-Arnold, A. (1991). The New York City Intensive Case Management training program: The first two years. *Psychosocial Rehabilitation Journal, 15*(1), 98-103.

Broskowski, A., & Marks, E. (1992). Managed mental health care. In S. Cooper & T. Lentner (Eds.), *Innovations in community mental health* (pp. 23-49). Sarasota, FL: Professional Resource Exchange.

Bryan, C. M. (1990). The uses of therapy in case management. *New Directions for Mental Health Services, 46,* 19-27.

Burchard, J. D., & Clarke, R. T. (1990). The role of individualized care in a service delivery system for children and adolescents with severely maladjusted behavior. *Journal of Mental Health Administration, 17*(1), 48-59.

Bush, C. T., Langford, M. W., Rosen, P., & Gott, W. (1990). Operation outreach: Intensive case management for severely psychiatrically disabled adults. *Hospital and Community Psychiatry, 41,* 647-649.

Bush, G. (1988). A family member looks at catastrophic case management. In K. Fisher & E. Weisman (Eds.), *Case management: Guiding patients through the health care maze* (pp. 38-42). Chicago: Joint Commission on Accreditation of Health Care Organizations.

Callahan, J. J. (1989). Case management for the elderly: A panacea? *Journal of Aging and Social Policy, 1*(1/2), 181-195.

Campbell, P. H. (1987). The integrated programming team: An approach for coordinating professionals of various disciplines in programs for students with severe and multiple handicaps. *The Journal of the Association for the Severely Handicapped, 12*(2), 107-116.

Capitman, J., Haskins, B., & Bernstein, J. (1986). Case management approaches in coordinated community-oriented long-term care demonstrations. *The Gerontologist, 26,* 398.

Capitman, J., Macadam, M., & Yee, D. (1988). Hospital-based care management. *Generations, 12*(5), 62-65.

Caplan, G. (1974). *Support systems and community mental health.* New York: Behavioral Publications.

Caragonne, P. (1980). An analysis of the function of the case manager in four mental health social service settings (Doctoral dissertation, University of Texas, 1980). *Dissertation Abstracts International, 41,* 3262A.

Carcagno, G. J., & Kemper, P. (1988). Evaluation of the National Long Term Care Demonstration: Overview of the Channeling demonstration and its evaluation. *Health Services Research, 23*(1), 1-22.

Case management could open insurance market. (1988, June 5). *Hospitals,* p. 118.

Castro, J. E. M. (nd). Puerto Ricans: Their uniqueness in the rehabilitation process. Unpublished manuscript.

Challis, D., & Davies, B. (1985). Long term care for the elderly: The community care scheme. *Journal of Social Work, 15,* 563-579.

Chamberlain, R., & Rapp, C. (1991). A decade of case management: A methodological review of outcome research. *Community Mental Health Journal, 27,* 171-188.

Chatman, V. S., & Turner-Friley, S. (1988). Providing long term health care to the minority aging poor: A case management approach. *Pride Institute Journal of Long Term Home Health Care, 7*(4), 10-13.

Christensen, E. W., (1979). Counseling Puerto Ricans: Some cultural considerations. In D. Atkinson, G. Morten, & D. W. Sue (Eds.), *Counseling American minorities: A cross-cultural perspective* (pp. 159-162). Dubuque, IA: William C. Brown.

Christianson, J. (1988). Purchase of services by case management agencies. *Generations, 12*(5), 19-22.

Clark, K. A., Landis, D., & Fisher, G. (1990). The relationship of client characteristics to case management service provision: Implications for successful system implementation. *Evaluation and Program Planning, 13,* 221-229.

Clarke, P. N., & Anderson, J. W. (1988). Case management contract: Collaboration for community care of the elderly. In K. Fisher & E. Weisman (Eds.), *Case management: Guiding patients through the health care maze* (pp. 51-55). Chicago: Joint Commission on Accreditation of Health Care Organizations.

Cohen, M., & Nemec, P. (1988). *Connecting with clients: Training module.* Boston: Boston University Center for Psychiatric Rehabilitation.

Cohen, M., Nemec, P., Farkas, M., & Forbess, R. (1988a). *Linking clients to services: Training module.* Boston: Boston University Center for Psychiatric Rehabilitation.

Cohen, M., Nemec, P., Farkas, M., & Forbess, R. (1988b). *Planning for services: Training module.* Boston: Boston University Center for Psychiatric Rehabilitation.

Cohen, M., Nemec, P., Farkas, M., & Forbess, R. (1988c). *Advocating for service improvement: Training module.* Boston: Boston University Center for Psychiatric Rehabilitation.

Cohen, R. (1983). Team service to the elderly. *Social Casework, 64,* 555-560.

Collard, A. F., Berman, A., & Henderson, M. (1990). Two approaches to measuring quality in medical case management programs. *Quality Review Bulletin, 16,* 3-8.

Collins, A. H., & Pancoast, D. L. (1976). *Natural helping networks.* Washington, DC: National Association of Social Workers.

Compher, J. V. (1983). Home services to families to prevent child placement. *Social Work, 64,* 360-364.

Commonwealth of Pennsylvania, Office of Mental Health. (1991). *Intensive case management training: Building for the future.* Pittsburgh, PA: Western Psychiatric Institute & Clinic, University of Pittsburgh.

Cornish, J., & Nelson, K. (1991). Families helping families. *Community Alternatives, 3*(2), 59-72.

Cross, T. L., Bazron, B. J., Dennis, K. W., & Isaacs, M. R. (1989). *Towards a culturally competent system of care: A monograph on effective services for minority children who are severely emotionally disturbed.* Washington, DC: Georgetown University Child Development Center.

Curtiss, F. R. (1989). Managed health care. *American Journal of Hospital Pharmacy, 46,* 742-763.

Dear, R. B., & Patti, R. J. (1981). Legislative advocacy: Seven effective tactics. *Social Work, 26,* 289-296.

Degan, K., Cole, N., Tamayo, L., & Dzerovych, G. (1990). Intensive case management for the seriously mentally ill. *Administration and Policy in Mental Health, 17,* 265-269.

DeLeon, P. H., VandenBos, G. R., & Bulatao, E. Q. (1991). Managed mental health care: A history of the federal policy initiative. *Professional Psychology: Research and Practice, 22,* 15-25.

DelTogno-Armansco, V., Olivas, G. S., & Harter, S. (1989). Developing an integrated nursing case management model. *Nursing Management, 20*(10), 26-29.

Dill, A. E. P. (1987). Issues in case management for the chronically mentally ill. *New Directions in Mental Health Services, 36,* 61-70.

Dincin, J. (1981). A community agency model. In J. A. Talbott (Ed.), *The chronic mentally ill: Treatment, programs, systems* (pp. 213-226). New York: Human Sciences Press.

Dobrish, C. M. (1987). Private practice geriatric case management: A new social work specialty. *Journal of Gerontological Social Work, 11*(1-2), 159-172.

Donabedian, A. (1966). Evaluating the quality of medical care. *Milbank Memorial Fund Quarterly, 44,* 166-206.

Dorwat, R. A. (1990). Managed mental health care: Myths and realities in the 1990s. *Hospital and Community Psychiatry, 41,* 1087-1091.

Downing, R. (1985). The elderly and their families. In M. Weil & J. M. Karls (Eds.), *Case management in human service practice* (pp. 145-169). San Francisco: Jossey-Bass.

Duchnowski, A. J., & Friedman, R. M. (1990). Children's mental health: Challenges for the Nineties. *Journal of Mental Health Administration, 17*(1), 3-12.

Dunst, C. J., & Trivette, C. M. (1988). An enablement and empowerment perspective of case management. *Topics in Early Childhood Special Education, 8*(4), 87-102.

Dunst, C. J., Trivette, C., Deal, A. (1988). *Enabling and empowering families: Principles and guidelines for practice.* Cambridge, MA: Brookline Books.

Dunst, C. J., Trivette, C. M., & Thompson, R. B. (1991). Supporting and strengthening family functioning: Toward a congruence between principles and practice. *Prevention in Human Services, 9*(1), 19-43.

Eastern Pennsylvania Psychiatric Institute/Medical College of Pennsylvania. (nd). *Case management trainer preceptorship.* Unpublished manuscript.

Echols, I. J., Gabel, C., Landerman, D., & Reyes, M. (1988). An approach for addressing racism, ethnocentrism, and sexism in the curriculum. In C. Jacobs & D. D. Bowles (Eds.), *Ethnicity and race* (pp. 217-229). Silver Springs, MD: National Association of Social Workers.

Edinburg, G., & Cottler, J. (1990). Implications of managed care for social work in psychiatric hospitals. *Hospital and Community Psychiatry, 41*(10), 1063-1064.

Emlet, C. A., & Hall, A. M. (1991). Integrating the community into geriatric case management: Public health interventions. *The Gerontologist, 31,* 556-560.

England, M. J., & Cole, R. G. (1992). Building systems of care for youth with serious mental illness. *Hospital and Community Psychiatry, 43,* 630-633.

Everett, F., Proctor, N., & Cartmell, B. (1983). Providing psychological services to American Indian children and families. *Professional Psychology: Research and Practice, 14,* 588-603.

Etten, M. J., & Kosberg, J. I. (1989). The hospice caregiver assessment: A study of a case management tool for professional assistance. *The Gerontologist, 29,* 128-131.

Fariello, D., & Scheidt, S. (1989). Clinical case management of the dually diagnosed client. *Hospital and Community Psychiatry, 41,* 1065-1067.

Fine, G. & Borden, J. R. (1989). Parents involved network project: Support and advocacy for training parents. In R. M. Friedman, A. J. Duchnowski, & E. L. Henderson (Eds.), *Advocacy on behalf of children with serious emotional problems* (pp. 68-77). Springfield, IL: Charles C Thomas.

Fiorentine, R., & Grusky, O. (1990). When case managers manage the seriously mentally ill: A role-contingency approach. *Social Service Review,64*(1), 79-93.

Fisher, G., Landis, D., & Clark, K. (1988). Case management service provision and client change. *Community Mental Health Journal, 24,* 134-142.

Fisher, K. (1987). Case management. *Quality Review Bulletin, 13,* 287-290.

Family Resource Council of North Carolina. (1992, July). *Developing a system of care for early intervention to promote infant mental health (IMH).* Paper presented at Developing Local Systems of Care for Children and Adolescents with Severe Emotional Disturbances, Breckenridge, CO.

Franklin, J. L. (1988). Case management: A dissenting view. *Hospital and Community Psychiatry, 39,* 921.

Franklin, J. L., Solovitz, B., Mason, M., Clemons, J. R., & Miller, G. E. (1987). An Evaluation of Case Management. *American Journal of Public Health, 77,* 674-678.

Freeman, S. J., Fischer, L., & Sheldon A. (1980). An agency model for developing and coordinating psychiatric aftercare. *Hospital and Community Psychiatry, 31,* 768-771.

Friedman, K. R., (1992, July). *Supervising case managers for systems of care.* Paper presented at Developing Local Systems of Care for Children and Adolescents with Severe Emotional Disturbances, Breckenridge, CO.

Friesen, B. J., Griesbach, J., Jacobs, J. H., Katz-Leavy, J., Olson, D. (1988). Improving services for families. *Children Today, 17*(4), 18-22.

Friesen, B. J., & Koroloff, N. M. (1990). Family-centered services: Implications for mental health administration and research. *Journal of Mental Health Administration. 17*(1), 13-25.

Gaitz, C. M. (1987). Multidisciplinary team care of the elderly: The role of the psychiatrist. *The Gerontologist, 27,* 553-556.

Garland, C., Woodruff, G., & Buck, D. M. (1988, June). *Division for Early Childhood white paper: Case management.* The Council for Exceptional Children, Reston, VA.

Gartner, A., & Riessman, F. (1977). *Self help in human services.* San Francisco: Jossey-Bass.

Geller, J. L., Fisher, W. H., Simon, L. J., & Wirth-Cauchon, J. L. (1990). Second-generation deinstitutionalization, II: The impact of Brewster v. Dukakis on correlates of community and hospital utilization. *American Journal of Psychiatry, 147,* 988-993.

Gemmill, R. H., Kennedy, D. L., Larison, J. R., Mollerstrom, W. W., & Brubeck, K. W. (1992). Case manager as advocate: Family advocacy in the military. In B. S. Vourlekis

& R. Greene (Eds.), *Social work case management* (pp. 149-165). New York: Aldine De Gruyter.

Getzel, G. S., Goldberg, J. R., & Salmon, R. (1971). Supervising in groups as a model for today. *Social Casework, 52*, 154-163.

Glasscote, R. (1978). What programs work and what programs not do work for chronic mental patients? In J. A. Talbott (Ed.), *The chronic mental patient: Problems, solutions, and recommendations for a public policy.* Washington, DC: American Psychiatric Association.

Goering, P. N., Wasylenki, D. A., Farkas, M., Lancee, W. J., & Ballantyne, R. (1988). What difference does case management make? *Hospital and Community Psychiatry, 39*, 272-276.

Goldman, H. H., Lehman, A. F., Morrissey, J. P., Newman, S. J., Frank, R. G., & Steinwachs, D. M. (1990). Design for the national evaluation of the Robert Wood Johnson Foundation Program on Chronic Mental Illness. *Hospital and Community Psychiatry, 41*, 1217-1221.

Goldman, H. H., Morrissey, J. P., Ridgely, M. S. (1990). Form and function of mental health authorities at RWJ Foundation program sites: Preliminary observations. *Hospital and Community Psychiatry, 41*, 1222-1230.

Goldman, H. H., & Ridgely, S. (Speakers). (1990, September). *Case Management models in the Robert Wood Johnson cities: An overview* (Cassette Recording No. MH06) Richmond, VA: Visual Aids Electronics.

Goldman, S. K. (1992). Ventura County, California. In B. A. Stroul, S. K. Goldman, I. S. Lourie, & C. Zeigler-Dendy (Eds.), *Profiles of Local Systems of Care for Children and Adolescents with Severe Emotional Disturbances.* Washington, DC: Georgetown University Child Development Center.

Goldstein, J. M., Bassuk, E. L., Holland, S. K., & Zimmer, D. (1988). Identifying catastrophic psychiatric cases: Targeting managed-care strategies. *Medical Care, 26*, 790-799.

Goldstrom I. D., & Manderscheid, R. W. (1983). A descriptive analysis of community support program case managers serving the chronically mentally ill. *Community Mental Health Journal, 19*, 17-26.

Graham, K., & Timney, C. B.(1990). Case management in addictions treatment. *Journal of Substance Abuse Treatment, 7*, 181-188.

Greene, R. R. (1992). Case management: An agenda for social work practice. In B. S. Vourlekis & R. Greene (Eds.), *Social work case management* (pp. 11-25). New York: Aldine De Gruyter.

Greene, R. & Lewis, J. (1991). Curriculum for case management for the frail elderly: A Delphi study. *Arete, 15*(1), 33-45.

Greene, V. L., & Monahan, D. J. (1984). Comparative utilization of community based long term care services by hispanic and anglo elderly in a case management system. *Journal of Gerontology, 39*, 730-735.

Grella, C. E., & Grusky, O. (1989). Families of the seriously mentally ill and their satisfaction with services. *Hospital and Community Psychiatry, 40*, 831-835.

Grisham, M., White, M., & Miller, L. S. (1983). Case management as a problem-solving strategy. *Pride Institute of Long Term Home Health Care, 2*(Fall), 21-28.

Grosser, C. F., Henry, W. E., & Kelly, J. G. (1969). *Nonprofessionals in the human services.* San Francisco: Jossey-Bass.

Grosser, R. C., & Vine, P. (1991). Families as advocates for the mentally ill: A survey of characteristics and service needs. *American Journal of Orthopsychiatry, 61*, 282-290.

Grunebaum, H., & Friedman, H. (1988). Building collaborative relationships with families of the mentally ill. *Hospital and Community Psychiatry, 39,* 1183-1187.

Grusky, O. (1990, September). *Quantifying case manager and client interactions.* Paper presented at Foundations for Success: A Blueprint for the Future. The First National Case Management Conference, Cincinnati, Ohio.

Guzman, L. P., & VandenBos, G. R. (1990). U.S. Hispanics: A complex and diverse population. In E. L. Olmedo & V. R. Walker (Eds.), *Hispanics in the United States: Abstracts of the psychological and behavioral literature, 1980-1989* (pp. ix-xi). Washington, DC: American Psychological Association.

Gwyther, L. (1988). Assessment: Content, purpose, outcomes. *Generations, 12*(5), 11-15.

Hanson, M. J., Lynch, E. W., & Wayman, K. I. (1990). Honoring the cultural diversity of families when gathering data. *Gathering family information: Procedures, products, and precautions. Topics in Early Childhood Special Education, 10,* 112-131.

Harding, C. (Speaker). (1990, September). *Hope, rational optimism, and empowerment.* (Cassette Recording No. MHOI). Paper presented at Foundations for Success: A Blueprint for the Future. The First National Case Management Conference, Cincinnati, Ohio. Richmond, VA: Visual Aid Electronics.

Hare, R. T., & Frankena, S. T. (1972). Peer group supervision. *American Journal of Orthopsychiatry, 42,* 527-529.

Hargreaves, W. A., Shaw, R. E., Shadoan, R., Walker, E., Surber, R., & Gaynor, J. (1984). Measuring case management activity. *Journal of Nervous and Mental Disease, 172,* 296-300.

Harkness, L., & Mulinski, P. (1988). Performance standards for social workers. *Social Work, 33,* 339-344.

Harris, M. (1986). Community Connections, Washington, DC. In P. Ridgeway, L. Spaniol, & A. Zipple (Eds.), *Case management services for persons who are homeless and mentally ill: Report from an NIMH workshop* (pp. 6-10). Unpublished manuscript. Boston University Center for Psychiatric Rehabilitation, Boston.

Harris, M. (1988). New directions for clinical case management. In M. Harris & L. Bachrach (Eds.), *Clinical case management: New Directions for Mental Health Services, 40,* 57-61.

Harris, M., & Bachrach, L. L. (1988). A treatment-planning grid for clinical case managers. In M. Harris & L. Bachrach (Eds.), *Clinical case management: New Directions for Mental Health Services, 40,* 29-38.

Harris, M., & Bergman, H. C. (1987). Case management with the chronically mentally ill: A clinical perspective. *American Journal of Orthopsychiatry, 57,* 296-302.

Harris, M., & Bergman, H. C. (1988a). Capitation financing for the chronic mentally ill: A case management approach. *Hospital and Community Psychiatry, 39,* 68-72.

Harris, M., & Bergman, H. C. (1988b). Misconceptions about use of case management services by the chronic mentally ill: A utilization analysis. *Hospital and Community Psychiatry, 39,* 1276-1280.

Harris, M. & Bergman, H. C. (1988c). Clinical case management for the chronically mentally ill: A conceptual analysis. In M. Harris & L. Bachrach (Eds.), *Clinical case management. New Directions for Mental Health Services, 40,* 5-13.

Harrod, J. B. (1986). Defining case management in community support systems. *Psychosocial Rehabilitation Journal, 9*(3), 56-61.

Hart, V. (1977). The use of many disciplines with the severely and profoundly handicapped. In E. Sontag, J. Smith, & N. Certo (Eds.), *Educational programming for the severely and profoundly handicapped* (pp. 391-396). Reston, VA: Division on Mental Retardation, The Council for Exceptional Children.

Haskell, M. A. (1969). *The new careers concept: Potential for public employment of the poor.* New York: Praeger.

Hatfield, A. B. (1981). Families as advocates for the mentally ill: A growing movement. *Hospital and Community Psychiatry, 32,* 641-642.

Hatfield, A. B., & Lefley, H. P. (1987). *Families of the mentally ill: Coping and adaptation.* New York: Guilford.

Hearn, G. (1969). Progress toward an holistic conception of social work. In G. Hearn (Ed.), *The general systems approach: Contributions toward an holistic conception of social work* (pp. 63-70). New York: Council on Social Work Education.

Henderson, M. G., & Collard, A. (1988). Measuring quality in medical case management programs. *Quality Review Bulletin, 14,* 33-39.

Herzberg, F. (1959). *The motivation to work.* New York: McGraw Hill.

Hobbs, N., Dokecki, P. R., Hoover-Dempsey, K. V., Moroney, R. M., Shayne, M. W., & Weeks, K. H. (1984). *Strengthening families.* San Francisco: Jossey-Bass.

Hodge, M. (1989). Supervising case managers. *Psychosocial Rehabilitation Journal, 12*(4), 51-59.

Hodge, M. (Speaker). (1990, September). *Practical approaches to relationship-building* (Cassette Recording No. TH32). Paper presented at Foundations for Success: A Blueprint for the Future. The First National Case Management Conference, Cincinnati, Ohio. Richmond, VA: Visual Aids Electronics.

Hoeman, S. P., & Winters, D. M. (1988). Case management for clients with high cervical spinal cord injuries. In K. Fisher & E. Weisman (Eds.), *Case management: Guiding patients through the health care maze* (pp. 109-115). Chicago: Joint Commission on Accreditation of Health Care Organizations.

Hogarty, G. E. (1979). Treatment of schizophrenia: Current status and future directions. In H. Pragg (Ed.), *Management of schizophrenia* (pp. 19-36). The Netherlands: Van Gorcum, Assen.

Holloway, F. (1991). Case management for the mentally ill: Looking at the evidence. *International Journal of Social Psychiatry, 37*(1), 2-13.

Honig, A., Tan, E. S., Weenink, A., Pop, P., & Philipsen, H. (1991). Brief reports: Utility of a symptom checklist for detecting physical disease in chronic psychiatric patients. *Hospital and Community Psychiatry, 42,* 531-533.

Horejsi, C., Bird, M., Bruno, W., Edwards, D., Pablo, J., & Redneck, D. (nd). *Risk assessment and the Native American family.* Unpublished manuscript.

Hoult, J., Reynolds, I., Charbonneau-Powis, M., Weekes, P., & Briggs, J. (1983). Psychiatric hospital versus community treatment: The results of a randomized trial. *Australian and New Zealand Journal of Psychiatry, 17,* 160-167.

Hughes, S. L., Mannheim, L. M., Guihan, M., McCarthy, M., Edelman, P., & Shortell, S. M., (1991). The national evaluation of the Living-at-Home program. In M. D. Bogdonoff, S. L. Hughes, W. G. Weissert, & E. Paulsen (Eds.), *The Living-at-Home program: Innovations in service access and case management* (pp. 22-49). New York: Springer.

Hughes, S. L., & Weissert, W. G. (1988). Living at home: Variations on a case management theme. *Generations, 12*(5), 66-67.

Humphreys, D., Mason, R., Guthrie, M., Liem, C., & Stern, E. J. (1988). The Miami Channeling program: Case management and cost control. *Quality Review Bulletin, 14,* 155-186.

Hunter College School of Social Work. (1990). *Training: Children's intensive case management schedule.* Unpublished manuscript.

Hurley, R. E., & Freund, D. A. (1988). A typology of Medicaid managed care. *Medical Care, 26,* 764-774.

Intagliata, F., & Baker, J. (1983). Factors affecting case management services for the chronically mentally ill. *Administration in Mental Health, 11*(2), 75-91.

Intagliata, J. (1982). Improving the quality of community care for the chronically mentally disabled: The role of case management. *Schizophrenia Bulletin, 8,* 655-674.

Intagliata, J., Willer, B., & Egri, G. (1988). The role of the family in delivering case management services. In M. Harris & L. L. Bachrach (Eds.), *Clinical case management* (pp. 39-50). San Francisco: Jossey-Bass.

James, W. H., Smith, A. J., & Mann, R. (1991). Educating homeless children: Interprofessional case management. *Childhood Education, 67,* 305-308.

Jerrell, J. M., & Hu, T. (1989). Cost-effectiveness of intensive clinical and case management compared with an existing system of care. *Inquiry, 26,* 224-234.

Johnson, D. (Speaker). (1990, September). *Spotlight: Suffolk County, Long Island, New York—Team case managers advocate for consumers.* (Cassette Recording No. TC85). Paper presented at Foundations for Success: A Blueprint for the Future. The First National Case Management Conference, Cincinnati, Ohio. Richmond, VA: Visual Aids Electronics.

Johnson, P. J., & Rubin, A. (1983). Case management in mental health: A social work domain? *Social Work, 28,* 49-55.

Kaczmarek, L., Goldstein, H., & Pennington, R. (1992). *Collaborative consultation: Inservice training for related service personnel in early interventions.* Grant funded by the U. S. Department of Education. Pittsburgh, PA: University of Pittsburgh Child Language Department.

Kahn, E. M. (1979). The parallel process in social work treatment and supervision. *Social Casework, 60,* 520-528.

Kamerman, S. B., & Kahn, A. J. (Eds.). (1990). "Innovations in Programs and Service Delivery." In Social Services for Children, Youth and Families in the United States [Special issue]. *Children and Youth Services Review, 12*(1/2), 113-143.

Kane, R. (1988). Case management: Ethical pitfalls on the road to high quality managed care. *Quality Review Bulletin, 14,* 161-166.

Kanter, J. S. (Ed.). (1985a). *Clinical issues in treating the chronic mentally ill.* San Francisco: Jossey-Bass.

Kanter, J. S. (1985b). Talking with families about coping strategies. In J. S. Kanter (Ed.), *Clinical issues in treating the chronic mentally ill* (pp. 7-19). San Francisco: Jossey-Bass.

Kanter, J. S. (1985c). Consulting with families of the chronic mentally ill. In J. S. Kanter (Ed.), *Clinical issues in treating the chronic mentally ill* (pp. 21-32). San Francisco: Jossey-Bass.

Kanter, J. S. (1985d). Psychosocial assessment in community treatment. In J. S. Kanter (Ed.), *Clinical issues in treating the chronic mentally ill* (pp. 63-75). San Francisco: Jossey-Bass.

Kanter, J. S. (1985e). Case management of the young adult chronic patient: A clinical issue. In J. S. Kanter (Ed.), *Clinical issues in treating the chronic mentally ill* (pp. 77-92). San Francisco: Jossey-Bass.

Kanter, J. S. (1987a). Points and viewpoints: Mental health case management: A professional domain? *Social Work, 32,* 461-462.

Kanter, J. S. (1987b). Titrating support in case management. *Tie Lines, 4*(4), 5-6.

Kanter, J. S. (1988). Clinical issues in the case management relationship. In M. Harris & L. L. Bachrach (Eds.), *Clinical case management* (pp. 15-27). San Francisco: Jossey-Bass.

Kanter, J. S. (1989). Clinical case management: definition, principles, components. *Hospital and Community Psychiatry, 40,* 361-368.

Kanter, J. S. (1990). Community-based management of psychotic clients: The contributions of D. W. and C. Winnicott. *Clinical Social Work Journal, 18*(1), 23-41.

Kanter, J. S. (1991). Integrating case management and psychiatric hospitalization. *Health and Social Work, 16,* 34-42.

Kaplan, K. (1992). Linking the developmentally disabled client to needed resources: Adult protective services case management. In B. S. Vourlekis & R. Greene (Eds.), *Social work case management* (pp. 89-105). New York: Aldine De Gruyter.

Kaplan, M. (1992). Care planning for children with HIV/AIDS: A family perspective. In B. S. Vourlekis & R. Greene (Eds.), *Social work case management* (pp. 75-88). New York: Aldine De Gruyter.

Katz-Leavy, J. W., Lourie, I. S., Stroul, B. A., & Zeigler-Dendy, C. (1992). Individualized services in a system of care. In B. A. Stroul, S. K. Goldman, I. S. Lourie, & C. Zeigler-Dendy (Eds.), *Profiles of Local Systems of Care for Children and Adolescents with Severe Emotional Disturbances.* Washington, DC: Georgetown University, Child Development Center.

Kaufman, A. V., DeWeaver, K., & Glicken, M. (1989). The mentally retarded aged: Implications for social work practice. *Journal of Gerontological Social Work, 14*(1/2), 93-110.

Kelker, K. A. (1988). *Taking charge: A handbook for parents whose children have emotional handicaps.* Portland, OR: Portland State University, Research and Training Center to Improve Services for Seriously Emotionally Handicapped Children and Their Families.

Kentucky Impact. (1990). *Big book of training.* Frankfort, KY: Cabinet for Human Resources, Department for Mental Health/Mental Retardation Services, Commonwealth of Kentucky.

Kenyon, V., Smith, E., Hefty, L., Bell, M., McNeil, J., & Martaus, T. (1990). Clinical competencies for community health nursing. *Public Health Nursing, 7*(1), 3-39.

Klee, L., & Halfon, N. (1987). Mental health care for foster children in California. *Child Abuse and Neglect, 11,* 63-74.

Klein, J., & Posey, P. (1986). Good supervisors are good supervisors anywhere. *Harvard Business Review, 64*(6), 125-128.

Knitzer, J. (1982). *Unclaimed children: The failure of public responsibility to children and adolescents in need of mental health services.* Washington, DC: Children's Defense Fund.

Knitzer, J., Steinberg, Z., & Fleisch, B. (1990). *At the schoolhouse door: An examination of programs and policies for children with behavioral and emotional problems.* New York: Author and the Bank Street College of Education.

Korr, W. S., & Cloninger, L. (1991). Assessing models of case management: An empirical approach. *Journal of Social Service Research, 14*(1/2), 129-146.

Kosberg, J. I., & Cairl, R. E. (1986). The cost of care index: A case management tool for screening informal care providers. *The Gerontologist, 26,* 273-278.

Krell, H. L., Richardson, C. M., LaManna, T. N. & Kairys, S. W. (1983). Child abuse and worker training. *Social Casework, 64,* 532-538.

Krieger, M. J., & Robbins, J. (1985). The adolescent incest victim and the judicial system. *American Journal of Orthopsychiatry, 55,* 419-425.

Kruger, L. J., Cherniss, C., Maher, C., & Leichtman, H. (1988). Group supervision of paraprofessional counselors. *Professional Psychology: Research and Practice, 19,* 609-616.

Krupinski, J., & Lippman, L. (1984). Multidisciplinary or nondisciplinary: Evaluation of staff functioning at a community mental health centre. *Australian and New Zealand Journal of Psychiatry, 18,* 172-178.

Kurtz, L. F., Bagarozzi, D. A., & Pollane, L. P. (1984). Case management in mental health. *Health and Social Work, 9,* 201-210.

Kurtz, L. F., Mann, K. B., & Chambon, A. (1987). Linking between social workers and mental health mutual-aid groups. *Social Work in Health Care, 13*(1), 69-78.

Lamb, H. R. (1980). Therapist-case managers: More than brokers of services. *Hospital and Community Psychiatry, 31,* 762-764.

Lamb, H. R., & Oliphant, E. (1979). Parents of schizophrenics: Advocates for the mentally ill. In L. Stein (Ed.), *Community support systems for the long-term patient* (pp. 12-16). San Francisco: Jossey-Bass.

Landsberg, G., Fletcher, R., & Maxwell, T. (1987). Developing a comprehensive community care system for the mentally ill/mentally retarded. *Community Mental Health Journal, 23,* 131-134.

Lebow, G., & Kane, B. (1992). Assessment: Private case management with the elderly. In B. S. Vourlekis & R. Greene (Eds.), *Social work case management* (pp. 35-50). New York: Aldine De Gruyter.

Lee, S. S., & Yee, A. K. (1988). The development of community-based health services for minority elderly in Boston's Chinatown. *Pride Institute Journal of Long Term Home Health Care, 7*(4), 3-9.

Lefley, H. P., Bernheim, K. F., Goldman, C. R. (1989). Conference report: National forum addresses need to enhance training in treating the seriously mentally ill. *Hospital and Community Psychiatry, 40,* 460-470.

Lefley, H. P., & Bestman, E. W. (1984). Community mental health and minorities: A multi-ethnic approach. In S. Sue & T. Moore (Eds.), *The pluralistic society: A community mental health perspective* (pp. 116-148). New York: Human Sciences Press.

Lehman, A. F. (1988). Financing case management: Making the money work. In M. Harris & L. L. Bachrach (Eds.), *Clinical Case Management: New Directions for Mental Health Services, 40,* 67-78.

Leukefield, C. G. (1990). Case management: A social work tradition. *Health and Social Work, 15,* 175-179.

Levine, I. S., & Fleming, M. (1985). *Human resource development: Issues in case management.* Rockville, MD: National Institute of Mental Health.

Lewis, D. A., Riger, S., Rosenberg, H., Wagenaar, H., Lurigio, A. J., & Reed, S. (1991). *Worlds of the mentally ill: How deinstitutionalization works in the city.* Carbondale: Southern Illinois University Press.

Like, R. C. (1988). Primary care case management: A family physician's perspective. *Quality Review Bulletin, 14,* 174-178.

Long, K. A. (1983). The experience of repeated and traumatic loss among Crow Indian children: Response patterns and intervention strategies. *American Journal of Orthopsychiatry, 53,* 116-126.

Loomis, J. F. (1988). Case management in health care. *Health and Social Work, 13,* 219-225.

Lorefice, L. S., Borus, J. F., & Keefe, C. (1982). Consumer evaluation of a community mental health service, I: Care delivery patterns. *American Journal of Psychiatry, 139,* 1331-1334.

Lowe, J. I., & Herranen, M. (1982). Conflict in teamwork: Understanding roles and relationships. *Social Work in Health Care, 3*(3), 323-330.

Lowe, J. I., & Herranen, M. (1982). Understanding teamwork: Another look at the concepts. *Social Work in Health Care, 7*(2), 1-11.

Lyon, S., & Lyon, G. (1980). Team functioning and staff development: A role release approach to providing integrated educational services for severely handicapped students. *The Journal of the Association for the Severely Handicapped, 5*(3), 250-263.

MacAdam, M., Capitman, J., Yee, D., Prottas, J., Leutz, W., & Westwater, D. (1989). Case management for frail elders: The Robert Wood Johnson Foundation's Program for Hospital Initiative in Long-Term Care. *The Gerontologist, 29,* 737-744.

Maguire, L. (1991). *Social support systems in practice: A generalist approach.* Silver Springs, MD: National Association of Social Workers.

Mahler, J., Blaze, E., & Risser, P. (Speakers). (1990, September). *Consumers as case managers* (Cassette Recording No. WH04). Paper presented at Foundations for Success: *A Blueprint for the Future.* The First National Case Management Conference, Cincinnati, Ohio. Richmond, VA: Visual Aids Electronics.

Mailick, M. D., & Ashley, A. A. (1981). Politics of interprofessional collaboration: Challenge to advocacy. *Social Casework, 62,* 131-137.

Mailick, M. D., & Jordan, P. (1977). A multimodel approach to collaborative practice in health settings. *Social Work in Health Care, 2*(4), 445-454.

Mandeville, P. F., & Maholick, L. T. (1969). Changing points of emphasis in training the community's natural counselors. *Mental Hygiene, 53,* 208-213.

Margolis, H., & Fiorelli, J. S. (1984). An applied approach to facilitating interdisciplinary teamwork. *Journal of Rehabilitation, 50,* 13-17.

Marks, J. L., & Hixon, D. (1986). Training agency staff through peer group supervision. *Social Casework, vol. 67*(7), 418-423.

Marlowe, H. A., Marlowe, J. L., & Willetts, R. (1983). The mental health counselor as case manager: Implications for working with the chronically mentally ill. *American Mental Health Counselors Association Journal, 5*(4), 184-191.

Mason, J. L. (1989). *The cultural competence self-assessment questionnaire.* Unpublished manuscript, Portland State University, Research and Training Center to Improve Services for Children and Youth With Serious Emotional Handicaps and Their Families. Portland, OR.

Mason, J. L., Young, T. M., Yoakum, K. S. (nd). *Therapeutic case advocacy training guide: Trainee's manual.* Unpublished manuscript, Portland State University, Research and Training Center to Improve Services for Seriously Emotionally Handicapped Children and Their Families, Portland, OR.

McAfee, J. K. (1987). Integrating therapy services in the school: A model for training educators, administrators, and therapists. *Topics in Early Childhood Special Education, 7*(3), 116-126.

McCormick, B. (1988). Case management plan "unbundles" managed care. *Hospitals, 62*(18), 45.

McGinnis, C. (Speaker). (1990, September). *Disabled adults: Meeting special needs of disabled adults with SSI case managers.* (Cassette Recording No. TC60). Paper presented at Foundations for Success: A Blueprint for the Future. The First National Case Management Conference, Cincinnati, Ohio. Richmond, VA: Visual Aid Electronics.

McGonigel, M. J., & Garland, C. (1988). The individualized family service plan and the early intervention team: Team and family issues and recommended practices. *Infants and Young Children, 1*(1), 10-21.

McGowen, B. G. (1987). Advocacy. In A. Minahan (Ed.), *Encyclopedia of Social Work* (pp. 89-95). Silver Springs, MD: National Association of Social Workers.

McRae, J., Higgins, M., Lycan, C., & Sherman, W. (1990). What happens to patients after five years of intensive case management stops? *Hospital and Community Psychiatry, 41,* 175-179.

Mechanic, D., & Aiken, L. (1987). Improving the care of patients with chronic mental illness. *The New England Journal of Medicine, 317*, 1634-1638.

Merrill, J. (1985). Defining case management. *Business and Health, 2*(8), 5-10.

Miller, L. L., & Miller, J. E. (1989). Selecting medical case management programs: The employer's/purchaser's perspective. *Quality Review Bulletin, 15*, 121-126.

Minahan, A. (1976). Generalists and specialists in social work—Implications for education and practice. *Arete, 4*(2), 55-67.

Modrcin, M., Rapp, C., & Chamberlain, R. (1985). *Case management with the psychiatrically disabled: Curriculum and training program.* Unpublished manuscript, University of Kansas School of Social Welfare, Lawrence.

Moeller, P. (1991). The occupational therapist as case manager in community mental health. *Mental Health Special Interest Section Newsletter, 14*(2), 4-5.

Moore, S. T. (1990). A social work practice model for case management: The case management grid. *Social Work, 35*, 444-448.

Morgenlander, K. H. (1990). *Capitated case management for Medicaid mental health patients: Thoughts concerning a demonstration project in Allegheny County.* Mimeo prepared for the Allegheny County Department of Mental Health, Mental Retardation, Drug and Alcohol Programs. Pittsburgh, PA.

Moxley, D. P. (1989). *The practice of case management.* Newbury Park, CA: Sage.

Nason, F. (1981). Team tension as a vital sign. *General Hospital Psychiatry, 3*, 32-36.

Nason, F. (1983). Diagnosing the hospital team. *Social Work in Health Care, 9*(2), 25-45.

National Alliance for the Mentally Ill. (1982). *Awakenings: Organizing a support/advocacy group.* Unpublished manuscript.

National Association of Counties. (1989). *Mental health fact sheet: Understanding what counties face in addressing the needs of young adults with the dual diagnosis of chronic mental illness and substance abuse.* Washington, DC: Author.

National Association of Social Workers. (1984). *NASW standards and guidelines for social work case management for the functionally impaired.* (Professional standards, Number 12). Washington, DC: Author.

National Institute of Mental Health. (1987). *Toward a model plan for a comprehensive, community-based mental health system* (DHHS Administrative Document). Washington, DC: Government Printing Office.

Netting, F. E. (1992). Case management: Service or symptom? *Social Work, 37*, 160-164.

Netting, F. E., & Williams, F. G. (1989). Establishing interfaces between community- and hospital-based service systems for the elderly. *Health and Social Work, 14*, 134-139.

Netting, F. E., Williams, F. G., Jones-McClintic, S., & Warrick, L. (1990). Policies to enhance coordination in hospital-based case management programs. *Health and Social Work, 15*, 15-21.

Newman, R., & Bricklin, P. M. (1991). Parameters of managed mental health care: Legal, ethical, and professional guidelines. *Professional Psychology Research and Practice, 22*, 26-35.

O'Connor, G. C. (1988). Case management: System and practice. *Social Casework, 69*, 97-106.

Olfson, M. (1990). Assertive community treatment: An evaluation of the experimental evidence. *Hospital and Community Psychiatry, 41*, 634-641.

Olson, D. G. (1988, Spring). A developmental approach to family support: A conceptual framework. *Focal Point, 3*, 3-6.

Orlin, M. (1973). A role for social workers in the consumer movement. *Social Work, 18*, 60-65.

Ozarin, L. P. (1978). The pros and cons of case management. In J. Talbott (Ed.), *The chronic mental patient: Problems, solutions, and recommendations for public policy* (pp. 165-170). Washington, DC: American Psychiatric Association.

Padilla, A. M., & Lindholm, K. L. (1983). *Hispanic Americans: Future behavioral science research directions.* Occasional Paper No. 17, University of California, Los Angeles.

Padilla, A. M., Ruiz, R. A., & Alvarez, R. (1975). Community mental health services for the Spanish-speaking/surnamed population. *American Psychologist, 30*(9), 892-905.

Panzarino, P. J., & Wetherbee, D. G. (1990). Advanced case management in mental health: Quality and efficiency combined. *Quality Review Bulletin, 16,* 386-390.

Paradis, B. A. (1987). An integrated team approach to community mental health. *Social Work. 32,* 101-104.

Parker, M., & Secord, J. (1988). Private geriatric case management: Current trends and future directions. *Quality Review Bulletin, 14,* 209-214.

Parks, S. H., & Pilisuk, M. (1984). Personal support systems of former mental patients residing in board-and-care facilities. *Journal of Community Psychology, 12,* 230-244.

Patterson, D. Y. (1990). Managed care: An approach to rational psychiatric treatment. *Hospital and Community Psychiatry, 41,* 1092-1095.

Perlman, B. B., Melnick, G., & Kentera, A. (1985). Assessing the effectiveness of a case management program. *Hospital and Community Psychiatry, 36,* 405-407.

Piette, J., Fleishman, J. A., Mor, V., & Dill, A. (1990). A comparison of hospital and community case management programs for persons with AIDS. *Medical Care, 28,* 746-755.

Piliavin, I. (1968). Restructuring the provision of social services. *Social Work, 13,* 34-41.

Pincus, A., & Minahan, A. (1973). *Social work practice.* Itsaca, IL: F. E. Peacock.

Pinderhughes, E. B. (1984). Teaching empathy: Ethnicity, race and power at the cross-cultural treatment interface. *The American Journal of Social Psychiatry, 4*(1), 5-12.

Pittsburgh Program for Affordable Health Care. (1989). *Model Case Management Program.* Unpublished manuscript. University of Pittsburgh, Graduate School of Public Health, Pittsburgh, PA.

Platman, S. R., Dorgan, R. E., Gerhard, R. S., Mallam, K. E., & Spiliadis, S. S. (1982). Case management of the mentally disabled. *Journal of Public Health Policy, 3,* 302-314.

Polinsky, M. L., Fred, C., & Ganz, P.A. (1991). Quantitative and qualitative assessment of a case management program for cancer patients. *Health and Social Work, 16,* 176-183.

Porporino, F. J., & Cormer, R. B. (1982). Consensus in decision-making among prison case management officers. *Canadian Journal of Criminology, 24,* 279-293.

President's Commission on Mental Health. (1978). *Report of the task panel on the nature and scope of the problems.* Washington, DC: Government Printing Office.

Procedures for the Bennington local interagency team. (nd). Bennington, VT.

Pulice, R. T., Huz, S., & Taber, T. (1991). Academic training and case management services in New York State. *Administration and Policy in Mental Health, 19,* 47-50.

Quick, T. L. (1986). *Inspiring people at work: How to make participative management work for you.* New York: Executive Enterprises.

Quinn, J., & Burton, J. (1988). Case management: A way to improve quality in long term care. In K. Fisher and E. Weissman (Eds.), *Case management: Guiding patients though the health care maze* (pp. 9-14). Chicago: Joint Commission on Accreditation of Health Care Organizations.

Raiff, N. R. (1990). *Children's intensive case management training curriculum.* Unpublished manuscript. University of Pittsburgh Medical Center, Western Psychiatric Institute and Clinic, Pittsburgh, PA.

Raiff, N. R. (1992). *Curriculum for community based child and adolescent case management training.* Pittsburgh, PA: University of Pittsburgh Medical Center, Western Psychiatric Institute and Clinic.

Raiff, N. R., & Ostrosky, R. (1992). *Final report to the Southern Human Resource Development Consortium for Mental Health.* Unpublished manuscript. University of Pittsburgh Medical Center, Western Psychiatric Institute and Clinic, Pittsburgh, PA.

Rapp, C. A. (1984). Information, performance, and the human service manager of the 1980s: Beyond "housekeeping." *Administration in Social Work, 8*(2), 69-80.

Rapp, C. A., & Chamberlain, R. (1985). Case management services for the chronically mentally ill. *Social Work, 30,* 417-422.

Rapp, C. A., Gowdy, E., Sullivan, W. P., & Wintersteen, R. (1988). Client outcome reporting: The status method. *Community Mental Health Journal, 24,* 118-133.

Rapp, C. A., & Poertner, J. (1980). Public child welfare in the 1980s. The role of case management. In K. Dea (Ed.), *Perspectives for the future: Social work practice in the '80s* (pp. 70-81). Silver Springs, MD: National Association of Social Workers.

Rapp, C. A., & Wintersteen, R. (1985). *Case management with the chronically mentally ill: The results of seven replications.* Unpublished manuscript. University of Kansas School of Social Welfare, Lawrence.

Richardson, L. M., & Austad, C.S. (1991). Realities of mental health practice in managed-care settings. *Professional Psychology: Research and Practice, 22,* 52-59.

Ridgway, P., Spaniol, L, & Zipple, A. (1986). *Case management services for persons who are homeless and mentally ill: Report from an NIMH workshop.* Unpublished manuscript. Boston University Center for Psychiatric Rehabilitation, Boston.

Rife, J. C., First, R. J., Greenlee, R. W., Miller, L. D., & Feichter, M.A. (1991). Case management with homeless mentally ill people. *Health and Social Work, 16,* 58-67.

Roberts-DeGennaro, M. (1987). Developing case management as a practice model. *Social Casework, 68,* 466-470.

Robinson, G. K., & Bergman, G. T. (1989). *Choices in case management: A review of current knowledge and practice for mental health programs.* Washington, DC: Policy Resources, Inc.

Rodriguez, A. R. (1989). Evolutions in utilization and quality management: A crisis for psychiatric services? *General Hospital Psychiatry, 11,* 256-263.

Roessler, R., & Rubin, S. E. (1982). *Case management and rehabilitation counseling: Procedures and techniques.* Baltimore, MD: University Park Press.

Romero, J. T. (1983). The therapist as social change agent. In G. Gibson (Ed.), *Our kingdom stands on brittle glass* (pp. 86-95). Silver Springs, MD: National Association of Social Workers.

Ronnau, J., Rutter, J., & Donner, R. (1988). *Resource training manual for family advocacy case management with adolescents with emotional disabilities.* Lawrence, KS: University of Kansas School of Social Welfare.

Rose, S. M. (1991). Acknowledging abuse backgrounds of intensive case management clients. *Community Mental Health Journal, 27,* 255-263.

Rose, S. M., Peabody, C. G., & Stratigeas, B. (1991). Undetected abuse among intensive case management clients. *Hospital and Community Psychiatry, 42,* 499-503.

Rosengren, W., & Litwak, E. (1970). *Organizations and clients.* Columbus, OH: Merrill.

Rothbard, A. B., Hadley, T. R., Schinnar, A., Morgan, D., & Whitehill, B. (1989). Philadelphia's capitation plan for mental health services. *Hospital and Community Psychiatry, 40,* 356-358.

Rothman, J. (1991). A model of case management: Toward empirically based practice. *Social Work, 36,* 520-528.

Rothman, J. (1992). *Guidelines for case management: Putting research to professional use.* Itasca, IL: F. E. Peacock.

Rubin, A. (1987). Case management. In A. Minahan (Ed.), *Encyclopedia of social work* (pp. 212-222). Silver Springs, MD: National Association of Social Workers.

Rubin, A. (1990, November). *Is case management effective for persons with serious mental illness? A research review.* Paper presented at the National Association of Social Workers annual meeting, Boston, MA.

Ryglewicz, H. (1982). Working with the family of the psychiatrically disabled young adult. In B. Pepper & H. Ryglewicz (Eds.), *The young adult chronic patient* (pp. 91-97). San Francisco: Jossey-Bass.

Ryndes, T. (1989). The coalition model of case management for HIV-infected persons. *Quality Review Bulletin, 15,* 4-8.

Sanborn, C. J. (Ed.). (1983). *Case management in mental health services.* New York: Haworth.

Sands, R. G., Stafford, J., McClelland, M. (1990). I beg to differ: Conflict in the interdisciplinary team. *Social Work in Health Care, 14*(3), 55-72.

Santa Clara County Mental Health. (1988). *Ethnic populations' mental health services in Santa Clara County: A long-term solution to community distress.* Unpublished manuscript.

Santarcangelo, S. (1992). *Summary of children and adolescents enrolled in Vermont's therapeutic case management program.* Paper presented at the National Conference on Case Management for Children with Emotional, Behavioral, or Mental Disorders. Portland, OR.

Saue, J. M. (1988). Legal issues related to case management. *Quality Review Bulletin, 14,* 239-244.

Schilling, R. F., Schinke, S. P., & Weatherly, R. A. (1987). Service trends in a conservative era: Social workers rediscover the past. *Social Work, 33,* 5-9.

Schinnar, A. P., & Rothbard, A. B. (1989). Evaluation questions for Philadelphia's capitation plan for mental health services. *Hospital and Community Psychiatry, 40,* 681-683.

Schneider, B. (1988). Care planning: The core of case management. *Generations, 12*(5), 16-19.

Schwartz, S. R., Goldman, H. H., & Churgin, S. (1982). Case management for the chronic mentally ill: Models and dimensions. *Hospital and Community Psychiatry, 33,* 1006-1009.

Seccombe, K., Ryan, R., & Austin, C. D. (1987). Care planning: Case managers' assessment of elders' welfare and caregivers' capacity. *Family Relations, 36,* 171-175.

Secord, L. J. (1987). *Private case management for older persons and their families: Practice, policy, potential.* Excelsior, MN: Interstudy Center for Aging and Long-Term Care.

Seltzer, M. M., Ivry, J., & Litchfield, L. C. (1987). Family members as case managers: Partnership between the formal and informal support networks. *The Gerontologist, 27,* 722-728.

Seltzer, M. M., & Mayer, J. B. (1988). A team approach for serving elders: Families as case managers. *Generations, 12*(5), 26-29.

Shaw, R. E., Hargreaves, W. A., Surber, R., Luft, L., & Shadoan, R. (1990). Continuity and intensity of case management activity in three CMHCs. *Hospital and Community Psychiatry, 41,* 323-326.

Sheehan, R. (1988). Implications of P.L. 99-457 for assessment. *Topics in Early Childhood Education, 8*(4), 103-115.

Sherman, P. S., & Porter, R. (1991). Mental health consumers as case management aides. *Hospital and Community Psychiatry, 42,* 494-498.

Shore, M. F., & Cohen, M. D. (1990). The Robert Wood Johnson Foundation Program on Chronic Mental Illness: An Overview. *Hospital and Community Psychiatry, 41,* 1212-1216.

Shuemen, S. (1987), A model of case management for mental health services. *Quality Review Bulletin, 13*(9), 314-317.

Silva, E. L. (1990). Collaboration between providers and client-consumers in public mental health programs. In T. A. Krupers (Ed.), *Using Psychodynamic Principles in Public Mental Health: New Directions for Mental Health Services, 46,* 57-63.

Simmons, K. H., Ivry, J., & Seltzer, M. M. (1985). Agency-family collaboration. *The Gerontologist, 24,* 343-346.

Sonsel, G. E., Paradise, F., & Stroup, S. (1988). Case-management practice in an AIDS service organization. *Social Casework, 69,* 388-392.

South Carolina Department of Mental Health. (1991). *Training curriculum for case managers.* Unpublished manuscript.

Specht, H. (1968). Casework practice and social policy formulation. *Social Work, 13,* 42-52.

Speaks, G. (Speaker). (1990, September). *Providing case management services for persons who are deaf* (Cassette Recording No. TO08). Paper presented at Foundations for Success: A Blueprint for the Future. The First National Case Management Conference, Cincinnati, Ohio. Richmond, VA: Visual Aids Electronics.

Spencer, P. E., & Coye, R. W. (1988). Project BRIDGE: A team approach to decision-making for early services. *Infants & Young Children, 1*(1), 82-92.

State of Hawaii. (nd). *Providing services with an interpreter.* (Pamphlet).

Stein, L. I. (1987). Funding a system of care for schizophrenia. *Psychiatric Annals, 17*(9), 592-598.

Stein, L. I. (1990). Comments by Leonard Stein. *Hospital and Community Psychiatry, 41,* 649-651.

Stein, L. I., & Test, M. (1980). Alternatives to mental hospital treatment. *Archives of General Psychiatry, 37,* 392-397.

Stein, L. I., & Test, M. (1982). Community treatment of the young adult patient. *New Directions in Mental Health Services, 14,* 57-67.

Stein, L. I., & Test, M. (1985). The Training in Community Living Model: A Decade of Experience. *New Directions in Mental Health Services, 26.*

Steinberg, R. M., & Carter, G. W. (1983). *Case management and the elderly: A handbook for planning and administering programs.* Lexington, MA: Lexington Books.

Stern, L., Serra, P., Borden, J, Williams, D., & Raiff, N. R. (1990). *Model children's case management programs—Spotlight on Pennsylvania.* Paper presented at Foundations for Success: A Blueprint for the Future. The First National Case Management Conference, Cincinnati, Ohio.

Stern, L., Serra, P., & Raiff, N. R. (1990). *Case management training as a joint venture: Developing a competency-based curriculum from the perspectives of families and professionals.* Paper presented at Going Back to the Future: Case Management With Children Who Have Severe Emotional Disturbance and With Their Families. Temple University, Philadelphia, PA.

Street, S., & Friedman, R. (1984a). *Overview of services for emotionally disturbed children: Interagency collaborations for emotionally disturbed children* (Vol I). Tampa: Florida Mental Health Institute.

Street, S., & Friedman, R. (1984b). *Planning for interagency collaboration: Interagency collaborations for emotionally disturbed children* (Vol II). Tampa: Florida Mental Health Institute.

Stroul, B. (1983). *Improving service systems for children and adolescents: Analysis of the NIMH Most in Need program.* Rockville, MD: National Institute of Mental Health.

Stroul, B. (1992a). Richland County, Ohio. In B. A. Stroul, S. K. Goldman, I. S. Lourie, & C. Zeigler-Dendy (Eds.), *Profiles of local systems of care for children and adolescents with severe emotional disturbances.* Washington, DC: Georgetown University Child Development Center.

Stroul, B. (1992b). Stark County, Ohio. In B. A. Stroul, S. K. Goldman, I. S. Lourie, & C. Zeigler-Dendy (Eds.), *Profiles of local systems of care for children and adolescents with severe emotional disturbances.* Washington, DC: Georgetown University Child Development Center.

Stroul, B., & Friedman, R. (1986). *A system of care for severely emotionally disturbed children and youth.* Washington, DC: Georgetown University Child Development Center.

Sue, D. W., & Sue, D. (1990). *Counseling the culturally different: Theory and practice.* New York: Pergamon.

Sue, S., Allen, D. B., & Conaway, L. (1978). The responsiveness and equality of mental health care to Chicanos and Native Americans. *American Journal of Community Psychology, 6,* 137-146.

Sullivan, W. P. (1987). Reconsidering the environment as a helping resource. Unpublished manuscript. University of Kansas, School of Social Welfare, Lawrence.

Sullivan, W. P. (1992). Reclaiming the community: The strengths perspective and deinstitutionalization. *Social Work, 37,* 204-209.

Summers, J. A., Dell'Oliver, C., Turnbull, A. P., Benson, H. A., Santelli, E., Campbell, M., & Siegel-Cause, E. (1990). Examining the individualized family service plan process: What are family and practitioner preferences? *Topics in Early Childhood Special Education, 10*(1), 78-99.

Taube, C. A., Morlock, L., Burns, B. J., & Santos, A. B. (1990). New directions in research on assertive community treatment. *Hospital and Community Psychiatry, 41,* 642-647.

Tessler, R. C. (1987). Continuity of care and client outcomes. *Psychosocial Rehabilitation Journal, 11*(1), 39-53.

Tessler, R. C., Bernstein, A. G., Rosen, B. M., & Goldman, H. H. (1982). The chronically mentally ill in community support systems. *Hospital and Community Psychiatry, 33,* 208-211.

Test, M. A. (1979). Continuity of care in community treatment. *New Directions for Mental Health Services, 26,* 29-39.

Texas Department of Mental Health and Mental Retardation. (1985). *Case management training curriculum.* Unpublished manuscript.

Thomason, T. C. (1991). Counseling Native Americans: An introduction for non-Native American counselors. *Journal of Counseling & Development, 69,* 321-327.

Thompson, K. S., Griffith, E. E. H., & Leaf, P. J. (1990). A historical review of the Madison model of community care. *Hospital and Community Psychiatry, 41,* 625-634.

Torres, M. S. (1988). Quality assurance of brokered service. *Quality Review Bulletin, 14,* 187-192.

Torrey, E. F. (1986). Continuous treatment teams in the care of the chronic mentally ill. *Hospital and Community Psychiatry, 37,* 1243-1247.

Trivette, C. M., Dunst, C. J., Deal, A. G., Hamer, A. W., & Propst, S. (1990). Assessing family strengths and family functioning style. *Topics in Early Childhood Special Education, 10*(1), 16-35.

Tsai, M., & Uemura, A. (1988). Asian Americans: The struggles, the conflicts, and the successes. In P. Bronstein & K. Quina (Eds.), *Teaching a psychology of people: Resources for gender and sociocultural awareness* (pp. 94-155). Washington, DC: American Psychological Association

Unzicker, R. (Speaker). (1990, September). *Overcoming obstacles to consumer empowerment* (Cassette Recording No. TH06). Paper presented at Foundations for Success:

A Blueprint for the Future. The First National Case Management Conference, Cincinnati, Ohio. Richmond, VA: Visual Aids Electronics.

Vaccaro, J. V., Liberman, R. P., Wallace, C. J., & Blackwell, G. (1992). Combining social skills training and assertive case management: The social and independent living skills program of the Brentwood Veterans Affairs Medical Center. *New Directions for Mental Health Services, 53,* 33-42.

VanDenBerg, J. (in press). Integration of individualized services into the system of care for children and adolescents with emotional disabilities. *Administration and Policy in Mental Health.*

Vigilante, F. W., & Mailick, M. D. (1988). Needs-resource evaluation in the assessment process. *Social Work, 33,* 101-104.

Vosler-Hunter, R. W. (1989). *Changing roles, changing relationships: Parent-professional collaboration on behalf of children with emotional disabilities.* Research and Training Center on Family Support and Children's Mental Health, Regional Research Institute, Portland State University, Portland, OR.

Vosler-Hunter, R., & Exo, K. (1987). *Working together: A training handbook for parent-professional collaboration.* Research and Training Center on Family Support and Children's Mental Health, Regional Research Institute, Portland State University, Portland, OR.

Vourlekis, B. S. (1991). Quality assurance indicators for monitoring social work in psychiatric acute care hospitals. *Hospital and Community Psychiatry, 42,* 460-461.

Vourlekis, B. S. (1992). The policy and professional context of case management practice. In B. S. Vourlekis & R. Greene (Eds.), *Social work case management* (pp. 1-9). New York: Aldine De Gruyter.

Vourlekis, B. S., & Greene, R. R. (Eds.). (1992a). *Social work case management.* New York: Aldine De Gruyter.

Vourlekis, B. S., & Greene, R. R. (1992b). Mastering the case manager role. In B. S. Vourlekis & R. R. Greene (Eds.), *Social work case management* (pp. 181-190). New York: Aldine De Gruyter.

Walden, T., Hammer, K., & Kurland, C. H. (1990). Case management: Planning and coordinating strategies. *Administration in Social Work, 14*(4), 61-72.

Warren, P. A., Dunn, L., & Jackson-Clark, A. (1991). The Medicare Alzheimer's project in Portland, Oregon. *Pride Institute Journal of Long Term Home Health Care, 10*(2), 20-27.

Wasylenki, D. A., Goering, P. N., Lancee, W. J., Ballantyne, R., & Farkas, M. (1985). Impact of a case manager program on psychiatric aftercare. *The Journal of Nervous and Mental Disease, 173,* 303-308.

Weick, A., & Pope, L. (1988). Knowing what's best: A new look at self-determination. *Social Casework, 69,* 10-16.

Weick, A., Rapp, C., Sullivan, W. P., & Kisthardt, W. (1989). A strengths perspective for social work practice. *Social Work, 34,* 350-354.

Weil, M., & Karls, J. M., (1985). *Case management in human services practice.* San Francisco: Jossey-Bass.

Weil, M., Zipper, I. N., & Dedmon, S. R. (1992, March). *Principles of training for child mental health case management.* Paper presented at the First National Children's Case Management Conference, Portland, OR.

Weiner, S. R. (1990). The benefits and drawbacks of managed care. *Hospital and Community Psychiatry, 41,* 1055.

Weisman, E. (1988). Managed care: Delivering quality and value. *Quality Review Bulletin, 14,* 372-374.

West, J. F., & Idol, L. (1990). Collaborative consultation in the education of mildly handicapped and at-risk students. *Remedial and Special Education, 11*(1), 22-31.

White, M. (1988). Case management: What is it? *Discharge Planning Update, 8*(1), 6-9.

White, M., & Goldis, L. (1992). Evaluation: Case managers and quality assurance. In B. S. Vourlekis & R. Greene (Eds.), *Social work case management* (pp. 167-180). New York: Aldine De Gruyter.

Williams, L. F. (1988). Frameworks for introducing racial and ethnic minority content into the curriculum. In C. Jacobs & D. D. Bowles (Eds.), *Ethnicity and race* (pp. 167-184). Silver Springs, MD: National Association of Social Workers.

Williams, P., Williams, W. A., Sommer, R., & Sommer, B. (1988). A survey of the California Alliance for the Mentally Ill. *Hospital and Community Psychiatry, 37,* 253-256.

Wilson, L. (1982). *The skills of ethnic competence.* Unpublished manuscript. University of Washington, Seattle.

Wimberly, E. T., & Blazyk, S. (1989). Monitoring patient outcomes following discharge: A computerized geriatric case management system. *Health and Social Work, 14,* 269-276.

Winton, P. J., & Bailey, D. B. (1990). Early intervention training related to family interviewing. *Topics In Early Childhood Education, 10*(1), 50-61.

Witheridge, T. F. (1989). The assertive community treatment worker: An emerging role and its implications for professional training. *Hospital and Community Psychiatry, 40,* 620-624.

Witheridge, T., & Dincin, J. (1985). The Bridge: An assertive outreach program in an urban setting. *New Directions for Mental Health Services, 26,* 65-76.

Woodruff, G., & McGonigel, M. J. (1987). Early intervention team approaches: The transdisciplinary model. In J. Jordan, J. Gallaher, P. Huntinger, & M. Karns (Eds.), *Early childhood special education: Birth to three* (pp. 163-182). Reston, VA: Council for Exceptional Children.

Woody, R. H., Woody, J. D., & Greenberg, D. B. (1991). Case management for the individualized family service plan under Public Law 99-457. *The American Journal of Family Therapy, 19*(1), 67-76.

Wright, R. G., Heiman, J. R., Shupe, J., & Olvera, G. (1989). Defining and measuring stabilization of patients during 4 years of intensive community support. *American Journal of Psychiatry, 146,* 1293-1298.

Wright, R. B., Sklebar, H. T., & Heiman, J. R. (1987). Patterns of case management activity in an intensive community support program: The first year. *Community Mental Health Journal, 23,* 53-59.

Wright, T. J. (1991, June). Psychiatric rehabilitation with African Americans. In L. Katz (Chair), *Psychiatric rehabilitation with persons from ethnic and racial backgrounds.* Symposium conducted in Baltimore, MD.

Young, T. M. (1990). Therapeutic case advocacy: A model for interagency collaboration in serving emotionally disturbed children and their families. *American Journal of Orthopsychiatry, 60,* 118-124.

Zgonc, A. M., & Jones-Smith, J. (Speakers). (1990, September). *Spotlight: Montgomery County, Ohio—Designing a case management system using the leadership concept* (Cassette Recording No. TC40). Paper presented at Foundations for Success: A Blueprint for the Future. The First National Case Management Conference, Cincinnati, Ohio. Richmond, VA: Visual Aids Electronics

Zimmer, J. G., Eggert, G. M., & Chiverton, P. (1990). Individual vs. team case management in optimizing community care for chronically ill patients with dementia. *Journal of Aging and Health, 2,* 357-372.

Zipper, I. N., Weil, M., & Rounds, K. (1991). *Service coordination for early intervention: Parents and professionals.* Chapel Hill: Carolina Institute for Research on Infant Personnel Preparation, Frank Porter Graham Child Development Center, University of North Carolina at Chapel Hill.

NAME INDEX

Aaranson, M., 12, 104
Abel-Boone, H., 77
Abrahams, R., 6, 13, 32, 130, 147, 150
Abramczyk, L. W., 8
Abramson, J. C., 62
Adams, A. C., 65
Aiken, L., 148
Allen, D. B., 67
Altshuler, S. C., 89, 130
Alvarez, R., 66
American Psychiatric Association, 33
Anderson, J. W., 32
Anthony, W. A., 84, 86, 103
Applebaum, R., 6, 9, 17, 28, 39, 45, 48, 49, 51, 53, 104, 110, 129, 130, 149, 150
Applebaum, R. A., 12, 15, 18, 113
Arana, J. D., 17, 135
Ashley, A. A., 8, 57, 91
Asper, R. D., 132
Atchley, S. J., 53
Austad, C. S., 147
Austin, C. D., 6, 9, 10, 12, 15, 17, 21, 28, 33, 39, 48, 131, 149, 150
Axelrod, S., 5

Bachrach, L. L., 5, 16, 18, 19, 36, 38, 60, 86, 106, 129, 133
Backer, T. E., 79
Bagarozzi, D. A., 9, 25, 48, 103
Bailey, D., 91, 93

Bailey, D. B., 81, 82
Baker, F., 21, 49
Baker, J., 43, 105
Ballantyne, R., 108, 133
Ballen, K., 119
Ballew, J. R., 9, 61
Barth, R. P., 9
Bassuk, E. L., 33, 152
Bazron, B. J., 66, 69, 70, 74
Beavers, J., 82
Bedell, J., 133
Behar, L., 7, 9, 140, 146
Beinecke, R. H., 48, 54
Bell, M., 21
Bennington, Vermont, 141
Benson, H. A., 81
Berger, V., 99
Bergman, G. T., 44
Bergman, H. C., 12, 16, 47, 49, 51, 53, 85, 86, 132, 148
Berkeley Planning Associates, 6, 28, 46, 105, 124
Berman, A., 19
Bernheim, K. F., 35
Bernstein, A. G., 38
Bernstein, J., 130
Bestman, E. W., 71
Biegel, D. E., 44, 79
Biestek, F. P., 77
Billig, N., 9, 106
Bird, M., 73
Blackwell, G., 88

Donabedian, A., 19
Donner, R., 19, 80
Donovan, R., 18, 105, 107, 109
Dorgan, R. E., 55
Downing, R., 28, 58, 133
Duchnowski, A. J., 139
Dunn, L., 43
Dunn, S., 147
Dunst, C. J., 81
Dzerovych, G., 9, 135

Eastern Pennsylvania Psychiatric Institute/Medical College of Pennsylvania, 127
Echols, I. J., 65
Edinburg, G., 146
Edwards, D., 73
Eggert, G. M., 133
Egri, G., 43, 80
Emlet, C. A., 43, 102
England, M. J., 139, 150
Etten, M. J., 33
Everett, F., 67
Exo, K., 83

Fariello, D., 15
Farkas, M., 33, 34, 37, 40, 43, 46, 54, 55, 57, 58
Feichter, M. A., 9
Fine, G., 59
Fiorelli, J. S., 100
Fiorentine, R., 21, 85
First, R. J., 9
Fischer, L., 13
Fisher, G., 21, 43, 48
Fisher, K., 147, 153
Fisher, W. H., 5
Fleisch, B., 143
Fleishman, J. A., 9
Fleming, M., 34, 48, 110
Fletcher, R., 15
Forbess, R., 33, 34, 37, 40, 43, 46, 54, 55, 57, 58
Forward, J., 17, 89, 130
Frank, R. G., 6, 150, 151
Frankena, S. T., 124
Franklin, J. L., 108
Fred, C., 9

Frederick, L. L., 77, 81
Freeman, S. J., 13
Freund, D. A., 148, 149
Friedman, H., 80
Friedman, R., 6, 19, 28, 140, 141
Friedman, R. M., 139
Friesen, B. J., 35, 79, 139

Gabel, C., 65
Gaitz, C. M., 93
Ganz, P. A., 9
Garland, C., 92-94, 96
Gartner, A., 111
Gaynor, J., 21
Geller, J. L., 5
Gemmill, R. H., 57
Gerhard, R. S., 55
Getzel, G. S., 122
Giemza, R., 131
Glicken, M., 15
Goering, P. N., 108, 133
Goldberg, J. R., 122
Goldis, L., 19
Goldman, C. R., 99
Goldman, H. H., 6, 10, 17, 38, 88, 117, 150, 151
Goldman, S. K., 143
Goldstein, J. M., 33, 152
Gordon, E., 44, 79
Gott, W., 46
Gowdy, E., 17
Graham, K., 9
Greenberg, D. B., 93
Greene, R. R., 8, 50, 57, 106
Greene, V. L., 33, 74
Greenlee, R. W., 9
Grella, C. E., 48, 80
Griesbach, J., 35
Griffith, E. E. H., 18, 132
Grisham, M., 4, 27, 44, 116, 131
Groenhout, J., 132
Grosser, C. F., 103, 111
Grosser, R. C., 79
Grunebaum, H., 80
Grusky, O., 43, 80
Guihan, M., 76, 137, 138
Guthrie, M., 6, 7, 41, 146, 149, 150
Guzman, L. P., 66
Gwyther, L., 28, 29, 87

SUBJECT INDEX

Abuse, 6, 9, 23, 33, 51, 74, 105, 147
Activities of daily living, 4
Administration, 5, 9, 89, 106, 115, 118, 150
Advocacy, 4, 13, 15-17, 22, 25, 51, 54-59, 66, 76, 77, 82, 85, 100, 113, 117, 124, 140, 154
Advocate, 16, 37, 55, 57, 58, 79, 80, 85, 116, 117, 142, 146
Aging, 2, 3, 6, 9, 10, 18, 19, 29, 47, 93, 106, 133, 137
AIDS, 9, 15, 147
Alcohol, 9, 33
Assertive:
community treatment, 13, 19
outreach, 72, 105, 117, 134
Assessment, 2, 4, 8, 10, 13, 16, 19, 22, 25, 28-30, 32-35, 37, 40, 45, 62, 66, 72, 73, 77, 82, 85, 87, 90, 92, 95, 96, 106, 110, 113, 116, 137, 138, 141, 143
Axis II, 64

Broker, 3, 5, 13, 14, 16, 47, 74, 85, 86, 116, 149
Brokering, 41, 43, 44, 57, 86, 103

Caregiver, 29, 33, 35, 38, 47, 61
Case assignment, 89, 117, 131

Children and Adolescent Service System Program (CASSP), 19, 137, 139-143, 146
Children, 2, 6, 7, 9, 19, 28, 39, 48, 60, 77, 83, 93, 95, 99, 139, 140, 142, 143, 145, 146, 149
Children and youth services, 9, 19, 28, 39, 48, 60, 77, 83, 93, 95, 99, 139, 140, 142, 143, 145, 146, 149
Child welfare, 7, 143
Churches, 43, 74
Client-focused, 5, 12, 79, 111, 117
Client outreach, 4
Clinical case management, 6, 10, 13, 16, 22, 28, 33, 45, 65, 71, 79, 84-90, 92, 100, 103, 132, 134, 143, 148, 153
Collaboration, 6, 16, 48, 57, 85, 86, 130, 136, 142, 147
Consultation, 8, 13, 16, 37, 39, 45, 58, 62, 73, 85, 89, 94, 96, 97, 99, 100, 110, 131, 134, 142, 143, 149
Consumer:
aide, 10, 12, 14, 17, 22, 29, 35, 37-39, 41, 45, 51, 53-56, 58, 63, 65, 77, 79, 82, 83, 92, 93, 95, 97, 99, 110, 111, 113-115, 133, 142, 149
case manager, 10, 12, 14, 17, 22, 29, 35, 37-39, 41, 45, 51, 53-56, 58, 63, 65, 77, 79, 82, 83, 92, 93, 95, 97, 99, 110, 111, 113-115, 133, 142, 149

ABOUT THE AUTHORS

Norma Radol Raiff, Ph.D., L.S.W., is Supervisor, Intensive Case Management Program, Western Psychiatric Institute and Clinic, University of Pittsburgh Medical Center. Her areas of specialty include public sector planning and evaluation and training. She has substantial experience in applied research and agency administration and has managed programs in aging, drug and alcohol, mental retardation, and mental health outpatient, case management, and emergency services. She has spearheaded consultative studies related to mental health services, equal opportunity in employment and education, domestic violence, and self-help and voluntarism. She is past president of the Pennsylvania Sociological Society and is active in the Pennsylvania Chapter of the National Association of Social Workers. She has presented numerous workshops and has written extensively on case management, applied research, and social work administration. She has been a national leader in developing materials to train intensive case managers and is recognized as a supporter of the family and self-help movements. She has also produced a child mental health training video, *If Only You Knew.*

Barbara K. Shore, Ph.D., A.C.S.W., M.P.H., is Distinguished Service Professor Emerita, University of Pittsburgh School of Social Work. She has been active in many aspects of social work, including the fields of aging, women, and children and youth. A former director of the doctoral program at the School of Social Work, she was also president of the Group to Advance Doctoral Education in Social Work, a national organization of doctoral programs. She was a founding member of the Pittsburgh Rape Crisis Center and the Persad Center, a mental health center serving sexual minorities. Currently she is Vice Chair of the

Allegheny County Mental Health/Mental Retardation Board and the Allegheny County Children and Youth Services. She has served on the national board of the National Association of Social Workers and is past president of the Pennsylvania Chapter of NASW, in addition to numerous boards and committees on the national, state, and local levels. She is co-author of *Building Informal Support Systems for the Elderly* and many articles and chapters in books. Among her many honors and awards, she has been named a Distinguished Daughter of Pennsylvania and Distinguished Alumni of the University of Pittsburgh School of Social Work.